WEiRD ViRGiNiA

STERLING

New York / London
www.sterlingpublishing.com

Weird
VIRGINIA

Your Travel Guide to
Virginia's Local Legends
and Best Kept Secrets

by
JEFF BAHR, TROY TAYLOR,
and LOREN COLEMAN

Mark Sceurman and Mark Moran,
Executive Editors

WEiRD ViRGiNiA

STERLING and the distinctive Sterling logo are registered
trademarks of Sterling Publishing Co., Inc.

Published by Sterling Publishing Co., Inc.
387 Park Avenue South, New York, NY 10016
© 2007 Mark Sceurman and Mark Moran
Paperback edition published in 2010.
Distributed in Canada by Sterling Publishing
c/o Canadian Manda Group, 165 Dufferin Street,
Toronto, Ontario, Canada M6K 3H6
Distributed in the United Kingdom by GMC Distribution Services,
Castle Place, 166 High Street, Lewes, East Sussex, England BN7 1XU
Distributed in Australia by Capricorn Link (Australia) Pty. Ltd.
P.O. Box 704, Windsor, NSW 2756, Australia

**STERLING ISBN 978-1-4027-3942-2 (hardcover)
978-1-4027-7841-4 (paperback)**

10 9 8 7 6 5 4 3 2 1

For information about custom editions, special sales, premium
and corporate purchases, please contact Sterling Special Sales
Department at 800-805-5489 or specialsales@sterlingpublishing.com.

Design: Richard J. Berenson
        Berenson Design & Books, LLC, New York, NY

CONTENTS

Our weird journey began a long, long time ago in a far-off land called New Jersey. Once a year or so, we'd compile a homespun newsletter called *Weird N.J.*, then pass it on to our friends. The pamphlet was a collection of odd news clippings, bizarre facts, little-known historical anecdotes, and anomalous encounters from our home state. The newsletter also included the kind of localized legends that were often whispered around a particular town but were seldom heard outside the boundaries of the community where they originated.

We had started *Weird N.J.* on the simple theory that every town in the state had at least one good tale to tell. The publication soon became a full-fledged magazine, and we made the decision to actually do our own investigating to see if we could track down where all of these seemingly unbelievable stories were coming from. Was there, we wondered, any factual basis for the fantastic local legends people were telling us about? Armed with not much more than a camera and a notepad, we set off on a mystical journey of discovery. Much to our surprise and amazement, a lot of what we had initially presumed to be nothing more than urban legends turned out to be real—or at least to contain a grain of truth that had sparked the lore to begin with.

After a dozen years of documenting the bizarre, we were asked to write a book about our adventures, and so *Weird N.J.: Your Travel Guide to New Jersey's Local Legends and Best Kept Secrets* was published in 2003. Soon people from all over the country began writing to us, telling us strange tales from their home states.

As it turned out, what we had perceived to be something of very local interest was actually just a small part of a larger and more universal phenomenon.

When our publisher asked us what we wanted to do next, the answer was simple: "We'd like to do a book called *Weird U.S.*, in which we could document the local legends and strangest stories from all over the country." So for the next twelve months, we set out in search of weirdness wherever it might be found in the fifty states. And indeed, we found plenty of it!

After *Weird U.S.* was published, we came to the conclusion that this country had more great tales than could be contained in just one book. Everywhere we looked, we found unwritten folklore, creepy cemeteries, cursed locations, and outlandish roadside oddities. With this in mind, we told our publisher that we wanted to document it *all* and to do it in a series of books, each focusing on the peculiarities of a particular state.

One state we definitely knew had a lot of weirdness to document was Virginia. Throughout our research into all the strange stories to be found across this country, some of the very oddest tales we uncovered hailed from Ol' Virginny. Case in point: Where else can you find a legend as unexpected and unusual as that of the Bunnyman—an ax-wielding homicidal maniac in a fuzzy rabbit costume? But as we would soon discover, the Bunnyman is just the tip of the iceberg when it comes to all the weirdness that the Old Dominion state has to offer.

So we set out to assemble a team of investigators to travel around the state and delve into all of its

mysteries, both past and present. The first author we invited to come along on this weird ride was Jeff Bahr. Jeff was a contributor to *Weird U.S.* and is a traveling gypsy of sorts, who rides extensively throughout the eastern states on his motorcycle in search of strange sites and stories. Next we recruited Troy Taylor, another *Weird U.S.* compatriot, who is perhaps the most prolific chronicler of American hauntings to ever put pen to paper. The third author we enlisted for the project was Loren Coleman, also a *Weird U.S.* alumnus, who has earned an international reputation as the premier cryptozoological expert in the world today. Loren has not only been tracking the bizarre beasts of his native state of Virginia for over forty years but has also been documenting its unexplained occurrences, ancient mysteries, and covert conspiracies.

Jeff, Troy, and Loren all have what we refer to as the Weird Eye. The Weird Eye is what is needed to search out the sort of stories we are always looking for. It requires one to see the world in a different way, with a renewed sense of wonder. And once you have it, there is no going back—you'll never see things the same way again. All of a sudden you begin to reexamine your own environs, noticing your everyday surroundings as if for the first time. And you begin to ask yourself questions like, "What the heck is *that* thing all about, anyway?" and "Doesn't anybody else think that's kind of *weird?*"

So come with us now and let Jeff, Troy, and Loren take you on a tour of the Old Dominion state, with all of its cultural quirks, strange sites, and oddball characters. It's a state of mind we like to call *Weird Virginia.*

– *Mark Sceurman and Mark Moran*

The Old Dominion state of Virginia is closely associated with classic American history. As one of America's original thirteen colonies and with some eight U.S. Presidents born here, such a role is highly merited if a bit dry and boring.

Sounds like a veritable snoozefest, right? Not so fast!

You see, as any weirdness hound will tell you, wherever there's legitimate history, there's bound to be some *weird* history. In the case of Ol' Virginny, such tantalizing tidbits are indeed plentiful. Consider the infamous Mermaid Tree, a scantily clad carved stump that represents one man's risqué fish fantasy come to life. How about death masks that feature the death-throe grimaces of the deceased, or the hyperhaunted Octagon House that many still fear to inhabit? Perhaps kitschy delights are more to your liking. Then feast your eyes upon Dinosaur Land, a roadside attraction just waiting to snare your greenbacks. More into the fear factor, you say? You might want to traumatize yourself at the Tombstone House—a dwelling made from . . . yep, you guessed it.

When it comes to Virginia, it seems the more one digs the more one finds.
So join us as we explore this heretofore underexplored state. The trip will cost little beyond the price of this book but will deliver you to bizarre places that most textbooks sidestep or avoid altogether. In our weird world, that's considered a real find. Happy hunting!
—Jeff Bahr

It's no secret that my life revolves around history, mystery, and hauntings. Having worked on other *Weird* projects that were spawned by the fevered imaginations of Mark Sceurman and Mark Moran, I was especially thrilled to be asked by the Marks to take part in *Weird Virginia.* There is probably no other state as mired in American history, strange mysteries, and hauntings as Virginia. It's a place that fits into the category of "just downright weird."

I still have memories of my first trip here. I must have been about ten, and my parents took the family (on one of our many station-wagon vacations from hell) to see Virginia's Natural Bridge. I never forgot the place and would drag friends and family members to see it many times over the years. I was not the only one who was impressed either, as this was apparently one of Virginia's first tourist traps, and George Washington himself even carved his initials in the stone there when he was still just a surveyor.

I would return to Virginia many times as the years went by and I discovered my true calling—writing about ghosts. A veritable who's who of American history haunts the place, from Abraham Lincoln to

Jefferson Davis and Robert E. Lee. A variety of former Presidents and Congressmen still wander the streets of Washington, and Civil War soldiers can be found roaming the remains of the battlefields from that bloody conflict. Virginia also boasts such classic hauntings as the Haw Branch Plantation and the Old House Woods. There is no question that it's a ghost hunter's paradise.

I hope you enjoy this weird trip through the cities, small towns, woods, and back roads of one of our nation's greatest, and weirdest, states. Who knows what may be lurking just around the next corner?
—*Troy Taylor*

Weird Virginia is built on my sixty-year relationship with the Commonwealth. I thank my parents, Anna and Loren, for my birth in Norfolk (yes, my father was in the navy). While I was growing up in the Midwest, the simple fact of my birthplace resulted in my remarkably intense interest in learning everything I could about the state, including a boyhood fascination with what I then saw as the mirror-image loyalty story of Robert E. Lee and his allegiance to Virginia. As a precocious kid, I assumed I would have to fight on the side of the Confederacy if a new War Between the States was declared, due to Lee's example. Luckily that never happened, and I wasn't forced to make that choice. Virginia, nevertheless, remained a core focus of what I see as my legacy.
—*Loren Coleman*

Local Legends

Virginia is a state so immersed in legend that there is no other place like it in America. Start with the fact that George Washington slept here, and so did Jefferson Davis—Presidents of different nations that existed on the same soil. Virginia is a place of weird events and strange tales that likely would have been forgotten, passed over by progress, if they had not captured the imagination of generations. Whether or not such stories are true will probably never be known, just like the real number of homes in which George Washington slept. But nearly every legend, no matter how outlandish and unbelievable it might seem, has a small kernel of truth at its heart. And while the legend itself may have changed many times over the years, that kernel of truth remains.

Phantom Lovers of the Great Dismal Swamp

It is one of the oldest legends in the state—and one of the most enduring. It is a tale that dates back to the earliest inhabitants of the region and was made famous by one of the great writers of the 19th century. And it is a story attached to a place nearly as legendary as the tale that haunts it: the Great Dismal Swamp.

One of the most secret spots in the East, the Great Dismal Swamp is a place that George Washington tried to drain and that Harriet Beecher Stowe was inspired by. Vast and ancient, the swamp sprawls unspoiled across the borders of Virginia and North Carolina. It has been home to outlaws, poets, ghosts, fugitives, and warring armies. Yet even today it appears untouched by history.

Many believe that the swamp is too poisonous for anything to live in, though others speculate that it was home to lions, alligators, demons, and ghosts. No single place is more connected to the legends of the Great Dismal Swamp than Lake Drummond, the mysterious body of water that lies in the dead center of the swamp. This freshwater heart of the region was named after William Drummond, a 17th-century governor of North Carolina who, the stories say, got lost in the swamp with a group of hunters. All but Drummond died. He eventually staggered out of the swamp—ragged, hungry, and filled with lurid tales of a lake deep in the wilderness.

Lake Drummond is ancient and almost magical. Gigantic cypress trees form odd-looking islands in the black shallow water. The wetland forest that surrounds it was created by the sea that departed after the last ice age and is made up of junipers, gum trees, and cypresses that loom over peat moss as much as ten feet thick. The water here is as strange as the swamp itself. European colonists found that for some reason the tea-colored water stayed drinkable longer than other water, and they filled casks with it for lengthy sea voyages.

No one can say how Lake Drummond originated. Some believe that it may have been created by the impact of a meteorite falling to earth. Others say that it was made by a large underground peat fire as long as 6,000 years ago. Native American legends tell of "the Fire Bird" creating the lake, adding to the eerie enigma of the place.

There is little sign of human habitation here these days, but man came and went in days gone by. During the 1920s and 1930s, small cabins on stilts surrounded the lake, catering to fishermen of all kinds. Guides would take tourists out onto the water, sometimes reciting the poem that made Lake Drummond famous—feeding the legend of the phantom lovers.

The first record of this tale dates back to 1803. At that time, Irish poet Sir Thomas Moore wrote a ballad that he claimed was an old Indian legend about a man driven mad by his lover's death. He seeks and finds her on Lake Drummond. According to the ballad, "She's gone to the Lake of the Dismal Swamp . . . Where, all night long, by a fire-fly lamp, she paddles her white canoe."

In this famous tale, the young man's lover died just weeks before they were to be married, fading away from some unknown illness. In the days and weeks that followed, the man fell into the depths of depression and finally went mad, obsessed with the idea that his beloved was still alive somewhere—just out of his reach. Her family had sent her away, he imagined, and she waited for him to come and rescue her. In vain, his friends and family tried to convince him that his lover had died, but he refused to hear it. He was sure that she was out there in the wilderness of the swamp, and one night he vanished into its depths. He wandered for days, living on roots and berries, stumbling lost and broken.

One evening, as night was falling, he came upon Lake Drummond, resting black and silent in the heart of Great Dismal. Out on the dark water, he saw the soft blinking of a firefly as it flitted back and forth. Convinced that the pale light was a signal from his lost love, he hurriedly made a raft of cypress branches tied together with vines.

The crazed lover rushed out onto the lake and paddled ferociously toward the point where he had seen the light. But the hastily constructed raft did not hold,

But oft, from the Indian hunter's camp,
This lover and maid so true
Are seen at the hour of midnight damp
To cross the Lake by a fire-fly lamp,
And paddle their white canoe!

—"A Ballad: The Lake of the Dismal Swamp"
Thomas Moore

and just as he reached the center of the lake, the bindings came apart and the young man sank down into the murky waters. He was never seen again.

According to the legend, though, he was reunited with his love in death. Their spirits found one another, and those who venture out to Lake Drummond today will still sometimes see a spectral light out on the water. Those who tell this old story say that the two lovers float side by side across the lake, in a white canoe, carrying a firefly lantern to light their way.

Curse of the Three Sisters

Looking out over the Potomac River between the Chain Bridge and the Francis Scott Key Bridge, the Weird traveler can see three large granite rocks, rising out of the water between the Virginia shoreline and the city of Washington. Legend has it that these rocks, dubbed the Three Sisters, are part of a Native American curse that persists to this day.

It is a curse so dire that few will cross the river at this point. Scores of people who have tried to do so have died in the attempt.

The story of the Three Sisters Rocks dates back more than 100 years before the first settlers came to Jamestown in 1607. At that time, Indian settlements and confederacies were scattered along Chesapeake Bay and on both sides of the Potomac River. The region was rich with farmland and game, and the villages flourished.

All was not peaceful here, however. There were often violent clashes between the Indians who lived in the region that is now Maryland and those settled along the Potomac in present-day Virginia. Northern Indians of the Iroquois tribes and the Susquehannocks raided across the river into the area of the Powhatan Confederacy, which was made up of several Algonquin tribes. The battles were frequent and bloody, and captives taken were usually killed or forced into slavery.

One day, after what had been a prolonged siege of his village, a Powhatan chief decided that the situation was quiet enough that he and some of his men could go out in search of food. The chief, though, refused to allow three of his young sons to come along. He did not believe they were old enough to defend themselves if the party encountered trouble outside the village.

The young men were disappointed, but soon devised a plan to impress their father. They would go out of the village in secret and bring back enough fresh fish to feed the women, children, and old men until the hunting party returned. Their self-appointed task was a dangerous one. The greatest abundance of fish was along the northern shore of the river, an area where Susquehannock warriors still might lurk. The boys were determined to prove themselves to their father, however, and they struck out, using one of the few canoes that had survived the recent fighting.

Unfortunately, the Susquehannocks had left behind a scouting party, and the boys had only been fishing for a short time before they were attacked. They were captured; and in full view of those who had stayed behind in the village, the chief's sons were tortured and murdered. Among those who watched the terrible scene were the three beautiful daughters of the village shaman, a respected tribal medicine man who, it was believed, received his powers directly from the Great Spirit.

The three young women were in love with the chief's sons and witnessed their deaths with great horror. Their terror and sadness soon turned to a wish for revenge, however, and they devised a plan of their own. The three sisters decided to cross the river and persuade the rival chief to give them to the warriors who had slain their lovers. They would hypnotize the murderers with their beauty and their father's great medicine, and then inflict on them a long, slow, agonizing death.

The sisters lashed together several logs to make a raft and then pushed out from the shore. Tragically, the river proved too fast and the current too strong. The raft was

> **Drawing from the supernatural powers inherited from their father, the sisters cursed the river. If they could not cross at that point, then no one would—ever.**

pulled downstream. The young women, still stricken by the sight of their lovers being killed, were thrown into a rage by their inability to navigate the river. Drawing from the supernatural powers inherited from their father, the sisters cursed the river. If they could not cross at that point, then no one would—ever.

The curse was forever sealed when the three sisters sank to their deaths in the swirling waters of the Potomac. The skies darkened as the young women submerged and a storm began to rage. Thunder rumbled and flashes of lightning illuminated the landscape. Then one deadly surge of energy snapped down and touched the waters where the sisters had vanished from sight.

The storm continued all night long, whipping the river into a frenzy. When the sun rose the following morning, the river was calm and the skies were clear. As the clouds rolled away, the Indians saw that three large granite boulders had appeared in the river where there had been none the day before. The three boulders had appeared at the same spot where the three sisters had gone to their deaths—cursing the crossing for all time.

To this day, the three rocks continue to take their toll on those who dare to defy the Curse of the Three Sisters. Law enforcement officials in the area add names to the list of the river's victims with each passing year, and among them are fishermen, swimmers, and boaters who attempted to cross the river at this point. Old-timers in the area say that if a moaning cry is heard drifting over the Potomac during a storm, there will soon be another drowning—another victim of the curse.

Old-timers in the area say that if a moaning cry is heard drifting over the Potomac during a storm, there will soon be another drowning—another victim of the curse.

Just an old Indian tall tale, you say? Consider this. In 1972, construction of a bridge that was supposed to span this river was interrupted by one of the worst storms in the region's history. Those who knew of the legend saw a strange parallel between the storms that came that summer and the storms that came after the curse was pronounced by the three sisters. The skies clouded over, rumbled with thunder, and flashed with lightning. The Potomac surged with whitecaps, and it was reported by some that fingers of lightning actually came down and touched the waters where the bridge supports were starting to be built. Floodwaters from this devastating storm swept away the construction framework for what would have been called, ironically, "The Three Sisters Bridge."

Needless to say, plans for the bridge were abandoned. Since that time, there have been no further efforts to try to span this legendary crossing, providing a continuing testimony to the power of an ancient curse.

The Light at Cohoke Crossing

In the Tidewater region of Virginia, near the town of West Point, literally thousands of people have come to a crossroads called Cohoke to witness something that seems to be from beyond this world. The Ghost Light at Cohoke Crossing seems to be the stuff of legend, but it is, to many people anyway, indisputably real. This weird light, which seems to come and go at will, has amazed some and been scoffed at by others. One thing is sure, though—there is no simple explanation.

There have been two explanations given as to why the light appears at the Cohoke railroad crossing, and neither of them is pleasant. One involves a railroad worker who was allegedly killed at the site during the 1800s.

In those days, every train was manned by a number of employees, each with his own tasks to perform to keep the train running on schedule. One such rail worker was the brakeman, who rode in the train's caboose. His job was to remain on watch in tunnels, at crossings, or at stations for any signs of trouble. He always carried a lantern with him so that he could signal the engineer if he needed to. When the train was stopped for loading, the brakeman would walk alongside the train and look for any problems.

Legend says that a train came to the crossing one night. It pulled to a stop and the brakeman climbed down from the rear platform of the caboose to begin his usual routine of checking the cars with his lantern. He had only gone a short distance when he spotted trouble. He leaned into the space between two freight cars and was caught off guard when the train suddenly lurched forward and knocked him off his feet. Somehow, his head passed into a space between two cars and then the space slammed closed, severing his head.

One of the other workers saw the brakeman's lantern

fall and ran to help him. A number of other men ran in the same direction, and the group was soon gathered around the man. Stunned, they lifted their coworker's body into the caboose so that he could be taken to the next station, but in all the excitement, no one thought to look for his head.

To this day, the ghost of the brakeman is said to walk the tracks at Cohoke Crossing. On certain nights, the bobbing light of a railroad lantern can be seen tracing the line of a long-forgotten freight train—as a phantom brakeman searches in vain for his missing head.

Many of those who believe in the validity of the ghost light still dismiss this story of the phantom brakeman, contending that such tales exist all over the country and rarely have any real history to back them up. In addition, many who have seen the light claim that it is much larger than any lantern. They claim that the light looks more like the headlight of a train. They offer an alternate explanation for the phenomenon, the lost train.

The legend goes that in 1864, after the battle of Richmond during the Civil War, a train was loaded with wounded Confederate soldiers and dispatched to West Point, VA, where the men could recuperate or be shipped farther south if their wounds were too critical. The train left Richmond but never reached its destination. It inexplicably vanished along the way and was never seen again. Some believe that it was attacked and destroyed by Federal troops, but others believe that its disappearance was more mysterious.

Many who come out to the crossing in search of the mystery light report that they have also seen the outline of a train in the distance, giving further credence to this explanation for the enigma. But whatever destination this train is headed for, it has never arrived there, for the eerie light persists to this day.

The skeptics' call is that the light is "marsh gas," "overactive imaginations," and sightings fueled by "liquid courage," but those who seek the light at Cohoke Crossing offer detailed accounts of what they have seen. Some claim to have seen it hundreds of times. Witnesses are usually in agreement as to its method of appearance. The shimmering ball first shows up far in the distance, perhaps several hundred yards down the tracks. It then silently starts to come closer, getting brighter and brighter as it draws nearer. In most cases,

The bobbing light of a railroad lantern can be seen tracing the line of a long-forgotten freight train—as a phantom brakeman searches in vain for his missing head.

A Visit to Cohoke Crossing

For some people, standing alone at midnight on a series of train tracks several states away from home would seem rather foolish. I just call it a night out.

I had arrived in the town of West Point a little ahead of schedule. One cannot witness ghost lights, even the famed Cohoke Crossing Lights, in broad daylight. Floating lights are ornery like that. So there I was with my tripod in hand. I stopped in a little Italian restaurant to wait out the setting sun. I mumbled to some strangers about the lights and everyone in the place erupted with their own stories of what they saw one time or another. This is a phenomenon the locals truly believe in.

Standing on the silent tracks in pitch black for several hours, I took numerous photos with extremely long exposures. The camera acts like a security blanket at times, taking the fear out of what you are witnessing through the viewfinder. And what I was witnessing was nothing. The longer I stood, the more my mind played tricks on me. I did notice lights appear and flicker out far down the tracks but I passed them off as odd reflections or perhaps my need for a hotel room. It wasn't until I got to that said place, later that night, and went through my shots that I noticed several with what looked like a form over the tracks. I shot with many angles with the same long exposures and the "shape" only appears in one direction and always over the track. None of the other shots seems to pick up anything of interest so I assume that the light is not an ambient reflection caught on film. In truth, I do not know what it is, but that, in the end, is half the fun.—*Ryan Doan*

the light is so bright that viewers are frightened away as it gets close to them. The only impediment to the light's appearance is when someone tries to chase it or, as has happened many times in the past, when someone shoots at it. This causes the light to disappear instantly. Also, even though many have tried, including national television shows and magazines, no one has yet been able to photograph it. In this way, the Cohoke Crossing Ghost Light remains as elusive as the source of the legend behind it.

The Curse Tree

The story of Jamestown is a familiar tale to anyone who made his way through eighth-grade history. We have all been regaled with the saga of Captain John Smith and Pocahontas, but there is a tale of Jamestown that is not so familiar. It is a compelling part of Virginia's history and a legend that still reaches out today from beyond the grave.

The Weird traveler who makes the journey to Jamestown Island will eventually be drawn to the site of the Jamestown Memorial Church, which was built in 1907 on the ruined foundations of the original church from 1617. Beyond the stone building is a small shady cemetery that contains only a scattering of graves. Among them are the grave sites of James and Sarah Harrison Blair.

Although James Blair is largely forgotten today, he was an important figure in Virginia history well into the 1700s. Born in Scotland, he served as a trusted counsel to the British governor, and later as the governor of the colony himself. Historians also consider him the driving force behind the founding of the College of William and Mary, the second oldest university in the country. On a more personal note, his tombstone points out that the "comliness [sic] of his handsome face adorned him . . . he entertained elegantly in a cheerful, hospitable manner without luxury . . . in affability, he excelled." It is because of these things, most believe, that the legend of the "Curse Tree" had its beginnings.

The other central figure in the story is a young woman named Sarah Harrison. She was a beautiful girl, age seventeen when the tale begins, and was the oldest daughter of Colonel Benjamin Harrison of the Wakefield Plantation. She was active in the plantation social circles of the day, thanks to the comfortable financial position of her father, and has been described as being beautiful,

headstrong, and full of life. No wonder then that Sarah found herself pursued by a number of handsome and eligible young suitors. A man named William Roscoe, just five years older than Sarah and a gentleman her parents heartily approved of, was the man who won her pledge of marriage. However, that marriage was not meant to be.

Just three weeks after her engagement became official, Sarah met the handsome and charismatic James Blair. She immediately fell in love with him, but her parents were not as impressed as she was. For one thing, Sarah was already engaged to a perfectly acceptable young man; and in addition, James Blair was thirty-one years old at the time, nearly twice Sarah's age. In those days, it was often a disgrace to the parents if a girl married someone so much older. Society viewed such marriages as born of the family's failing finances, an attempt to marry their daughter off to a wealthy man.

But Sarah, headstrong as she was, could not be swayed, resulting in a bitter rift between the girl and her parents. They argued, threatened, and pleaded with her to stay away from Blair, but Sarah's mind was made up. According to legend, William Roscoe died from a broken heart after Sarah left him. She and Blair were soon married, although her parents refused to attend the wedding and would have nothing to do with the newlyweds.

They refused to give up on trying to ruin the marriage, however. They sought to have the union annulled and even went so far as to draw up legal papers in the matter. It was during a trip to seek out an attorney that fate stepped into the affair. During this journey, Colonel Harrison, his wife, Hannah, and their youngest daughter were caught in a horrific storm and their carriage was struck by lightning. All three were instantly killed. They never got the chance in life to separate Sarah from James Blair.

That couple went on to live happily together as

husband and wife. Sarah died in 1713 at the age of forty-two, never having been forgiven by her relatives. She was denied burial in the Harrison family plot and was buried in a stone crypt just outside it, in a small cemetery on Jamestown Island.

James Blair went on to live another thirty years, making many contributions to the growth and prosperity of the Virginia colony. When he died in 1743, he was laid to rest in another stone crypt just six inches to the left of the tomb of his wife. The two lovers, it seemed, would rest side by side for eternity.

As the sycamore grew larger, it shattered the bricks between the Blair crypts and caused Sarah's stone to separate from her husband's.

But in 1750, seven years after James was interred next to Sarah, fate once more had a hand in the story. It was in that year that a small sycamore tree began to grow next to the crypt of James Blair—between his tomb and that of his wife's. Nothing was done to prevent the tree from growing or to protect the tombs. As the sycamore grew larger, it shattered the bricks between the Blair crypts and caused Sarah's stone to separate from her husband's. The tree pushed Sarah's stone into the nearby Harrison plot, a short distance from the graves of her parents and her sisters. This left Blair's crypt all by itself to one side, separated from that of his wife. And so, the legend went, Sarah's parents, who could not destroy her marriage to Blair while they were alive, finally managed to separate the lovers after their death.

The story of the Curse Tree has been widely told since that time and it should end on that note, but it doesn't. Several years ago, the old sycamore tree, which had grown to considerable size, died and was cut down—although the broken bricks and shattered tombs were left as they were, pushed apart. Soon after, a new sycamore sapling began to grow in the same spot where the original tree once stood. It still flourishes here in the graveyard today. It is, the legend continues, the hand of the Harrisons as they continue to reach out from the other side, pushing their daughter away from the man she loved.

Woman in Black

She seemingly appeared from nowhere, and those who saw her said that she was stunningly beautiful, although few of them could look her in the eyes. A quick glance was all that the strongest could ever manage. Whenever she materialized from the shadows, she brought with her a feeling of horror; and when she spoke, icy needles of fear pierced the hearts of her listeners. One man who encountered her described her as tall and handsome, with "dancing eyes." Many others said that she was dressed completely in black and wore something "like a black turban on her head." She wore it in such a way that it was drawn around her face and under her eyes, creating a black mask. To complete this gothic and menacing costume, she had a long black cloak pulled around her body. She never caused anyone physical harm. It was merely her presence that inspired such fear. She would draw herself out of the shadows and then melt back in the same way that she came, leaving no part of herself behind.

This chilling woman was the legendary "Woman in Black" who terrorized Roanoke for a short time in March 1902. The *Roanoke Times,* the newspaper of the day, was quoted as saying: "Her name was on every lip; strong men trembled when her name was spoke; children cried and clung to their mother's dresses; terror reigned supreme!"

Pretty scary stuff, but why did this woman cause such a disturbance in the city? As the newspaper pointed out, "Just why the 'Woman in Black' should be so terrible has never been known. She made no attack on anyone. It was probably due to the unexpected appearance in places unthought of, and at hours when the last person the city expected to be about should be a woman.

"Just what her mission may be," the *Times* continued, "has not exactly been figured out; but of one thing there seems to be a unanimity of opinion, and that is, she has a proclivity for attacking married men, if 'attack' is the proper word."

The newspaper gave a detailed accounting of one such occurrence that purported to be a firsthand report from a "prominent merchant" in Roanoke. The man stated that he had been at his store late one evening, taking care of assorted chores. He was unable to leave his business until well after midnight and was walking home, deep in thought, when a woman in a black cloak suddenly appeared just behind him. She whispered his name, sending cold chills down his spine, and he quickly increased his pace. As he started to walk faster, the woman walked faster as well. Finally he began to run and, eerily, the woman kept pace with him. Strangest of all was the fact that she almost seemed to glide along behind him, never showing any signs that she was making an effort to keep up.

After several blocks, she spoke to him. Her voice was the same smooth whisper in which she had earlier spoken his name. "Where do you turn off?" she asked of him.

"Twelfth Avenue," the merchant choked out.

Suddenly, the man froze in his tracks and stumbled. The woman's hand had appeared on his shoulder. He could feel the soft pressure of it, burning and freezing his flesh at the same time. He tried to shake it off, but she refused to let go. He was unable to bring himself to lift his own hand and push hers away.

She spoke again in a low, musical voice that seemed to hint at amusement. "You are not the first married man that I have seen to his home this night," she murmured.

The merchant began to run again and soon reached his front gate. He slammed it open and rushed through, sure that the woman would now leave him in peace. To his shock, though, the woman clung to his shoulder as he violently thrashed his way along the walk. He planned to dash through his front door and then slam it behind him, cutting off the woman's passage into his home. He prayed silently that he could do this in time.

The merchant reached for the door handle, twisted the lock, and started to push his way into his house—and the fiery cold pressure on his arm vanished! He looked behind him and the woman in black was no longer there. How she had disappeared, he didn't know. All he knew was that the monster was gone. He hurried into the house and tightly locked the door behind him.

Two others who experienced visitations with the mysterious woman were a young telegraph operator and a hotel porter. Both men were married, and in both cases she appeared to them late at night on deserted Roanoke streets. Each of them said that she approached them in total silence and that she had called them by name. The porter admitted to being terrified by the apparition and ran all the way to his home. The telegraph operator stated that she had called after him to wait for her, but like the porter, he ran hard for several blocks before making it to his house.

Whoever the woman in black may have been, she stayed in Roanoke only a few days, and soon the reports of her ceased. A short time later, there were stories of her nighttime activities in the town of Bluefield. And curiously, in that same month of March 1902, another newspaper story appeared about the woman—or at least one just like her. This story, however, told of a

sighting in the town of Alma, NE.

The story was headlined "Two Prominent Men See Ghost!" and reported that the spirit form of a young woman was walking the streets of Alma, appearing from the shadows in alleyways and rushing past lone pedestrians. The newspaper added, "The Alma ghost is remarkable in that instead of being garbed in the proverbial white, it walks about clothed in deep black."

Was this the same woman in black who came to Roanoke, still appearing to men as they walked late at night? And if it was, had she been seen in other places as well? We may never know; but for now, we can chalk it up to one more mysterious tale in the annals of Virginia legend.

Curse of the Hope Diamond

The most famous cursed item in the world is undoubtedly the Hope Diamond, which now resides at the famed Smithsonian Institution in Washington, DC. The diamond once belonged to a Colorado gold heiress named Evalyn Walsh McLean, who became obsessed with it during her honeymoon with the *Washington Post's* Ned McLean. The legend of this infamous diamond will be forever entwined with the history of Washington and is one of the weirdest stories ever to be told here. For those unfamiliar with the tale, it is one of madness, tragedy, death, and scandal, and even the fall of a U.S. President.

Evalyn Walsh first met Edward "Ned" McLean in 1908 in Denver while he was there covering the Democratic National Convention for his father's newspaper. The election that year went to Republican William Howard Taft, but neither of them cared. They were only interested in each other. Evalyn Walsh was the beautiful daughter of a mining man who had struck it rich, and Ned McLean was the dashing heir to the *Washington Post* empire. The two were immediately attracted to one another and were married that same year.

The privileged young couple celebrated the event by traveling to exotic places around the globe for "a happy whirlwind of worldwide travels," as the newspaper described their honeymoon. It was in Turkey that Evalyn first set her eyes on the most seductive and amazing gemstone she had ever seen. She was completely captivated by the shimmering blue diamond, even though it was hanging around the neck of a sultan's favorite harem girl. Years passed before she heard of the diamond again, but she never forgot it.

When Evalyn read that the sultan had been assassinated and his favorite wife murdered, she set out to track down the stone and buy it. The story about the unlucky sultan—how his life had fallen apart and ended in ruin after acquiring the diamond—didn't seem to bother her. Apparently, such stories had been told to the sultan as well, but he had scoffed at them, just as Evalyn did.

For one who did not believe in the ominous stories, though, it was strange that Evalyn arranged to have a priest bless the stone after it came into her possession. But many wondered if a mere blessing could erase centuries of death and terror.

The legend of what came to be known as the Hope Diamond claimed that it had originally been part of the eye of an Indian idol, discovered in a lost tomb in the jungle. The idol's eye was stolen and then sold to a French soldier of fortune named Tavernier. He smuggled it into Paris, but soon after died a slow and horrible death after being attacked by a pack of wild dogs. Later, the stone turned up as part of the French

crown jewels, although it was said that Louis XIV probably wished that he had never acquired the cursed diamond. Legend holds that his eldest son, eldest grandson, and his great-grandson all fell victim to its curse in the same year. It was even said that the stone was used to bribe the commander of a foreign army brought to Paris to save Louis XVI and Marie Antoinette, when they were imprisoned during the French Revolution. The royal couple, as most know, lost their heads over this piece of business.

After that, the diamond vanished for many years, to resurface later in Amsterdam. Perhaps to escape the curse, it was recut by a jeweler named Fals. But the spell remained. Fals would die a poor and shattered man, betrayed by his son, who stole the diamond from him.

Henry Thomas Hope, a London banker, acquired the huge stone in 1830, and it gained the name "Hope" that it still bears today. Strangely, the curse spared Hope but revived again when it passed into the hands of Catherine the Great of Russia, who lived a well-known life of grief and tragedy. The curse remained strong in the new century. A merchant sold it to the wealthy sultan who graced his harem favorite with the diamond. As we know, the sultan met an unfortunate fate, placing the diamond into the possession of Evelyn Walsh McLean.

The first two people to handle the stone after Evelyn

acquired it died unexpectedly. Her mother-in-law and a friend of her mother-in-law, Mrs. Robert Goelet, both touched the stone and passed away within a few months of each other.

Regardless, Evelyn still insisted that she did not believe in the curse, though she refused to allow her children to handle the diamond. But that was not enough to save her young son Vinson. When the boy was only nine, an out of control automobile struck and killed him in front of the family's home. His death put a terrible strain on the McLeans' marriage, and reports of their public bickering began to appear in Washington's society columns.

Among the many friends of the wealthy couple was President Warren G. Harding. Legend has it that Harding's life began to change for the worse after he came into contact with the Hope Diamond. Rumors of corruption swirled during Harding's tenure, leading his administration to be remembered as one of the most crooked to occupy the White House. He dropped dead in San Francisco in 1923 while still in office, after a blood clot made its way to his heart. Many believe that Harding's connection with the Hope Diamond led to his tragic fall from losing the goodwill of the American people, suffering health problems, and his untimely death.

Ned McLean himself was alleged to have been intricately involved in the scandals surrounding the Harding presidency, and the resulting stress from the accusations pushed him into heavy drinking. He was often reported as being falling-down drunk at public events. These stories would begin a decade of newspaper articles that chronicled the McLeans' public fights and separations. Ned's drinking and strange behavior eventually reached the breaking point for his wife, who began working to have him committed to an asylum. In 1933, twenty jurors in Washington granted her wish. Ned McLean was declared insane. He was hospitalized for eight years before a heart attack ended another life that was ruined by the Hope Diamond.

Edward McLean's death did not prevent him from having one last bit of revenge. In July 1941, it was revealed that he had cut Evalyn out of his will and had left more than $300,000 to a woman named Rose Davies, a companion from what were termed "cheerier days."

During this same time, the McLeans' daughter, who led a troubled life of her own, died, taken by an overdose of sleeping pills. Evalyn Walsh McLean had now survived her husband, her son Vinson, and her only daughter. She had weathered many trials, and it looked as though her most prized possession was slipping through her fingers. Newspaper reports uncovered the fact that she

What has become of the curse? Does the ironically named Hope Diamond wait even now for one more victim?

was willing to put up the Hope Diamond as collateral for a loan needed to bail the *Washington Post* out of trouble. She would not live long enough to lose it entirely, though. Not long after, Evalyn fell and broke her hip; and while suffering from that, she contracted another illness, from which she never recovered. In April 1947, only days after her death, the *Washington Daily News* asked, "Who will be the next to risk wearing the 'unlucky' diamond?"

New York diamond merchant Harry Winston acquired the stone after Evalyn's death and claimed that he did not believe in the curse. A short time later, however, the diamond was placed on what Winston called "permanent loan" to the Smithsonian. One article about the "loan" stated that he decided to get rid of the diamond because his wife kept nagging him to let her wear it.

The stone would be safely ensconced inside the Smithsonian, but many believe that it claimed its final victims before it reached its destination. Harry Winston shipped the diamond to Washington by way of registered mail—much to the misfortune of the unknowing mail carrier. According to the reports, a truck crushed the mail carrier's leg soon after he delivered the stone to the museum. Shortly after that, his wife died of a heart attack, his family dog hanged itself by jumping through a basement window while still tied to a leash, and his suburban Washington home was gutted by fire.

What has become of the curse? Does the ironically named Hope Diamond wait even now for one more victim? As long as it remains safely behind glass at the Smithsonian, we'll probably never know. But if you are ever offered an opportunity to even come near this weird gem—walk quickly the other way! Best not to find out the hard way if this is one legend that is more truth than fiction!

Ancient Wonders and Unsolved Mysteries

Mysteries surrounding the origins and meanings of prehistoric structures, such as Easter Island's great statues, Stonehenge's stone pillars, or even the pyramids of Egypt, have fired the imaginations of generations of wonderers and thinkers. These bizarre relics in exotic locations naturally lend themselves to thoughts of ancient people of greater wisdom than us mere moderns. But few North Americans have considered the mysteries of the "ancients" near their own towns.

The Commonwealth of Virginia is rich in history. From the shores of the Atlantic to the foothills of the Appalachians, hundreds, perhaps thousands, of years of events have left their imprint on the landscape. Some are well known, but Virginia also has hidden enigmas that have been overlooked by the public and some investigators. It's up to the crew at *Weird Virginia* to uncover the lost wonders of this very special state.

Fairy Crosses

Charles Fort, the American intellectual writer and pursuer of the Weird, gave us the word Fortean to cover all matter of unexplained phenomena. Fort had a special interest in Virginia. The state produced a wealth of objects that fascinated him, one of which he described in his *Book of the Damned*, chapter 12.

"Near the point where the Blue Ridge and the Allegheny Mountains unite, north of Patrick County, Virginia, many little stone crosses have been found. . . ." The crosses were made, Fort suggested, by a race of tiny beings. "Exquisite beings . . . in their diminutive way they were human beings."

The objects Charles Fort was discussing are called staurolites by geologists but are better known to the general public as fairy stones or fairy crosses. They are tiny naturally formed crosses, long regarded by mountain folk as powerful talismans. In the May 19, 1906, edition of *Harper's Weekly,* we are told that the fairy stones range in weight from one-quarter of an ounce to an ounce, but an earlier article in *Scientific American* (December 17, 1898) said that some of them are no larger than the head of a pin. They seem to appear in three basic forms—Roman, Maltese, and St. Andrews, as if depending on the whim of their tiny creators.

Forty-four miles west of Martinsville, fairy stones are found in a fifty-acre field on the top of Bull Mountain in Patrick County. It was the Bull Mountain appearances that Fort was mostly familiar with, but other nearby discoveries of the fairy crosses have also been made. One source for the tiny crosses is Fairy Stone State Park, eighteen miles northwest of Martinsville. In 1933, Junius B. Fishburn, former owner of the *Roanoke Times*, donated the 4,537 acres that make up the park today. The Depression era's Civilian Conservation Corps dug its lake and created much of the infrastructure still being used there. The park's natural beauty and outdoor recreational prospects, in addition to its rare mineral crosses, make it a regional favorite.

Legend of the Fairy Stone

Fairy Stone State Park's literature and Web site share the following story about the origin of the little crosses.

Many hundreds of years before Chief Powhatan's reign, fairies were dancing around a spring of water, playing with naiads and wood nymphs, when an elfin messenger arrived from a city far away. He brought news of the death of Christ. When these creatures of the forest heard the story of the Crucifixion, they wept. As their tears fell upon the earth, they crystallized to form beautiful crosses.

For many years people held these little crosses in superstitious awe, firm in the belief that they protected the wearer against witchcraft, sickness, accidents and disaster. Fairy stones are staurolite, a combination of silica, iron and aluminum. Staurolite crystallizes at 60 or 90-degree angles, hence the stone's cross-like structure. Found only in rocks once subjected to great heat and pressure, the mineral was formed long, long ago, during the rise of the Appalachian Mountains. The stones are most commonly shaped like St. Andrew's cross, an "X," but "T" shaped Roman crosses and square Maltese crosses are the most sought-after.

Fortean writer Ivan Sanderson (*Pursuit*, April 1971) accepted the staurolite analysis and minimized the idea that there was anything more to the crosses than that they were so-called penetration twins, where two crystal bars have randomly intergrown at crossed angles. However, Charles Fort was not so sure that all of the crosses were of the same mineral composition. Whatever their origin, Fortean investigators today understand the rarity of the "fairy crosses" and Fort's fascination with them is enough to capture their attention.

The crosses are said to be most potent if you find them yourself. The lucky person who stumbles on one of the little fairy stones will have a talisman for warding off evil, bringing good luck, and enhancing love. However, sinister things happen to those who lose their fairy crosses, and owners should treat them carefully. While purchased crosses are said to be less special, there is a thriving business in fairy crosses in the Blue Mountain area.

Natural Chimneys

If there were a book called *Thoroughly Odd Items Not Generally Associated with Virginia,* Natural Chimneys in Mt. Solon would be one of its main features. The weird formations are a rare eastern example of a western mainstay. That they achieve this uncommon feat in a rocky package of mystery and raw beauty comes as mere icing on the cake. Truth is, you'd be wasting your time to look for anything remotely like these strange chimneys anywhere else in the state.

So just what are natural chimneys? Well, in geologic terms, these turretlike towers are remnants from the Paleozoic Era. And less technically, they resemble chimneys when viewed from afar. Each is composed of sediment-based layers of limestone that have been pushed upward for well over 500 million years. But this only accounts for the physical makeup of the towers and not the odd feelings that they sometimes bring to those who stand beneath them.

There are seven towers in all, ranging in height from 65 to 120 feet. On a bright, sunny day, they instill feelings of warmth, grandeur, and majesty to those fortunate enough to gaze upon them. Perhaps for this reason, the medieval-fortress-like Natural Chimneys are flanked by a sea of campsites, with the warmer seasons finding scores of happy people flitting merrily beneath them. To add to the weirdness, the tower to the extreme left of the grouping (when viewed head-on) is canted some thirteen and a half feet from vertical, an angle that precisely equates with Italy's Leaning Tower of Pisa.

Taking advantage of the amphitheatre-like setting, jousting competitions have long been held here. One annual contest staged each August traces back to 1821, which makes it North America's oldest by a wide margin. Today's jousters take aim at innocuous steel rings, not people, which we suppose is far more civilized if not nearly as much fun to observe.

In stark contrast to its sunny days, the Natural Chimneys assume a different mood as dusk arrives, particularly when the tourists retreat for the day. Then, under subdued light, the deserted turrets take on a rather unsettling appearance as they turn from white to a deathlike gray in hue. This scary phenomenon is increased by stories of ghosts and the like, with the most prevalent one being a headless knight returning to exact revenge on a victorious rival in a long ago jousting contest. Still, Natural Chimneys are odd enough all by their lonesome, with or without such ghostly attachments. Majesty by day, terror by night—what's not to like?

Natural Bridge

Once owned by none other than Thomas Jefferson, present-day Natural Bridge and its surrounding acreage are now a thriving privately held tourist venture in west-central Virginia. A naturally occurring phenomenon, this baby is 215 feet tall. That means you can fit the entire Statue of Liberty beneath it (less its pedestal) and still have sixty-four feet of air swimming between it and the bridge! At night, there is a sound-and-light show that uses Natural Bridge's stone walls as its backdrop. Since the place is spooky enough at night, this interplay enhances the fear factor tenfold as shadows and nuances in the rock can easily be mistaken for hobgoblins and the like. Go alone on a starless and moonless night, and every flicker of light will make you think that you've seen a ghost.

But maybe the weirdest thing of all is that this place has graffiti done by none other than George Washington, the Father of our Country. To explain, it seems ol' George made himself a tidy living in his pre-general/presidential days by performing land surveys. Apparently he was asked to do such a survey here, and when he finished, he "signed" his work by chiseling his initials into the wall directly beneath the Natural Bridge. His mark is still visible in the rock today! The fact that these initials sit some twenty feet up the stone wall speaks mightily to Washington's physical prowess and agility.

Clarksville Ancient Ironworks

For those who know guns, the name Griffin & Howe may be familiar. The company is recognized as having produced some of the finest sporting rifles ever built in America and provided celebrities like Teddy Roosevelt and Ernest Hemingway with their hunting and safari needs during the heyday of such treks. Griffin & Howe was once associated with Abercrombie & Fitch Co., which today is more known for cool suburban adolescent clothing than it is for its past safari outfitting.

The "Howe" in the name was James V. Howe, the cofounder of the company and a Virginia machinist turned firearms metalworker. In his later years, he developed a deep interest in history, especially in finding traces of those ancient metalworkers who had come before him.

It was back in the 1940s and '50s when James V. Howe began finding ancient iron workings around his farm homestead near the Roanoke River at Jeffress. Looking farther afield, Howe found other ironworks fifty miles to the east, in Brunswick County. The site near his home, which he found initially, became known as the Clarksville Ancient Ironworks. The ironworks he found there would stir debates for decades.

In the ancient ironworks he was exploring, Howe discovered a variety of items, including threaded nuts, chisels, swords, and other weapons. In addition to the iron items, Howe recovered a number of bronze objects. His find caused him some puzzlement because bronze is an alloy of copper and tin, and these metals are not indigenous to this area. So he acknowledged that the metals found in the bronze must have been brought from someplace else to this ironworks.

The area itself shows other signs of strangeness.

Local author John W. Tisdale, owner of the Rosseechee Manor House in Clarksville, has penned in his local historical pamphlets various curiosities about the surroundings. These include the fact that near where Howe found his ancient ironworks items there was a "barren acre" — where nothing would grow — near the now flooded town of Springfield. Also, it was here local residents found two odd stone objects in the shape of Maltese crosses.

The discovery of the Clarksville Ancient Ironworks was met with a dazzling display of entrenchment tactics from establishment archaeology. Howe was mystified by his findings, but he was downright outraged and flabbergasted by what institutions that he invited to help him explain the find did or, rather, didn't do.

In 1951, the Smithsonian Institution conducted an elementary dig at the site. The specialists from the District of Columbia found various pieces, and yet refused to perform any carbon-14 dating. Howe experienced the same thing, over and over again, when he asked other researchers to date materials. The artifacts from these ironworks, including a fantastic bronze cup, continue to rest unstudied at the Smithsonian. Their fate is one of being ignored on a shelf, labeled "Origin Uncertain."

In his book *They All Discovered America*, historian and amateur archaeologist Charles M. Boland noted that the Clarksville bronze cup is almost identical to the Roman Pompeian cups displayed in Italy's Museum of Naples.

Today, forty-five feet of water covers the area of these remarkable findings. James V. Howe's original site is beneath water. More than fifty years after its discovery, it is neglected as much as that amazing bronze cup that was turned over to the Smithsonian.

The artifacts from these ironworks, including a fantastic bronze cup, continue to rest unstudied at the Smithsonian.

Ancient Romans in Virginia?

The artifacts found at the Clarksville Ancient Ironworks force us to ask, did the Romans once pay a visit to Virginia? Or have collectors from the 17th and 18th centuries lost or buried items that are confusing the picture? The puzzle becomes more complex as we travel about the state and see that other Roman objects have been found.

But first a note about locations involved in this story. By 1634, the English colony of Virginia consisted of eight shires, or counties, with one being Elizabeth City Shire, which included an area on both sides of Hampton Roads. The northern portion is now incorporated into the independent city of Hampton. In September 1833, as cited by Fortean researcher Jim Brandon, workers were boring for water near "Elizabeth" (an area perhaps located in present-day Hampton). Thirty feet below the surface, they discovered what appeared to be a Roman coin.

The coin, about the size of a modern American quarter, was oval and it was not familiar to local residents. Historian W. S. Forest said the characters pictured on the coin appeared to be Roman, like a hunter or warrior. Brandon noted that similar out-of-place finds of such Roman coins have occurred in San Luis Obispo, CA; Boise, ID; and Peoria County, IL.

Origins of the Great Dismal Swamp

The Great Dismal Swamp is a marshy wetland that goes from Norfolk, located on the Elizabeth River, through southeastern Virginia's Coastal Plain into northeastern North Carolina. It has been known as a miniversion of the Bermuda Triangle, on the level of other states' mystery triangles, like the Coudersport Triangle (linked to the Black Forest) in Pennsylvania or the Bridgewater Triangle (aligned with the Hockomock Swamp) in Massachusetts. Reports of ancient mysteries, as well as sightings of giant snakes and Bigfoot, have been associated with the Great Dismal Swamp.

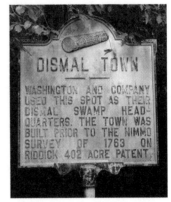

The discoverer of the Great Dismal Swamp is lost in time, but archaeological finds indicate that humans have been here for about 13,000 years. William Drummond, a future governor of North Carolina, was the first European to explore the lake—the highest point in the Great Dismal Swamp—to which he gave his name.

Lake Drummond, a strange oval of water on top of a hill, is one of only two natural lakes in Virginia, and it conceals mysteries that still baffle scientists today. How it was created is unknown. Is it the result of a giant meteorite? Was it made by a large underground peat burn about six thousand years ago? The local First Nations have their own explanation. They have a tradition that says Lake Drummond is the work of a phoenixlike creature, the Fire Bird.

What's Buried in Bacon's Secret Crypt?

A *secret crypt*, said to be buried near a local church in Williamsburg, may hold answers to an old mystery and plans for a new world order. The hidden crypt is supposedly located next to the Bruton Parish Episcopal Church, today to be found in the restored tourist area of Colonial Williamsburg. The only problem is that although it's been around since the late 1600s and has been actively sought since 1938, no one has found it. Most of the background for the hidden vault tales comes from Marie Bauer Hall's book, *Foundations Unearthed*. Her husband was Manley Palmer Hall, a famous 33rd-degree Mason, author, lecturer, and mystic. His most famous book is *The Secret Teachings of All Ages: An Encyclopedic Outline of Masonic, Hermetic, Qabbalistic and Rosicrucian Symbolical Philosophy* (1928).

Marie Hall writes that the secret vault is a ten-foot cubicle, buried sixteen feet below the cemetery of the Bruton Parish Church, which sits right on the main street of this restored area of the city. You don't need a treasure map for this one. She writes that the crypt is to be found ninety feet northwest of the church's door and ten feet west of the grave marker of Ann Frank, the wife of Graham Frank. The name itself is a clue, as "Ann Graham" is a hint to the fact that anagrams lead to this treasure.

Marie Bauer Hall received permission in 1938 to dig in the churchyard, but found nothing. Her desire to conduct deeper excavations was forestalled by Williamsburg and Episcopal Church officials, and so the crypt, if it exists, sits undiscovered.

What is the secret vault reported to contain? The contents are not minor trinkets, please note. Hall wrote that the crypt held the master plan for nothing less than a new world order, the answer to who really wrote Shakespeare's plays (it was Sir Francis Bacon), some plays written by Bacon, and, last but not least, a map of other secret Rosicrucian vaults throughout Europe filled with other similar all-telling documents.

Hall believed the secret crypt was buried there by Nathaniel Bacon in 1676, preceding Bacon's Rebellion, the first uprising by the colonists against the British in America. The causes of the unrest were poor economic conditions, made harsher by an uncanny series of natural disasters including floods, hailstorms, drought, and hurricanes that left Virginia reeling.

For a short time, Nathaniel Bacon was actually in charge of Virginia, but it all ended on October 26, 1676, when he suddenly died of the "Bloodie Flux" and "Lousey Disease" (body lice). According to what is known today, Bacon's rebel supporters burned his body and it was never found, very much reflecting the fate of his secret vault.

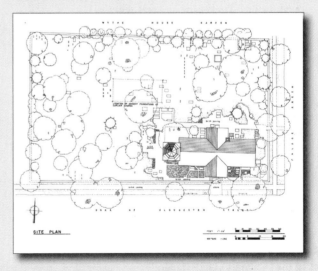

The crypt is to be found ninety feet northwest of the church's door and ten feet west of the grave marker of Ann Frank.

Riddle of the Beale Ciphers

One of Virginia's stranger stories issues from around Roanoke, specifically in the rolling hills between Lynchburg and Roanoke. It is a tale that keeps treasure seekers coming back to the area. Is there gold hidden away there? And what does it have to do with the mysterious Beale Ciphers?

Most of the information on the Beale Ciphers, or Beale Cryptograms—as puzzling today as they were over a hundred years ago—comes down to us from a single pamphlet published in 1885 entitled "The Beale Papers."

The story goes that the treasure was buried around 1821, after first being obtained by Thomas Jefferson Beale. In 1822, while in Lynchburg, Beale entrusts his friend Robert Morriss with a small box. Beale says that he's heading out west to hunt wild game, but if he doesn't come back, Morriss should assume that he's dead, and open the box. Beale is never seen again.

Twenty-three years later, in 1845, Morriss opens the box. Inside is a letter from Beale stating that on a trip out west he found thousands of pounds of gold and silver, and buried it in Bedford County, Virginia. Along with the letter are three coded cipher texts, papers with strange numbered sequences scrawled on them. It's a cryptographic code, and Beale's letter states that Morriss must decipher it to find the treasure. Unfortunately, he did not provide the key to the code.

In 1862, Robert Morriss, who presumably had no luck deciphering the codes, passed the cryptographs to his friend James Ward. Ward theorized that the key must be a commonly known document. After trying many documents, he discovered that by numbering each word of the Declaration of Independence in ascending order, then taking the first letter of each numbered word, he could decode a portion of the cryptograms. Ward decoded a few pages, which describe the amazing contents of the treasure. The text of the message, which is technically cypertext #2, reads as follows.

I have deposited in the county of Bedford, about four miles from Buford's, in an excavation or vault, six feet below the surface of the ground, the following articles, belonging jointly to the parties whose names are given in number "3," herewith:

The first deposit consisted of one thousand and fourteen pounds of gold, and three thousand eight hundred and twelve pounds of silver, deposited November 1819. The second was made December, 1821, and consisted of nineteen hundred and seven pounds of gold, and twelve hundred and eighty-eight pounds of silver; also jewels, obtained in St. Louis in exchange for silver to save transportation, and valued at US$13,000.

The above is securely packed in iron pots, with iron covers. The vault is roughly lined with stone, and the vessels rest on solid stone, and are covered with others. Paper number "1" describes the exact locality of the vault, so that no difficulty will be had in finding it.

The problem is that the Declaration *isn't* the key for the section of the cryptograms that describe the *location* of the treasure. No other historical document seemed to work, and Ward got so frustrated trying to solve the cryptograms that he took the mystery public. In 1885, he published *The Beale Papers,* in which he set out the cryptograms and the story of Thomas Beale. For a mere fifty cents, anyone who could decipher the cryptograms had a shot at finding the loot.

But is the story true? Intriguingly, there is no concrete proof that Thomas Beale ever existed. Ward is likewise relatively unknown in local archives. There is some evidence about Morriss, however. According to the *Lynchburg Virginian* of May 21, 1861, one Robert Morriss was the companion or husband of Sarah Morriss, who passed away at the age of seventy-seven. Perhaps Morriss was really "Ward"? Perhaps they merely kept low profiles? Or perhaps the whole thing is a hoax.

In April 1972, Fortean author Jim Brandon tells us, the Beale Ciphers Symposium was held in the Univac Auditorium in Washington, DC. Brandon wrote that "according to Carl Hammer, director of computer sciences at Univac Corporation, two positive facts have been established. The remaining Beale Ciphers are real messages, not hoaxes; and they really are code, of a kind similar to the already translated letter."

Weird Virginia met with computer science professor Clay Shields of Georgetown University to ask him what he thought our chances might be of deciphering the Beale Cryptograms and becoming fabulously wealthy.

Weird Virginia: Professor Shields, what method would one use to decode a message that has no key?

Clay Shields: Most decryption of ciphers of this type depends on the fact that languages use letters in different frequencies. And so what you do is you examine all of the numbers and you look for numbers that repeat. And then based on that, you try to match those repetitions to repetitions in the English language.

WV: How was the code broken for the one Beale cryptogram that was decoded, and by whom?

CS: It was apparently broken by James Ward, the man who published them.

WV: And how did he stumble upon the correlation with the Declaration of Independence?

CS: He said that he tried to solve it for twenty years, and eventually got around to trying that. And there's one little problem with his decryption, which is the copy of the Declaration of Independence that he printed in his pamphlet wasn't quite correct. But it turns out whoever encrypted it made exactly the same mistakes. When they numbered the words as he did.

There's also a few things in the letters that are slightly off. Mostly words that hadn't appeared in the English language when they were supposedly written, but *were* in common use by 1885 (when the pamphlet was published). Like the words "improvise" and "stampede," two words that weren't in common use in the 1820s but showed up in Beale's letters which were dated then.

WV: So do you believe there ever was any treasure?

CS: I think it was a hoax. I'd love for someone to prove me wrong and show up with a couple of tons of precious metal to laugh in my face. But I don't think it's going to happen. But if you go online, you can find people that will sell you software that will help you decrypt these.

Of course you have to ask yourself, if the people selling this code-cracking software know how to decipher the ciphers, then why don't they just figure out the location of the treasure and go dig it up for themselves?

A Hoax Perpetrated by Edgar Allan Poe

The title "The Beale Papers" contains the letters EAP twice, which is well known. I have noticed that in the decoded number 2 cipher, as it starts out "I hAvE dEPOsited in the county of [etc.]" there is I EA POE, and in the first word of the last sentence "PApEr number one describes the . . .", there is the EAP thing again.

I think Poe created this Beale story as the greatest hoax he ever wrote and somehow it got published at the later date. Like ole George Burns used to say, "It might not be a true story, but it's true that it's been a good story."

P.S. The location is not in Virginia! The location, true or FALSE, as stated in the cipher is a little farther north and west of Virginia.—*Solobear*

Fabled People and Places

here are people and places in this world that may exist, or they may not. We all know about that mysterious location somewhere over the horizon, but no one has directions to it. Or that odd person your friend's cousin's friend knows, but both cousin's friend and the odd person can't be precisely located. Legends and rumors spread and become so extensive that truth is hard to separate from myth.

Other fabled places — or people -- definitely exist, or once did, but for one reason or another, their storied past has become so legendary that it is hard to decipher where their true history ends and myth begins. In some cases the truth is stranger, and harder to swallow, than the fiction.

This chapter is dedicated to those places and people -- the ones that many have heard about but few have actually seen for themselves. The places and people with a past, or even a present, that is so secretive or shameful or fantastic that the stories seem unbelievable. But don't be too quick to write them off as mere tall tales or conspiracy theories. Some of them are all too true!

The Melungeons: Lost Tribe of Appalachia?

We all learned the story of the discovery of the "New World" in grade school history classes. Jamestown was mentioned; Plymouth Rock was covered in spades. But the elementary school version of our nation's history overlooks some of the most interesting stories in our collective heritage. For example, it does not explain the existence of European-influenced settlements that may have existed before Jamestown and Plymouth Rock. Nor does it account for the people who inhabited them—the Melungeons.

Who, or what, are the Melungeons, you ask. That is a question that has left many historians scratching their heads for years.

As early settlers and explorers ventured farther westward into North America, they encountered isolated bands of people living in desolate areas in the Appalachian Mountains where modern Virginia, North Carolina, and Tennessee converge. These people identified themselves as Melungeons. These local inhabitants were not Europeans, nor were they Native Americans, although they displayed features suggestive of both races. They spoke broken English, and in some cases, Elizabethan English, mixed with Indian dialects. Physically, they varied in appearance. Many had the dark skin of Native Americans, but some had red hair or blue eyes. They grew beards like Europeans and lived not in Native American–style dwellings, but in log cabins. They were regarded as a tri-racial isolate. All that could be said for certain was that there were various bloodlines— Caucasian, African, and Native American—present within the population.

The question of who these people were then, and are today, has never been fully answered. Besides the general lack of recorded facts regarding their origins, family histories were often intentionally hidden or obscured by the reclusive Melungeons. And for good reason. In the South, where racial antagonism ran high, Melungeons were considered people of color. Many families hid their Melungeon ancestry to retain the rights to own land and vote. These practices further obscured the already cloudy history of these mysterious people.

One popular theory has it that the Melungeons were the descendants of the settlers of the Lost Colony of Roanoke. The story of Roanoke is a famous one. Settled at roughly the same time as Jamestown, the colony thrived for a few years. Then, seemingly without explanation, every member of the colony simply vanished. The search party that discovered the disappearance found the word "Croatoan" carved into a tree at the abandoned settlement and assumed the pilgrims had fled to the Croatoan Indian tribe nearby. Efforts to locate them, however, were unsuccessful, and their fate remains unknown to this day. Some speculation has it that they fled to the Appalachian Mountains and the Melungeons are their descendants.

Another theory says that the Melungeons are the survivors of the wreck of a Portuguese ship that disappeared in the 1700s. Early records say that the Melungeons claimed they were "Portyghee." Some believe that these Portuguese sailors fled to the mountains after the shipwreck and formed a society with Native Americans and runaway slaves. Many popular Melungeon surnames could conceivably have once been Portuguese: Brogan could have been Braganza, Mullins could have been Mollen, etc.

The origin of the term *Melungeon,* which was considered derogatory until the late 20th century, is disputed as much as the people's ancestry. Some believe it could be derived from the Afro-Portuguese word *melungo,* which means shipmate. Others say that it might

first New World settlements. They say that groups of Carthaginians fled their homeland when it fell to Rome in 146 B.C. Some may have crossed the Strait of Gibraltar into Portugal and continued their flight, eventually winding up in Appalachia. This theory is supported by the existence of a stone tablet found in Brazil in 1872 that chronicles the landing of a ship there in 531 B.C.

In his book *The Melungeons: The Resurrection of a Proud People: An Untold Story of Ethnic Cleansing in America,* author Brent Kennedy suggests that Portuguese sailors brought Turkish slaves to America in the 1500s, who then took up with female Cherokee Indians— resulting in the first Melungeons. He also asserts that Abraham Lincoln, Elvis Presley, and Ava Gardner may have had Melungeon blood. Unfortunately, Kennedy, who says he is part Melungeon himself, offers little in the way of hard evidence to support his claims, and critics have charged that his research is based more on the prevailing mythology of the Melungeons than on any historical facts.

Like the so-called "Jackson Whites" or Ramapo Mountain people of New Jersey and New York, the Melungeons have struggled for years to be recognized as a unique and distinct culture of Indian descent but of mixed ethnicity. These days many southern families can trace their heritage back to some vestige of Melungeon connection. There are some unique genetic traits that are said to be dead giveaways

be a version of the French word *mélange,* meaning mix, or the Turkish *melun jinn,* meaning cursed soul.

But perhaps the Melungeons have even more of a right to be here than we do. Some historians have theorized that they were on this continent for more than a thousand years before what we consider to be the

There are some unique genetic traits that are said to be dead giveaways of Melungeon ancestry: a curvature of their front teeth into a shovel-like formation, a lump on the back of the head . . . and an occasional sixth finger on one or both of the hands.

of Melungeon ancestry: a condition known as shovel teeth, a curvature of their front teeth into a shovel-like formation, a lump on the back of the head known as a cranial ridge, and an occasional sixth finger on one or both of the hands.

Though in the past there may have been a stigma attached to those of Melungeon descent, today there are communities with Melungeon populations who celebrate their unique heritage and culture. Some, it is said, still speak a hybrid version of Elizabethan English, centuries after the tongue died out elsewhere.

History books and grade school lessons may be telling us only half the story. It's possible that the history of the first true European settlers in what would one day become America can be traced back to the mysterious people known as Melungeons.

In 2001, Melungeon scholar Brent Kennedy teamed up with British DNA expert Dr. Kevin Jones to study the DNA of over a hundred people claiming to be of Melungeon heritage. In the course of making their hit show "Weird U.S." for the History Channel, Mark Moran and Mark Sceurman had an opportunity to speak with Brent and Kevin about their research.

Mark Moran: Brent, how did you get involved with tracing the lineage of the Melungeon bloodline?

Brent Kennedy: Well, growing up in these mountains, it didn't take a genius to figure out that my family had a different ethnic look than the Scots Irish and the English that they were supposed to be. Things of that nature. Other genetic work that I've been involved in set me off in the late '80s and '90s to figure out who I was and also possibly, if I could, who and what a Melungeon is.

MM: So how did you go about conducting your research?

Kevin Jones: Members of the Melungeon population donated either hair or cheek cell samples, from which it is very easy to get their DNA. The results showed that the Melungeons did reflect a multiracial heritage. There is Native American,

African American, as well as European ancestry. Perhaps the most interesting thing is that some people's ancestry appears to reflect a non–Northern European origin and possibly a Mediterranean, Turkish, Indian-subcontinent ancestry.

Mark Sceurman: Have there been any famous Melungeons coming out of this heritage?

BK: Yeah, I think there have been a lot of famous Melungeons, but the reality is that as Melungeons and their descendants moved westward and went with the expanding nation, there are probably a lot of Americans in all walks of life descended from Melungeons whether they know it or not.

MM: Closet Melungeons!

BK: Yes, and many of them are starting to come out of the closet.

Midgetville: A Cadre of Little People in Vienna?

One of the most enduring archetypes in world mythology is the idea that small people inhabit secret pockets of the earth, separate from the world of average-sized people. The Irish tell stories of Leprechauns. Native Hawaiians speak of the Menehune. It's hard to find a culture with a rich tradition of folklore that does not have a legend or two about a diminutive group of people.

The modern folklore of the United States is no different—although this mythology deals not with leprechauns or fairies, but actual little *people*. There are dozens of sites across the country purported to be enclaves of homes inhabited only by little people (or midgets, to the less politically correct). Stories abound, saying that these temperamental tinies separate themselves from everyday society and construct small homes on their own scale, where they can live on their own terms. Long Island has Tinkertown, Utah has Hobbitville, Maryland and Delaware share Zoobieville, and Virginia has Midgetville.

We first heard about the existence of Midgetville in VA when we received this short but sweet letter many years ago:

> I'm from Arlington, VA. In high school we all knew about 'Midgetville,' where a bunch of rich, retired midget actors from "Wizard of Oz" built a completely scaled down neighborhood of suburban excellence.
>
> But since building the town in an isolated, hard-to-find place, the residents had gone insane and their inbred children had insatiable desires for mischief and blood. They wait in the trees in front of their home and jump down on lost motorists and bite their eyes. —*Dyna Moe*

After hearing this, we couldn't resist learning all we could about our state's Midgetville. What we found were stories of a fabled, strange, and ultimately beloved place.

The basics of the story are as follows: In Vienna, there is a small area off Cedar Road upon which stand a number of houses that are remarkably small. These houses, the stories say, were built *by* little people *for* little people. Some say they were *Wizard of Oz* actors, others claim they were formerly traveling performers with the Ringling Brothers Circus. Regardless, after years of derision and scorn, some group of little people chose to construct homes and a neighborhood on their own scale—smaller houses, lower doorknobs and countertops, and so on. And they attempted to build their neighborhood in seclusion to avoid the prying eyes of the "normals." Still, people sought them out to gawk, mock,

or taunt them. As the story goes, this insular society decided to defend itself, and unruly visitors are met with a shock when the area's little inhabitants fight back by hopping into their cars and chasing the invaders out, throwing rocks at them, or even firing guns at them. Through the past few decades, it has become a rite of passage for Virginia teenagers to spend weekend nights seeking out Midgetville.

In truth, Midgetville is an area of dirt roads and gravel paths upon which stand a group of peculiarly small cabins. Apparently the current owners are trying to sell the property to developers, who would knock down the little houses and erect condos. Community activists are attempting to block this move, saying that the cottages sit in a historic district.

A Local Fills in the Details on Midgetville

Along Northern Virginia's Old Dominion trail (formerly the Old Dominion train line) are nearly 15 houses on the remaining 14 acres of the Wedderburn Estate that are rumored to have housed retired and ailing little people, former circus performers. The houses, which now stand in ruin, are no larger than a typical one-car garage, yet they have a far more elaborate floor plan. Each consists of a living room, kitchen, and bedroom spread across two floors. Each tiny house is equipped with a wood-burning stove, and although the apparent midget commune is long deserted, the smell of burning wood still lingers in the air.

How did these mysterious houses become associated with circus midgets? Legend has it that in 1892, the Bailey family of Ringling Brothers and Barnum and Bailey Circus fame, who owned several hundred acres of neighboring land (now named Bailey's Crossroads on behalf of the family) commissioned newspaper tycoon A. J. Wedderburn to build the tiny houses as a retirement facility for circus-performing little people. The houses are buried in the thick woods of the area, and Bailey thought this secluded area a fine place for the little people to escape the jeers and mockery of society. It was here that the midgets lived peacefully for many years, until the area became more and more populated and their hiding place was stumbled upon by common folk more frequently.

Several generations of little people are rumored to have lived in these appropriately sized houses after the original Barnum and Bailey retirees left. Sometime in the late 1970s, the tenants decided that the jeers of many a high school student were too much for them and hired some security—a mentally handicapped gentleman with a shotgun who would chase and threaten trespassers. Although this midget guardian no longer guards the now boarded-up houses, the rocking chair post where he spent many of his days still sits on one of Midgetville's tiny front porches.

In 2004, rumors that the Wedderburn land would be developed into multimillion-dollar town homes were thrown around; but today, no development signs can be seen on the estate. Although several of the locals who live in the surrounding areas deny the legends of Midgetville, there is no denying that the grove of tiny houses certainly is mysterious and filled with the untold secrets of the past.—*Melody Johnson, Falls Church*

Legend has it that in 1892, the Bailey family of circus fame commissioned A. J. Wedderburn to build the tiny houses as a retirement facility for circus-performing little people.

She's Seen the Midgets!

I've been to Midgetville plenty of times . . . mostly on bored high school nights. The majority of the times that I went there, what I found was a desolate, eerily quiet neighborhood of little homes—but not much else. To my joy and surprise, going in the day once yielded better results. I kid you not when I say that I saw from a distance a family of midgets sitting in lawn chairs outside of their home. Needless to say, when I approached closer, they disappeared into their house. So I never got an up close and personal look and never had a conversation with them, but I can vouch firsthand for the fact that at least at one point, some midgets did call Midgetville home.—*Anita Jameson*

Mentally Challenged Caretaker Protects His Little Friends

The scariest story I heard relating to Midgetville had nothing to do with midgets—it had to do with the crazy, psycho, mentally retarded security guard they hired and entrusted with their lives. From what I understand, they employed him with one job—to keep the curious away. He looked at the midgets not just as his employers, but as his friends—so when people would bother them, coming through late at night flashing their high beams and honking their horns, he saw it as his duty to protect his little buddies. This has led to many stories of people being roughed up, attacked, and scared s---less. I think a lot of people go to Midgetville laughing, thinking that if trouble hits they can handle a few little people. Not many reckon for a run in with a mentally unstable, highly volatile security guard who will go to any length to stop them!—*Joe Bee*

Military Myths and Mysteries

Because of the close proximity of the state to our nation's capital, Virginia is an epicenter for rumors of clandestine activities carried out by various sneaky agencies of our government. Numerous sites here are said to house more than meets the naked eye. To name a few . . .

The Shadow Government

What would happen if the unthinkable occurred, a nuclear weapon dropped on Washington, DC, our nation's capital? If the bulk of our nation's legislators were wiped out in one fell swoop, how could the federal government survive?

For decades, stories spread that there was a "shadow government" located just outside the area that might be affected by such a nuclear strike. It was said that this mysterious phantom bureaucracy was located on a secret military base somewhere in Virginia, and that each day, dozens of people reported to work there. These people represented facets of the federal government, but they were essentially dummies—exercising no power, but maintaining operations on a daily basis in case an all-out disaster decimated the federal government and its leaders.

While it seems impossible that such a large-scale operation could go on for years in secrecy, in recent years it has come to light that such an operation is, in fact, in existence, and has been for some time. A 1991 CNN report was the first to bring the project, which is known as the "continuity of government" plan, to light. In researching government waste, CNN stumbled upon something known as the National Program Office. This innocuous moniker was the name for the organization in charge of administrating what was in effect a shadow government.

The Constitution and legislation have defined a chain of command for ascendancy to the United States presidency. If the President dies, he is succeeded by the Vice President. If the Vice President has died as well, the Speaker of the House of Representatives assumes the presidency. After the Speaker of the House, the President pro tempore of the United States Senate is in line. From there, a clear-cut guide exists of which Cabinet members should lay claim to the presidency in the case of a disaster.

The National Program Office's shadow government was created by executive order and works outside the boundaries of the United States Constitution. It lays out a plan in which a President can simply be instated in the government's highest office in the case of disaster, superseding any chain of command laid out through previous legislation. If this plan was ever implemented, Congress itself would be dissolved and without power until further notice. This would allow the government to continue seamlessly in the face of a massive disaster,

most specifically a nuclear strike, without wasting any time sorting out who from the established chain of command was still alive and available to run the country.

These accounts of the shadow government strike fear in some, but they seem logical to others. Most of its structure was established during the Reagan administration, when President Reagan signed a secret order in 1982. It was reported that the programs relating to the shadow government had been largely dismantled after the Clinton administration deemed it unnecessary due to the end of the Cold War. The events of September 11, 2001, proved otherwise.

The shadow government was activated for the first time in its history by President George W. Bush after the events of September 11, 2001. A March 2002 *Washington Post* article detailed how over 100 civilian employees were stationed in secret government bases outside of Washington in the event of further terrorist attacks.

According to that *Post* article: "The civilian cadre present in the bunkers usually numbers 70 to 150, and 'fluctuates based on intelligence' about terrorist threats, according to a senior official involved in managing the program. It draws from every Cabinet department and some independent agencies. Its first mission, in the event of a disabling blow to Washington, would be to prevent the collapse of essential government functions.

"Assuming command of regional federal offices, officials said, the underground government would try to contain disruptions of the nation's food and water supplies, transportation links, energy and telecommunications networks, public health and civil order. Later it would begin to reconstitute the government."

It's a safe bet that few Americans realize there is a group hidden away in bunkers ready to go to work should the government become temporarily disabled.

Mount Pony

Security purposes will never allow the location of current shadow government bases to be accurately determined, but one former base was right here in Virginia, at Mount Pony in Culpeper. At first glance, the peaceful landscape here seems interchangeable with just about any other in its downright normality. Yet it is in Culpeper that the Federal Reserve chose to shield a bundle of cash from nuclear attack.

Despite the probability that thousands, perhaps millions, would be wiped from the face of the earth if nuclear madness came to pass, we Americans, ever the scheming optimists, saw fit to draw up contingency plans. Assuming *some* people would live through the initial conflagration, ever-ballooning radiation cloud, and frigid nuclear winter, our intelligentsia further reasoned that this brave new society would need some hard cash to jump-start things. On December 10, 1969, these forward thinkers made a huge deposit under a section of lush Virginia farmland. And just in case you're wondering, we're *not* talking fertilizer!

One hundred feet longer than a football field and impervious to such pesky things as nuclear airbursts and encroaching radiation, Mount Pony's bunker was put at the ready. Lead-lined throughout and covered with up to four feet of coddling mother earth, the installation soon played host to its star attraction: a one-*billion*-dollar store of folding U.S. currency. Now that's what we call a payload of post-nuke seed money.

While the money vault of Mount Pony was an impressive 23,000 square feet, the facility itself was an even more impressive 140,000 square feet. A large portion of this base was dedicated to serving as a continuance of government. The base was equipped to house, feed, and clothe up to 540 people for thirty days. A set of lead-lined radiation-proof shutters could close off the base from the

surface in just a few seconds, allowing those 540 people to live radiation-free during their stay there (unless they wound up in an above-ground cold-storage facility, rumored to be used to keep radiation-contaminated bodies on-site).

Things went quietly at Mount Pony until 1988, when a decision to remove the cash was reached. Whether or not the soon-to-collapse Soviet Union (long our chief adversary) played a part in this, we can't say, but one thing's for certain: Culpeper's net worth went down quickly, and a brave new era in weirdness had come to an abrupt halt.

PRIVATE PROPERTY
NO TRESPASSING

NO
Solicitation

In 1997, the facility was handed over lock, stock, and bunker to the Library of Congress. Their future plan involves the safe storage of priceless motion picture, television, and recorded-sound collections. It's a worthwhile proposition even if the bunker's bounty won't be nearly as sexy this time around.

Mount Weather

While Mount Pony has been decommissioned, Virginians shouldn't fear that they are being left out of the secret government game. One of the sites believed to be a currently active "continuance of government" unit is Mount Weather in Bluemont.

The aboveground sections of Mount Weather are home to offices of the Federal Emergency Management Agency. It's said that below the surface of this base is a huge facility that could serve as the home base for the White House itself in the event of an attack on Washington. Mount Weather and a facility known as Raven Rock in Waynesboro, PA, are considered sister facilities designed to house the executive branch of the government. In the event of a catastrophe, another nearby military base in PA will send helicopters to evacuate White House officials and immediately bring them to Raven Rock and Mount Weather.

Mount Weather was code named High Point

West Portal

Main Support Compound

H-3 Presidential Helicopter

Mount Weather Special Facility

East Portal

during the Eisenhower administration, when it is believed to have been established. According to one *TIME* magazine article, the director of Mount Weather was given a stern directive from Eisenhower himself upon its establishment: "I expect your people to save our government," he said. The mountain on which the military base stands is rumored to be almost entirely hollowed out and is large enough inside to contain an entire city, including a subway, system of roads, and sidewalks. It is widely believed that Mount Weather is where Vice President Dick Cheney took refuge after the attacks of September 11, 2001. Many conspiracy theorists' suspicions of Mount Weather were given some validation on 9/11 when a line of government cars, limousines, and police vehicles made their way from Washington directly to—Mount Weather.

Stations A and B, Warrenton

Warrenton is home to two military bases that are shrouded in secrecy. Known only as Station A and Station B, their true use remains unknown and speculated upon by many.

Both stations are operated by an unknown federal agency. Station A is on Route 802, while Station B is on Bear Wallow Road. These roads are only a few miles apart on Viewtree Mountain. Many electronic and communications devices are visible at both bases, but their specific purpose is unknown. The grouping of stations is known as the Warrenton Training Center.

Theories abound about what happens at the bases and, more pertinently, underneath them. Their close proximity to each other has led to speculation that they are connected underground, and that a sprawling underground complex has been carved into the mountain.

While even the existence of this underground facility is unverified, conspiracy theorists have guessed that it may be a research facility dedicated to UFOs and alien life. Although the veil of secrecy surrounding the Warrenton stations may mean we will never know the truth, it is a fascinating theory.

The Spooks of Langley

Langley is a small community, technically a part of McLean, that serves as a commuter base for those who work in Washington, DC. It is also the headquarters of the Central Intelligence Agency, the CIA, an organization to which conspiracy theorists have attached hundreds of stories. Some of these stories are outright fantasy, but some are much truer than we'd like to believe. And some of the strangest tales are set right in the heart of Langley.

Many rumors revolve around the seven subterranean levels that are said to exist beneath the town. Supposedly, the experiments carried out in Langley's subterranean base, which was rechristened the George Bush Center for Intelligence in 1999, revolve around using mind control. We can't say whether these rumors are true or not, but there is historical precedence for the Central Intelligence Agency performing similar experiments in the past. One example of this was Project MKULTRA, a sinister program started in 1953. Dozens of drugs were tested in this program. At one point, a plan was even developed with the aim of drugging Fidel Castro to gain control of his mind and overthrow his regime. In 1972, the CIA ordered that many documents regarding MKULTRA be destroyed, so to this day, specifics regarding the program are scarce.

Perhaps someday the activities taking place in the underground portions of Langley will come to light. In the meantime, we sent Chris Gethard, one of our writers and photographers, on a photo mission to Langley, wondering if anything weird would show up.

We thought Chris would be smart enough to leave the CIA's main national headquarters off his assignment list. Obviously, this is not the sort of place you can poke around in at will. Well, what Chris lacks in common sense, he makes up for with an adventurous spirit. He filled us in on what happened when he attempted to drive up to the main gate of the CIA.

Don't Visit Langley on Your Own!

I wasn't thinking. I just remembered that when I was a little kid, my parents once took me on a tour of the FBI facility in Quantico. I figured the CIA would have something similar. So one early summer afternoon, I dragged my girlfriend along as we drove out to Langley. As soon as we made the turn into the driveway, I knew I'd made a huge mistake. Signs were posted telling us not to enter, but unfortunately, there was no place to turn around.

I drove up to the gate, where there was a barrier and a loudspeaker. A voice came over and asked me what I was doing there. I didn't know what to say, so I said, "I thought maybe you guys offered tours. I know I shouldn't be here, just tell me where I can turn around." Instead, the voice informed me that I was trespassing on federal property, and that I should drive ahead, park behind the white concrete bunker, roll down the windows, put my hands on the wheel, stay in the car, and not make any sudden movements.

Needless to say, I complied.

Two federal agents walked toward our car. The one guy approached me and again reiterated that I was indeed trespassing on federal property. I apologized, and he collected our licenses. He radioed our names in, as well as the license number of my car. It looked like we were about to get a hefty fine.

Then my girlfriend started saying that she would sweet-talk this guy out of the ticket—that he was a human being and would understand if she could just explain it to him.

I told her it seemed to be a little more serious, and that she should probably look to her right. It was then that she saw the other federal agent holding an M-16 machine gun about a foot away from her face.

After they searched around our car a bit, they let us go with a stern warning, and the advice that we should definitely call ahead before visiting any more federal facilities. Needless to say, I will.—*Chris Gethard*

George Washington Masonic Temple

Stories of Freemasonry and its far-reaching influence have existed for centuries. Some claim that Freemasonry is a simple fraternal organization, not unlike a local Elks club. Others see it as a front for something far more powerful and evil. These people say that upper-level Freemasons form the core of the Illuminati, an organization of the world's power brokers intent on dictating the direction of the world and eventually leading a one-world government themselves.

The Freemasons have supposedly sunk their teeth into the United States government since its very inception. And since Washington, DC, is the capital and northern Virginia is the seat of numerous government agencies and was home to many early leaders of our country, it has long been said that the area is an important center of American Freemasonry.

Adding fuel to the rumors is the fact that the most famous figure in American history is also one of the most famous figures in Masonic history. He is our country's first President, George Washington. Not only was he an avowed Freemason (portraits exist of him sporting his Masonic garb, an apron of which still exists today), he was of such influence that the Washington Masonic Temple in Alexandria is named after him as well.

Located at 101 Callahan Drive in Alexandria, the temple presents itself as an architectural achievement and monument to Washington. Their official Web site, www.gwmemorial.org, states that "the George Washington Masonic National Memorial was constructed entirely with voluntary contributions from members of the Masonic Fraternity. The Memorial Association is the only unified effort of all of the Grand Lodges in the United States. . . . Each Grand Lodge is a sovereign body in its own territorial jurisdiction but the love and reverence for George Washington by the Masons in this country is amply demonstrated by the collective effort of all of the jurisdictions to keep this Memorial to Washington, the Mason, a living reality."

In other words, this lodge is a quaint place of triumph that displays the ability of separate lodges to come together to achieve a goal.

Those suspicious of Freemasonry say that this is exactly the reason this place should not be trusted. Rumors abound that this lodge is the central headquarters for high-level Freemasonry. Those skeptics say that the many Grand Lodges coming together is not just a sign of harmony in building a memorial, but a sign of harmony in building a central meeting place to house their most secretive, evil meetings.

Legend says that the most powerful Freemasons in the world convene regularly at this temple, just a mile outside the nation's capitol. Who knows what nefarious schemes they're calculating, and just how many strings they're pulling?

Octagon House of Marion

What can be said about a house with eight sides? Plenty, if that house happens to be the Octagon House in Marion. This unique brick structure has been doing its multifaceted thing since 1856, a lengthy stretch of time that not only assures the home's rich local history, but gives it a few ghosts to boot.

As odd as it may seem, octagon houses were once plentiful. Dubbed "poor man's mansions" during their mid-19th-century heyday, these oddball structures fascinated people not only for their peculiar shape, but for their generous interior space as well. Since eight walls present a rather grand opportunity for furniture placement, these houses likely won over their share of interior decorators.

This particular octagon house, however, has a dark side attached to it. It was originally built by Abijah Thomas, a textile-plant owner and slaveholder, and one of its seventeen rooms (appropriately tagged the "dark room") is reportedly haunted. Opinions about this phenomenon vary, but the chief theory behind such frightful stirrings involves mistreated slaves. Indeed, due to such past injustices, blood is said to drip down the octagon house's interior walls, and shackles can sometimes be heard jangling about with nary a *living* soul in sight. "If walls could talk" goes the popular saying. In this case, they very well might!

These days the octagon house is in transition. An enterprising local man has obtained ownership and is hoping to fully restore this long-vacant property. We wish him the best, as his newly acquired house represents the end of a dying breed. At the same time, however, we cannot shake a nagging feeling that we've carried with us since standing beneath the octagon house's thirty-two boarded-up windows.

On the gray, overcast day of our visit, no matter where we stood on the abandoned grounds, a palpable "presence" followed us. Was it the knowledge of paranormal activity having its way with our imaginations? Hardly. Until we arrived, we knew little of the home's history and nothing at all about its alleged ghosts. Was it the lingering life force of past slaves attempting to scare us away from unspeakable tortures doled out within? We'll let you decide.

Engineering the Master Race

Sometimes the fabled places we visit are benign, with frivolous tales to tell. Too often they're not. Lynchburg's State Colony for Epileptics and Feebleminded has a stranglehold on the latter. Within its stark, institutional walls, unthinkable atrocities once took place under the banner of "progress." While this chapter in human folly stands as a substantial blemish on the Old Dominion's past, it is one mega-weird tale that needs to be told, if only to ensure that it will *never* happen again.

Imagine for one moment the possibility of a superrace. Using genetic cleansing methods, all members of such a group would be free from transferable abnormalities and defects, both mental and physical. This was the ambitious goal of Virginia doctors like Dr. H. E. Jordan (slated to become Dean of the Department of Medicine at the University of Virginia) and Dr. Joseph DeJarnette (director of Virginia's Western State Mental Hospital, 1905–1943). On paper the idea looked promising, not just to these well-stationed Virginians but to other Americans as well. Sterilization of any "lesser" beings would ensure that their pitiful genes would not be repeated.

Dr. Joseph DeJarnette

However, this controversial movement (called eugenics, from the Greek word meaning well-bred) came with serious quandaries attached. Should Virginians really be in the business of human breeding? Beyond this, what would give *any* individual the deity-like right to make such a call on behalf of another? Like most dilemmas involving personal human rights, this one remained unanswered, then as now. Still, the eugenics movement marched forward with the State Colony for Epileptics and Feebleminded leading the charge. Sometimes, as we now know, to lead is not necessarily to win.

For proof that Virginia was at the very forefront of this mixed-up movement, let's examine the evidence. Adolf Hitler kicked off his "Law for the Prevention of Offspring with Hereditary Diseases" in 1933. Many believe that he dreamed up this lunacy by his lonesome or with the help of Gestapo cronies. The truth is *Der Führer* would have had to look no further than Virginia's eugenics movement as a template for creating his superrace.

From 1927 until 1956, with full legal backing, American doctors routinely sterilized thousands of poor unfortunates at the Lynchburg facility. This, at least, is the official operational time frame. Evidence suggests, however, that forced sterilizations were carried on into the 1970s, and perhaps beyond. Statewide, the estimated tally for this misguided abomination hovers around the eight thousand mark.

Virginia wasn't alone in such insanity. Thirty states in all backed the eugenics movement. Big-name colleges like Harvard, Columbia, and the University of Virginia offered accredited courses that extolled the benefits derived from this new "cleansing" wave of the future.

Today the renamed Central Virginia Training Center (rechristened with much political correctness in 1983) is still the largest psychiatric institution in Virginia, housing some 650 people afflicted with mental disorders. Presumably this slick, modern facility no longer performs state-backed gonad snipping.

A strange footnote to this story occurred in 2002 when Virginia Governor Mark Warner called the eugenics program "a shameful effort," which the state government should never have been involved in. "We must remember the Commonwealth's past mistakes in order to prevent them from recurring," Warner nobly added, stopping just short of a full apology. (No doubt to protect the state from sweeping lawsuits and settlements.) Warner's words represented the absolute end of an uncommonly hurtful, strange, and dare we say *weird* era.

Eugenics for the Kiddies

As I was lollygagging about in the city of Staunton, something caught my Weird Eye. I was on a winding access road, heading for Staunton's Frontier Culture Museum, when an imposing brick structure high on an adjacent hillside came into view. It had obviously been abandoned for some time, and yet the place was eerily inviting. The markings above its Georgian Revival columns cryptically read, Peery Building, 1938.

What I subsequently learned about this place, once the DeJarnette Sanatorium, rocked me to the core. For here at this fast-crumbling institution, innocent children once played a central role in the twisted eugenics movement.

Defectives will breed defectives
And the insane breed insane
Oh, why do we allow these people
To breed back to the monkey's nest
To increase our country's burdens
When we should breed from the good and the best
Oh, you wise men take up the burden
And make this your loudest creed
Sterilize the misfits promptly
All not fit to breed.
—Dr. Joseph S. DeJarnette 1920

Functioning as director at Staunton's Western State Mental Hospital during the early portion of the 20th century, "Sterilization DeJarnette" (his adopted nickname) pushed strongly for the compulsory sterilization of mental defectives. The DeJarnette Sanatorium operated from 1932 until 2001. It is not known with certainty just how many forced sterilizations of children took place under its roof or precisely when they ceased, but whatever the figure, a gross injustice had indeed been foisted upon people who could not fend for themselves.

Today, one can almost hear the lingering screams of fear and oppression echoing throughout the sanatorium's hallways. These are offset rather creepily by frilly, friendly nursery rhymes scribbled inside on its dayroom walls. This bizarre contrast exists largely because of the institution's varying incarnations. In 1980, only one year after sterilizations had officially ceased in the state of Virginia, the facility became a genuine *caring* hospital. At this stage, the DeJarnette Sanatorium had morphed into the DeJarnette Center for Human Development, without doubt a cleverly orchestrated stroke to distance it from its dark past. In 2001, the center was relocated and renamed once again. This time it completely removed the DeJarnette stigma by calling itself the Commonwealth Center for Children & Adolescents. This pleased many critics, including Valerie L. Marsh (executive director of the Virginia chapter of the National Alliance for the Mentally Ill), who once

quipped, "Leave it to Virginia to name a hospital after someone who systematically tortured vulnerable people. I'm embarrassed and ashamed."

The original DeJarnette Sanatorium now stands as a rat-infested shell of its former self, a tangible and oversized reminder of a path badly chosen. Virginia, it's plain to see, misplaced its moral compass during the eugenics debacle. But we shouldn't pile on too quickly with snap judgments. We must remember the prevailing climate of the times and the nodding approval of others residing in even loftier places. A classic example of eugenics' nutty mainstream popularity occurred in 1927 when the celebrated Supreme Court Justice Oliver Wendell Holmes Jr. wrote, "It's better for all the world, if instead of waiting to execute degenerate offspring for crime or to let them starve for their imbecility, society can prevent those who are manifestly unfit from continuing their kind. Three generations of imbeciles are enough." If ever there has been a weird statement that stands completely upon its own merits, this is certainly the one. You can't make this stuff up, folks!–*Jeff Bahr*

Unexplained Phenomena

Virginia is full of mysterious events and odd happenings for which science can find no credible explanation. Maybe it's because of the state's links to the earliest days of the country or its proximity to federal power; but for whatever reason, odd things seem to happen here. Body parts fall from the sky; poltergeists invade homes and throw tomatoes; and a virtual fleet of UFOs flies over the skies, some of them in the shape of amoebas. And that's just for starters.

It's a wide array of the strange and the wicked that we'll explore in this chapter. Some things are mere rumors, whispers of incidents that may or may not have happened. Others are well documented, though their meanings may not be known yet. It is not our place to seek out logical explanations. We merely point the way for the adventurous. So come along, sightseer, on the journey through weird Virginia.

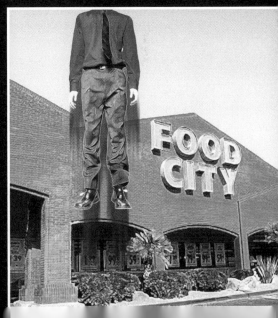

Gasser of Botetourt

The *fraternity* of Gassers is a small one. Perhaps the most famous is the Mad Gasser of Mattoon, Illinois, who carried out his vaporous deeds in September 1944. In this case, a tall, darkly dressed "Gasser" would peer into the windows of Mattoon homes, then shoot in a sweet-smelling gas that would incapacitate the residents. One day the attacks just stopped, but not before police found a cloth that appeared to have some of the gas on it and bizarre imprints of what appeared to be a woman's high-heeled shoes on the ground beneath the bedroom window at the site of the last attack.

It was later discovered that the FBI had quietly sent agents into Mattoon to try to identify the type of gas the prowler was using. It's possible that this incident serves as a true-life example of the FBI having an *X-Files*–type unit in operation as early as 1944. Or it may be that the unit was established as far back as 1934. That was the year the Botetourt Gasser visited Virginia.

The wave of Gasser incidents in Botetourt County occurred from December 1933 through early February 1934. The first recorded incident took place at a farm near Haymakertown during the night of December 22, when three separate attacks into one house sickened nine people inside. The victims suffered from nausea, headaches, face puffiness, and tightening of throat muscles. A nineteen-year-old female had convulsions for weeks afterward. Eyewitnesses said they saw a man fleeing in the darkness, but police found only one clue: the track of a *woman's* heel under the window apparently used by the Gasser to deliver the gas.

Now where would we hear that in the future? Ten years later in Mattoon, Illinois!

Other nighttime gas attacks occurred over the next two weeks. Eyewitnesses thought they saw a 1933 Chevrolet speeding away from one attack, but nothing came of it. In another attack, a mother, while with her baby, heard strange mumblings behind a rattling window shade. The next thing she knew, the room filled with gas as she felt her body grow limp. In another incident, farmer F. B. Duval said he saw a man escaping to an automobile parked on a rural road. Duval and a sheriff's deputy looked around soon after, and found prints of a woman's shoes.

Panic grew, and some concerned homeowners even began to shoot at innocent people who dared approach their homes. Author Jerome Clark discusses the final incident as follows, in *The Encyclopedia of Strange and Unexplained Physical Phenomena*.

> One of the last gassings was reported near Lithia in nearby Roanoke County. Afterwards the victim found discolored snow with a sweet-smelling, oily substance in it. When analyzed, it turned out to consist of sulfur, arsenic, and mineral oil — something like the components, authorities thought, of insecticides. A trail of footprints led from the house to the barn, but none led away from the barn. The tracks, according to press accounts, (were) a "woman's tracks."

Michael T. Shoemaker wrote of the case in 1985, in *Fate* magazine. He noted how similar the Illinois and Virginia cases were: "In both Mattoon and Botetourt, the principal physical effects were the same. A sickeningly sweet odor, nausea, paralysis, facial swelling and unconsciousness. Doctors confirmed these effects and, moreover, in both cases doctors smelled the gas. Both gassers made repeat attacks on one family, multiple attacks in one night, and assaults on unoccupied houses. The pattern of explanation was also similar, progressing from pranksters to lunatics to hysteria. Tantalizing but useless clues were found, including (with Shoemaker's emphasis) *a woman's print beneath a window.*"

The Botetourt Gasser case was debunked in a study of the news articles about the case conducted by Robert Bartholomew, Ph.D., and Simon Wessely, M.D. Their paper, "Epidemic Hysteria in Virginia: The Case of the Phantom Gasser of 1933–1934," was published in the *Southern Medical Journal* in 1999. The researchers concluded that the reports were a kind of mass hysteria that coincided "with heightened awareness of environmental pollution and triggered by imaginary or exaggerated contamination threats."

Environmental concerns in the 1930s? Investigators of the unexplained are skeptical of the paper and still wonder who put on a pair of high-heeled women's shoes and shot a strange gas into the homes of innocent Virginians.

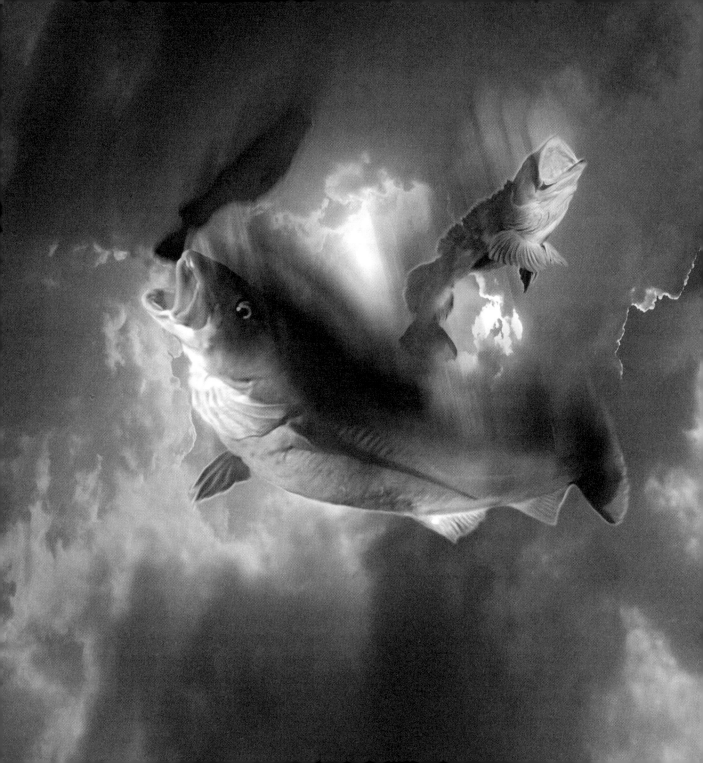

Fortean Falls

Anyone interested in the weird must have some familiarity with the works of Charles Hoy Fort (1874–1932), an American writer and researcher of strange phenomena. Fort compiled — with wit, challenges, and a sense of humor — hundreds of accounts of odd, inexplicable, or weird events, mostly extracted from newspapers and scientific journals.

Fort was especially fond of collecting old scientific journal and newspaper items of organic objects falling from the heavens. Today they're called "Fortean falls," and here's a small bucketful of some uniquely Virginian ones.

During the spring of 1850, several men saw a strange small cloud moving over the south bank of the Pamunkey River in Hanover County. Soon, to their surprise, they saw pieces of flesh and liver falling from it, covering a five-yard area. Eyewitness G. W. Bassett, a physician, returned the next morning with an associate, and they collected about twenty pieces of the fragments of flesh. Each weighed an ounce or under, and Bassett preserved them "for the future inspection of the curious," wrote Henry Winfred Splitter, in *Fate* magazine in 1953.

Norfolk supposedly experienced a foot-long catfish fall in 1853, noted Fort. Jerome Clark, who reinvestigated the case, found it could have been the rain of codfish discussed in the *Norfolk Argus* in 1853. The fish, each said to have been one foot long, fell throughout different sections of Norfolk and the nearby fields during a hailstorm. "Hundreds were picked up in the morning," the papers reported. The fish fall was "a fact which is attested by hundreds of citizens of that place," wrote the *Daily Alton Telegraph* of Illinois, on May 30, 1853.

It was rocks from the skies that appeared around September 26, 1889, wrote the *Statesville Landmark* of North Carolina: "Culpeper, Virginia, is perplexed on account of a rock-dropping mystery. Rocks fall around, apparently from the heavens, and the phenomenon excites much interest."

In Fincastle, rocks of several tints fell into the garden of S. B. Smith on May 5, 1895, at 7:00 p.m., wrote Jerome Clark in his *Unnatural Phenomena*. "They seemed to fall in clusters of about 15 and were of different colors, some of brilliant hue, others pale and black, and in a brief time would dissolve into smoke. Others would seem to sparkle brilliantly and disappear."

A "heavy downfall" of dry oak leaves fell for several hours at Winchester on April 22, 1904, according to the *Bluefield Daily Telegraph* of West Virginia, on April 28, 1904.

Jackson Road's Spook Light

Spook lights are not Unidentified Flying Objects, but appear to be permanently fixed lights that may indicate some haunted attachment to an old railroad bed, valleys, ridges, or specific geological locations. Most spook lights are long-term phenomena at a special place, like the famous Brown Mountain light in North Carolina. Some are mere fleeting will-o'-the-wisps, once thought to be the light representing a bog's supposed haunted entity but now sometimes believed to be swamp gas.

Virginia briefly hosted a spook light, beginning on March 5, 1951, at Suffolk in Nansemond County. After several people saw what was labeled "The Light" in the vicinity of Jackson Road, investigating Deputy Sheriff Hurley Jones also saw it. He described it as resembling a single automobile headlamp heading right toward the viewer.

Jackson Road resident Jeston Reid, who was sixty-two years old, told investigators his father had seen the spook light some seventy-five years earlier. And area resident Raleigh Outland said he had seen it all his life. He noted it sometimes stayed "right in the middle of the road, about five feet off the ground," and at other times it veered off to the side of Jackson Road.

The local head of the state troopers, Sergeant W. S. Dameron, said, "It's a bright light that looks exactly like a train coming down a track."

Over three hundred cars showed up in March 1951 to look for an answer to the mystery of The Light. More serious investigations discovered that the old Jackson and Whaleyville Railroad ran down the strip that has since been renamed Jackson Road. Deputy Sheriff Beale recalled that a railroad flagman was killed on the line sometime in 1912, and many folks believed it was the flagman with his lantern that was haunting the old railroad bed. But general agreement in the county is that the light had been seen long before that event occurred.

> Near relatives of spook lights can be found at two other sites in Virginia. The first of these are the phantom trains at Staunton and Otto River, and the second are the phantom ships at Lake Drummond and Rappahannock River.

The "Norfolk" Experiment

In 1954, Morris Jessup was living in Washington, DC, and writing about ancient and contemporary unsolved mysteries. Jessup had studied at the University of Michigan to just shy of his doctorate, and would go on to study astronomy and archaeology after he left the Midwest. His first book, *The Case for the UFO,* was published in 1955, the first book ever to use the term UFO in its title. The text covered flying saucers, of course, but also falls from the skies, disappearances, and other anomalies.

In October of the same year, Jessup received two letters from a person who said his name was Carlos Miguel Allende. In one of these letters, Allende told a bizarre story of a World War II experiment that used Albert Einstein's unified field theory to make a ship disappear. His exact wording said the experiment caused the "complete invisibility of a ship, Destroyer type, and of its crew, While at Sea Oct. 1943." He also said the ship and crew were teleported from Philadelphia to reappear in Norfolk and other ports.

And so began the saga of the strange event now called the Philadelphia Experiment, though it could just as easily have been called the Norfolk Experiment.

After the two letters, Jessup heard no more of Allende. Or so he thought. Then in 1957, the Office of Naval Research (ONR) in Washington, DC, invited Jessup to come for a visit. The ONR had been sent a heavily annotated paperback edition of *The Case for the UFO,* and the writing style of some of the notes appeared to match Allende's. The mysterious Allende also mentioned again the teleporting incident. Between the letters and the book, the ONR had pieced together talk of time warps, men getting caught within the metal of the deck when it reappeared, and even a name for the ship: the U.S.S. *Eldridge.*

Convinced that the Allende material held "clues to the nature of gravity," some ONR officers took it on themselves to reprint Jessup's book. Republished by Varo Mfg. Co., this edition of *Case* became legendary, as did what it contained. Perhaps it was more official than some readers think, but never mind; the Philadelphia Experiment folklore was launched.

The navy received so many requests for information on the Philadelphia Experiment that it eventually created a press release that said it had searched its records and found no document that confirmed the event, nor did the navy have any interest in attempting such an achievement.

To debunk the story, the press release explains the *Eldridge*'s activities, as recorded in its deck log and war diary from August to December 1943. The ship, the press release says, traveled from the New York Naval Shipyard to Bermuda, then back to New York. It then left New York Harbor on November 1 as part "of the escort for Convoy UGS-23 (New York Section)." The convoy, including the *Eldridge,* entered the Naval Operating Base at Norfolk on November 2. The ships left for Casablanca and arrived back in New York Harbor on December 17. The *Eldridge* left there again for Norfolk on December 31, and during this entire time frame, the press release says, the "*Eldridge was never in Philadelphia.*"

And even though the ONR printed copies of the annotated *Case,* the press release says the ONR "has stated that the use of force fields to make a ship and her crew invisible does not conform to known physical laws . . . and that while Albert Einstein was a part-time consultant with the Navy's Bureau of Ordnance in 1943 and 1944, "there is no indication that (he) was involved in research relevant to invisibility or to teleportation."

Throughout the 1960s and '70s, Allende would surface from time to time, making outrageous claims. He wrote letters to *Weird Virginia* author Loren Coleman during this time, telling him how best to "capture a Bigfoot." By the 1980s, researchers Jerome Clark, Jacques Vallee, and Robert Goerman had discovered that Carlos Allende was in reality an eccentric born Carl Meredith Allen in Springdale, PA, in 1925. No evidence has ever been found that the tale he told is true.

But the myth persists. Since Allende's first report of the Philadelphia Experiment, a cottage industry in books, movies, and TV shows has told the story. On second thought, maybe Norfolk is lucky to have been omitted from the name of this fabulous fabrication.

Morris Jessup disappeared in 1958 and was found in his car, dead from carbon monoxide poisoning, on April 20, 1959, in Dade County Park, Florida. Local authorities ruled his death a suicide.

Jerome Clark bemoans the fact that Jessup's vanishing and death has been linked by "the fringe literature" with the Philadelphia Experiment. "One theme of the new mythology is that government agents killed Jessup because he knew too much," Clark wrote in *The Encyclopedia of Strange and Unexplained Physical Phenomena*.

Old Dominion UFOs

Unidentified Flying Objects

have invaded the skies of Virginia for centuries, although they weren't described as the disks, globes, and black triangles we hear of today. Throughout early America, witnesses reported strange sightings in the heavens in frames of reference to the things they knew. As Jerome Clark states in his classic encyclopedia *The Emergence of a Phenomenon,* "People reported many appearances in the sky as strange and credited anything out of the ordinary with a supernatural origin. A strange sight could be a supernatural being or, more often, a message from such beings. In those days the heavens were telling the will of the gods."

It wasn't until the age of mechanical advancements that technological phenomena were reported with increasing frequency in Virginia. This shift from the mystical to the mechanical can clearly be seen in the first important cases from the state to be mentioned in UFO literature.

"An Automobile Without Wheels," read the headlines in the Edwardsville, Illinois, *Intelligencer,* for May 3, 1909, about one sighting. The item was small but revealing: "The spectacle of a mysterious airship, occupied by a man and woman, [at] Sewall's point, was witnessed by more than fifty persons in that vicinity. Those who saw the strange aircraft stated that it resembled an automobile without wheels." Needless to say, airships and aircraft of this kind did not exist at the time.

On September 29, 1929, four hundred miles off the coast of Virginia, a steamship crossing the Atlantic Ocean was overflown by a giant, glowing, mysterious airship, origin unknown. The captain was so shocked by the event, he immediately contacted officials, who could not explain the observation or identify such an airship.

But it was with the onset of the modern era of "flying saucers"—a word coined by a news reporter after a famous 1947 UFO sighting near Mt. Rainier in Washington State—that Virginia began to be overrun with the unexplained craft in the skies.

Why Virginia?

Before we revisit some of Virginia's more famous UFO cases, a comment about the significance of the state in the scheme of things. In 1952, at the height of UFO sightings in this country, the United States Air Force set up Project Blue Book. The group's stated purpose was to study reports of UFOs and determine if they were a threat to national security. However, the Washington, DC, citizen watchdog group NICAP (National Investigations Committee on Aerial Phenomena) discovered that the Blue Book was merely a public relations front. NICAP discovered this not from some crazy conspiracy nut, but from no less an authority than Brigadier General C. H. Bolender. In a memo dated October 20, 1969, General Bolender stated, "Reports of unidentified flying objects which could affect national security . . . are not part of the Blue Book system." The memo acknowledges that actual responsibility for UFO reports was held by a covert and classified operation located in Langley, Virginia—home to the Central Intelligence Agency. This explains why some important case files have never been found in the Blue Book archives; and as most people know, the CIA has a knack for keeping things quiet.

UFOs over the White House

Perhaps we should not be surprised that Virginia figures so prominently in the world of UFO sightings. After all, the state is a breath away from the seat of power of the mightiest country in the world, a logical target for beings from outer space. And that may explain what happened on one summer night in 1952.

On July 14 of that year, a Pan American Airways DC-4 was flying over the Chesapeake Bay at 8,000 feet. The night was clear, and at 8:12 p.m. the pilots were startled to see eight craft, seemingly from another world, fly by their own plane. The craft performed maneuvers as they paced the jet before climbing at a graceful 45-degree angle and disappearing. The accounts given by Captain William B. Nash and First Officer William H. Fortenberry of this sighting have remained among the most credible in UFO history, even though an air force investigation declared their sighting "unexplained." As time would soon tell, it was only a hint of what was to come.

At 11:40 p.m. on Saturday, July 19, 1952, radar operators at Washington National Airport noticed seven "pips" or "blips" on the radar over Washington, DC, about fifteen miles south-southwest from their location. The blips traveled at 100 to 130 m.p.h. and quickly accelerated to incredible speed—sometimes in excess of 7,200 m.p.h. The radar operators at the airport confirmed their sightings with other sites' radar personnel, then contacted the military at Andrews Air Force Base.

In a scene that seemed out of a science fiction movie, the military attempted to scramble aircraft from Newcastle AFB in Delaware, while more sightings occurred fast and furiously. The tower at Washington National saw an orange disk at about a 3,000-foot altitude. And a Capital Airlines pilot, Captain S. C. Pierman, saw a fiery blue-white object flash across the horizon, followed a few minutes later by six bright white tailless, fast-moving objects whizzing by him against a pitch-black sky.

When two F-94 night fighter planes, delayed for two hours by runway repairs, finally made it to the target area, they could find nothing. That did not mean the UFOs were gone. Visual sightings from the ground and further radar blips—around radio towers, over DC and Virginia, and circling the area—were reported throughout the night.

Blips showed up on the radar again on July 26. F-94s would be dispatched, fly around for a few minutes, not see anything, and return to their base. As soon as they returned, the blips reappeared on radar. But the last time they flew out, the pilots turned around and visually saw four mysterious lights. In one report, a pilot yelled out, "They've surrounded my plane—what should I do?" Then the lights disappeared.

On July 29, Air Force Intelligence took an official position and said nothing really happened; it was only "temperature inversions."

In the annals of UFOlogy, this is seen as one of the biggest cover-ups of all time. The radar operators and pilots knew all about temperature inversions, well-known phenomena over Washington, DC, and all felt what they saw was not some kind of weather phenomenon. Even Project Blue Book discounted the "temperature inversion" explanation.

The Virginia–DC area remained on edge for months, and incidents in the following year didn't help matters. On February 3, 1953, a USMC F-9F fighter pilot chased a rocketlike object with a red glow at the rear for four minutes over the Virginia–North Carolina state line. And on December 31, 1953, at Quantico Marine Base in Virginia, marines saw the landing of a round unknown object that pulsated and throbbed, emitting red lights.

UFO Attack

The media in the '50s tended to think of flying saucers as invaders from outer space. But in this next case, dubbed "the UFO Attack of October 19, 1959," the attack was not by the flying saucer. It all began in a town called Poquoson, near Langley Air Force Base. Virginia UFO investigator Larry Bryant told the story to *Weird Virginia's* Loren Coleman.

No, it came from the trembling hands of a 12-gauge-shotgun-toting fifteen-year-old named Mark George Muza, Jr. He and his fourteen-year-old hunting companion, Harold Moore, Jr., had ventured out that afternoon into an old USAF restricted bombing range near their homes off Ridge Road.

Somewhere about a mile into the Big Marsh, Muza heard a whirring sound, "like a flock of wild birds," coming from above. Separated from Muza by about a hundred yards, the other boy watched in amazement as a roughly four-foot-diameter flying saucer slowly descended from about a hundred feet to some fifty feet above Muza's head. At that point, the terrified youngster aimed his gun at the craft and, over the course of about ninety seconds, pumped three shots into it. All three blasts—especially the third, heavy-duty slug—produced a ricochet that, to Muza, sounded as if metal were scraping metal.

Apparently unaccustomed to such a hostile greeting, the saucer finally ceased its wobbly descent and proceeded to spin as a toy top, zooming straight up, out of sight.

Years after the incident, Bryant would lament that from evidence found in archives, it was clear that "no one at Langley had chosen to investigate the case."

The Flap of January 1965

Jacque Vallee's "UFO Sighting Database" is a concise listing of worldwide events, and as we reviewed it for *Weird Virginia*, it quickly became apparent that something special was happening in Virginia throughout the first month of 1965. Here are Vallee's notes.

Jan. 14, 1965: Norfolk. James Myers saw an object rise from the ground, appearing as a bright, circular silvery craft.

Jan. 19, 1965: Brands Flats. A workman cutting wood on the Augusta archery range saw two saucer-shaped objects, 30 m and 6 m in diameter, hovering in the sky. The smaller one landed, a door opened, and three pilots emerged. They looked human, but had a reddish-orange skin and staring eyes. One of them had "a long finger on his left hand." Their clothes were the same color as the craft, whose open door showed a strange light inside. The object was so highly polished that "I would bet on a clear day you could not see it at five thousand feet." The occupants spoke sounds that were not understood and reentered the object. The door outline could not be seen when it was closed.

According to ufologist Jerome Clark, the Brands Flats case is one of the most important in Virginia. Clark identifies the workman as William Blackburn, a resident of Waynesboro, Virginia. He was working at the Augusta County Archery Club off Route 250 near Brands Flats, when at approximately 5:40 p.m. he encountered these "beings." Clark states there is "no evidence that Blackburn hoaxed his report."

Jan. 23, 1965: Williamsburg. A 31-year-old man driving a '64 Cadillac was at the intersection of U.S. Highway 60 and State Route 14 when the engine failed, and he had to stop by the side of the road. He then observed an object about 1.2 m above ground. It was shaped like a mushroom or an electric bulb, 25 m high, 8 m in diameter, made noise similar to a vacuum cleaner, had a metallic gray color, a red-orange light on one side, and a blue one on the other. It took off against the wind toward the west, at high speed.

Jan. 25, 1965: Marion. Woody Darnell, his family and several neighbors saw a stationary object on the ground. It took off with a shower of sparks. Several trees were found uprooted at the site.

Aliens in Aisle Five

Are people still seeing UFOs in Virginia? Of course, and some of these are close encounters of the third kind: those that involve reports of apparent UFO occupants or aliens. Take, for example, a sighting that occurred on April 28, 2006, in Vansant. While driving by the Food City store, an eyewitness was startled to see, hovering only five feet above the store, a flying disk. The witness saw more than a UFO, however, as he reported that a gray thin figure came out of the disk, grabbed a man on the ground by the neck, and abducted the poor soul onto it. The craft's door snapped closed and the disk flew away.

What are we to make of such a report? Delusion, prank, fantasy, or reality? Whatever happened, we have to consider and investigate. Including our last example: flying amoebas!

Jellyfish UFOs

In his book *Sky Creatures: Living UFOs*, researcher Trevor James Constable wrote about "UFO amoebas" or "amoebae-like life forms existing in the plasma state" in outer space. Ivan T. Sanderson, a zoologist, played with the notion that UFOs might be living creatures in his book, *Uninvited Guests*. Jerome Clark calls them "space animals."

As strange and bizarre as this sounds, we leave you with this last UFO case, from Springfield. It was the summer of 2003, and Norm Gagnon was with his wife, driving east on the Franconia Springfield Parkway. At 11:00 a.m., near the Springfield Metro, the couple saw two weird formations in the blue sky, which Gagnon wrote about online [hometown.aol.com/facadefx/JellyfishUFO.html].

> At first I thought they were hot air balloons but then I observed that they were much like vapor clouds, and somewhat thick in consistency since both objects were casting a shadow. The shape of these UFOs were rather identical from one another, their tops were circular in shape, as domes, and both had what appears to be 'trails' at their bases, similar to tentacles from a jellyfish, almost organic in texture. Both objects were motionless as they floated above and they emitted no sound . . . *Sorry to say that I didn't have my camera handy.*

So perhaps UFOs aren't really a problem for astrophysicists or military investigators but instead fall within the realm of some new science called cryptoastrobiology.

Portsmouth Poltergeist

Mrs. Charles Daughtery had never seen anything like it in her hundred years of life ("give or take a few years," she said). Just after she finished making the bed in her Portsmouth home, the covers and the mattress suddenly flew off and blew in her direction! It was Thursday, September 6, 1962, the day her once peaceful home would change in ways that would alter her perceptions of the world forever.

It had been a quiet afternoon until the bedcovers began to behave so erratically. Following that, a bedroom dresser suddenly crashed over to the floor. Then a vase flew off the mantel in the parlor and smashed a window seven feet away. A bottle of insecticide sailed from a shelf next to the washing machine and struck Mrs. Daughtery on the back of the head. Moments later, a kitchen cabinet popped open and salt and pepper shakers jumped out and landed on the counter. They vibrated for a moment and then danced down the countertop to music it seemed only they could hear.

Mrs. Daughtery's thirteen-year-old great-great-grandson . . . was dumped out of a chair as his schoolbooks literally flapped around the room like angry birds.

Mrs. Daughtery's thirteen-year-old great-great-grandson, Cleveland Harmon, who lived with her and her husband, was dumped out of a chair as his schoolbooks literally flapped around the room like angry birds.

Finally, as most people do when they are facing something beyond their understanding, the Daughterys called the police. Officers arrived a few hours after the first incident, around 7:00 p.m., and were puzzled (and more than a little skeptical) about the events being described. Convinced that a prankster was preying on the elderly couple, the officers sent for a police dog to inspect the premises. The dog found nothing, but his handler was struck hard on the leg by some sort of object. No one discovered what it was or where it came from. Mrs. Daughtery warned him, "You stay around here, you get hit by a lot of stuff."

The elderly Mrs. Daughtery believed that at her age (she had been born into slavery around 1862) she had seen everything, but her "housebreaking ghost" was just getting started. The strange happenings would continue over the course of the next few evenings, totally disrupting her life and those of her great-great-grandson and her ninety-year-old husband, Charles.

On the following Friday and Saturday evenings, the strange events began around 4:00 p.m. and continued for several hours. They started with the bang and clatter of objects being thrown around the house. Pipes, tobacco tins, books, vases, lamps, and just about anything that was lying around loose was fair game. The items moved suddenly and with great speed and force. A stool jumped from the floor to shatter a ceiling light. A skillet hurtled from the stove to a chair by a window. On Sunday, things were a little less lively. The poltergeist contented itself with throwing ripe tomatoes, with excellent aim. Two pieces of the fruit struck Charles Daughtery and young Cleveland Harmon right in the center of their chests! The police were again summoned but again left without filing any reports on the strange events. In this time period, most police departments would not have taken the bizarre reports seriously, especially if they came from an elderly African American couple. Within a few days, though, the officers would be wishing that they had listened to the story more closely!

Talk of the strange happenings began making the rounds of the neighborhood, and soon the rumors reached the ears of a local reporter, Joseph V. Phillips, who worked at the *Norfolk Virginian-Pilot*. Not believing in such nonsense, Phillips went to the house to see for himself and took a photographer along with him. Neither expected to see anything out of the ordinary; both were soon in for a shock.

Phillips arrived at the same time as a nurse named Marion Bivens, who had come to check on Mr. Daughtery's high blood pressure. She and Phillips were leaning against a buffet in the dining room, talking, when the nurse suddenly cried out and asked the reporter if he had felt the piece of furniture move. He had not, and frankly blamed the outburst on an overactive imagination.

But just moments after Mrs. Bivens stated that the buffet had moved, Phillips saw a vase he had recently handled suddenly jump off the mantel in the living room and hit the wall in the hallway at the front of the house. It had to round a corner to land at that spot and Phillips knew that he had seen no one touch the vase, and that no one could have thrown it to make it travel in such a manner. The reporter ran into the living room, only to discover that no one was there. He started back into the dining room, and as he crossed into the room, a cup that had been sitting on the buffet landed at his feet. The photographer had seen it land there as well.

Phillips was shocked, to say the least, saying, "I didn't believe in ghosts—until today!" All the people present had been in his full view when the cup crashed on the floor, he said, and "I felt my hair stand on end. Then I saw an empty tobacco can fly toward me from the buffet. It was in the air when I saw it. It crashed and rolled to the floor at my feet."

Phillips may have been unnerved by these events, but Mrs. Daughtery remained calm in the face of the unknown. "I'm not nervous," she told the reporter,

"and I'm not afraid of ghosts." She was, however, scared of the crowds that began to appear outside of her home after Phillips's story appeared in the local newspaper. The police estimated that nearly 10,000 people visited the neighborhood, 600 to 700 at a time. The visitors milled about and asked to be let inside the house to see the ghost. It got so bad that twelve patrolmen and two police dogs were kept on duty outside the home for several days.

On September 9, the Daughterys, who had not been frightened away by the ghost, decided to move out of the house until order had been restored to the neighborhood. They hoped that if they left, the crowds would lose interest. Within a few days, a lone patrolman, still on duty in front of the house where excited thousands had come just days before, finally reported that it was "all quiet."

On September 11, a contingent of scientists arrived in Portsmouth from the Duke University Institute of Parapsychology in Durham, North Carolina, including Dr. T. J. Pratt of Duke and William G. Roll from the Psychical Research Foundation, also in Durham. Dr. Roll would later lament that the researchers arrived too late to really ascertain what had been happening in the Daughtery house. When they came, the family was still staying with relatives, although they did agree to come back to the house for interviews and for study. Roll stated that there were a few occurrences that took place that may have been caused normally, but there was no way to be sure.

The experiments didn't last long. When some of the curiosity seekers learned that the Daughterys had returned home, they showed up again, asking to come inside. The frenzy reached the point where several onlookers actually broke into the house and threw some of the household furniture out the windows! Such severe damage was done that the Daughterys finally moved out of the house completely.

It was a sad ending to the case, which still raises

the question "what could have caused the bizarre outbreaks?" According to the Reverend Fred Jordan, a practicing Spiritualist since the 1920s, it may have been an "earthbound spirit who has been provoked into physical manifestations by recent events in the household." He further explained that the spirit had picked the Daughtery house because "Mrs. Daughtery has mediumistic powers that she is not aware of. The powers are physical—chemical—as well as spiritual. Without the presence of a medium, a spirit could not make his presence physically known."

After visiting the house, Dr. Pratt said he felt the reports were fairly typical of other poltergeist cases he had studied: Objects had been reported to move about and a teenager was present. In this case, like many others, it was noted that the boy was unhappy and disturbed and this may have been the cause of the violent, seemingly supernatural actions. However, no details were ever released about Cleveland Harmon. We can only guess what circumstances led to the young boy living with his very elderly great-great-grandparents.

Regardless of the theories, the startling events that occurred in Portsmouth remain unexplained.

Strange Caves

Virginia has not one but two caves that claim to be the location of strange moaning or crying sounds. Is the source of these sounds natural or unnatural? Your guess is as good as ours.

Buck Hill Caverns

These legendary caverns are said to be somewhere in the area of the small town of Bell's Cove. Legend says that deep within the caves, explorers stumbled upon what appeared to be a massive bottomless shaft. And as they began to explore the area, they were shocked to hear the sound of female cries, screams, and sobs coming from deep within the shaft. They left in fear. Nobody seems to know the exact location of this eerie, seemingly haunted shaft, or who or what was causing the strange sounds.

Devil's Slide Cave

Near the town of Tazewell is Devil's Slide Cave. Frequented by cavers, it has come to be known not just for its depths and the challenges it offers but also for a strange, inexplicable phenomenon. Visitors often report hearing moanlike sounds coming from deep within. The source of these cries is unknown— but what is known is that the cave is a constant source of curiosity for all who encounter it.

For some of us who were born in the intriguingly strange state of Virginia, there has always been a special pull to the unexplained, especially to the weird beast stories that are told, from the craggy foothills of Appalachia to the windy shores of the Atlantic Ocean. The normal Virginia presents many faces to its inhabitants and visitors, so should we be surprised that weird Virginia does an excellent job of hiding many creatures in its woods, lakes, and rivers?

Bizarre Beasts

Throughout the state, residents regularly report to unbelieving wildlife officials that they have encountered strange unknown critters. Not escaped zoo or circus animals, these beasts appear to inhabit that nether land of cryptids, animals yet undiscovered or underacknowledged by local law enforcement officers. Still, these bizarre creatures, whatever they are, haunt those who see them.

Legend of the Wampus Cat

The mountains of western Virginia, Tennessee, and Kentucky are populated by people whose occupations range from farmers to coal miners to businessmen and -women. But no matter what their line of work, many of these country folks have tales of the paranormal to tell. One of the oldest of these is the story of the Wampus Cat.

One version of the story is an old Indian legend. It was said a young Native American woman was married to a man she did not trust. Though he seemed loyal and loving to her at home, she was not sure what he did on the many occasions when he was away from her. In those days, it was customary for the men of the tribe to hunt, while the women took care of things around the encampments. The women themselves were forbidden to hunt. One night, the woman in the story placed the hide of a mountain cat on her body and snuck out to spy on her husband during one of his hunting trips. As the men gathered around their campfire, the woman watched them. She became fascinated with the stories and the magic that were presented to the men of the tribe by their medicine man. But she was so transfixed that she became careless and didn't notice that one of the Native American hunters had spotted her and was slowly creeping toward her. The poor woman was caught, and for her crime of trespassing on the male's territory she was transformed into what is known as the Wampus Cat. The woman was doomed to be forever half woman and half mountain cat. A ghastly creature to the eye, she walks upright, but has the snout and ears of a feline.

The Wampus Cat is still said to prowl the hills of Virginia, looking for animals to steal. When the moon is full, you can hear her howling. If you are camping in the woods and hear her wail, be warned. She is near and may come to visit you.

But this is not the only tale of the Wampus Cat.

The Dreaded Wampus Cat

There are many stories, all varied, concerning the origin of the dreaded Wampus Cat. I know of it only because we did a brief study of local urban legends in my high school history class (I am now in college). Anyhow, several primary characteristics appear in all the stories. The Wampus Cat has been spotted by hunters and lumberjacks, all of whom claim it to be too large for a bobcat and too far from home to be a mountain lion; it walks erect on its hind legs; and it has a piercing scream that resonates whenever it is near.

The origin of the tale perhaps comes from Cherokee folklore of a woman who dressed herself up in the skin of a mountain lion to spy on the men of her tribe. She was caught and cursed by the medicine man and transformed into half woman, half cat. Other stories tell of a witch in the woods attempting to transform herself into a cat, but local villagers caught her halfway through her transformation. She fled, but was stuck in the half woman, half cat transformation forever.

Regardless of the origin, the tale still lives on today. Farmers still have tales of their livestock unexpectedly disappearing or mysteriously dying.—*Billy Griffith*

A Wampus Among Us

I've got a bit of weirdness to pass on. I was camping deep in the Blue Ridge Mountains of Virginia with a friend. Note that this is illegal; you are only allowed to camp in approved spots in the area, but since we weren't going to light a fire we knew we could get away with it. The plan was to get some nice nature pics from the more obscure parts of the park and hike back out the next day, no big deal.

The day went fairly normally, no problems, no bears, boars, or cottonmouths. We found a level spot close to dusk and started to set up camp. Mind you it was a minimal camp. One small tent, and we heated the food over Sterno. We hung all our soiled cans and stuff in a bag ten feet off the ground to discourage a bear visit. A little while later, as the sun was setting quickly, we were overcome by a smell. It was like smelling a skunk in the distance, not exactly unpleasant but you know you don't want to be any closer. And the smell was very musky, not like rotting meat or anything, way different from anything else we'd ever smelled.

Anyway, we were sitting outside the tent slightly after dark, reviewing the pics we shot, when we heard something circling the small clearing we were in. We talked for a moment and decided it was most likely a boar—the mountains are loaded with feral pigs—and decided to scare it off by strutting around and making loud threatening noises. This turned out to be a mistake. Whatever it was got quiet, but not completely. We could still hear it if we stopped to listen. It was circling more slowly now.

Honestly, at this point I was a little freaked out. With all the noise we were making, whatever it was should have been scared off. Sure there are scattered reports of big cats in the region and bears are abundant, but our tactics would have sent either of these things scurrying into the night. We decided to build a fire because fire usually trumps any wildlife except moths.

There was a danger in this action. Like I say, we were camping illegally and the fire could lead to detection. At this point, I was unsettled enough to risk the massive fine. The problem was that we lacked firewood. Sure, there was an entire forest around us but something was circling out there. We took turns shining the flashlight into the woods in essence "covering" each other as we went for tinder.

After we had amassed a small pile, I shined the beam on some nice-looking rotted wood, and while my friend went to fetch it, I went about lighting the fire. At this point what actually happened becomes unclear. My friend maintains I moved the beam, while I think he ventured out of the illuminated area. In any event, at the moment the kindling caught, which was very quickly, my friend screamed.

I grabbed the flashlight and turned it directly on my friend. This is what I saw: A thing, definitely not a primate, no Bigfoot or anything and not a bear. But it was holding my pal with a hand. The closest thing I could call it was a walking cat. About five feet tall and thick. As soon as the light hit it, it hissed, like a cat, and took off—on two legs! My friend had five small puncture wounds in his arm and scratches on his head. He maintained that the thing was trying to bite his throat.

We kept a blazing fire going through that sleepless night—screw the possible federal charges! When morning rolled around, we hiked out. Whatever the thing was made no sense to me so I asked around with the old-timers in the area.

Here's the weird part—the Indians and early white folks to the area did have a legend called the Wampus Cat. The white folks said it was a witch stuck in mid-transformation between a human and cat, but the Cherokee legends just labeled it as a cat that would kill you once you saw it.

I guess I'm nuts, but I swear we were almost killed by a walking cat.—*Letter via e-mail*

> A thing, definitely not a primate, no Bigfoot or anything and not a bear . . . was holding my pal with a hand. The closest thing I could call it was a walking cat. About five feet tall and thick.

Lions and Pumas and Cougars

Mountain lions, also known as eastern cougars or pumas, have not been seen in the state of Virginia for more than a hundred years, at least officially. And yet there have been 121 reported sightings of the big cats just since 1970, according to the Virginia Department of Game and Inland Fisheries.

Wildlife biologist Rick Reynolds, who works for the Department of Game, is skeptical of the reports. "There hasn't been a confirmed record of mountain lions in Virginia since 1880," Reynolds says. "But that doesn't mean that there aren't some that have been obtained and kept illegally and then released."

So what are the large feline creatures that Virginians report so frequently to skeptical authorities? Are they zoo animals who escaped their captors and somehow made their way into the mountains? Or are they some throwback to another time, cryptozoological creatures not known to mainstream science? Or perhaps they're descended from the few survivors who managed to escape Virginia's industrialization, endangered species that need our protection.

Since 2005, staff members at Cougar Quest, an independent organization based in Winchester, have been investigating the appearances of the mystery cats. The organization says they have collected more than sixty accounts of cougar or mountain lion sightings in Virginia, dating back to the 1970s.

Interestingly, many of the mystery sightings take place in or around Fairfax County, not exactly a wilderness, but perhaps a good source of sustenance for the big cats, what with all the garbage cans and small pets in the area. One of the first witnesses, George Correll, saw one of the giant cats during the first week of February 1971. Manhunts began as the cats began to be seen more frequently, and then the sightings slowly stopped. No more data was released. Then in the spring of 1998, Virginia Game Department personnel began to receive another string of reports of "cougar" sightings in the county.

In one case, Harley Nygren was out trying to corral his little dog, Dillon, on his neighbor's property when he had a close encounter with a seventy-five-pound mountain lion. Nygren, seventy-three, a retired federal worker, said he and the cat eyed one another from a distance of about ten feet.

"A nice kitty," Nygren said, as he escorted a Fairfax County wildlife specialist through a blackberry thicket near his home on Carrington Lane in Tysons Corner to the secluded site where he had spotted the khaki-colored cougar. For wildlife biologist Earl Hodnett, Nygren's tale was the tenth "convincing account" he had received of the mystery cat loose in the suburban wilds of this town that May.

The most famous phantom cat report of recent years in Virginia comes from Craigsville, at the foot of the Appalachian Mountains. The story was told in the August 9, 2004, edition of the Staunton, VA, *News Leader.*

"It all started when Joe Rowland rolled into his driveway off Augusta Springs Road after a trip to town. He scanned the yard for wildlife, as he always does. Deer sometimes graze between the hay bales; rabbits often skip into the flowerbeds. On July 19, 2004, Rowland saw a lump of tan fur in a low place, and initially took it to be a deer. But as he got closer, he saw it was a big cat. Exclaiming, 'Oh my God!' he darted into his house for a digital camera. He tiptoed into the field, getting about 60 feet from the beast, when it raised its head and looked straight at him.

"As the beast took three leaps into the protection of the cornfield, Rowland took a big step backwards and raised his camera above his head. In the house, he quickly printed a picture for his friend Roy Thompson, who checks game at the IGA. There, the pair hovered over the copier machine, peering at blown-up images and comparing them with the store's collection of mounts. It looked too pale to be a bobcat, and too feline for a small bear. Rowland wondered, Could it be a mountain lion?"

The article also reported another sighting, of a six-foot-long cat with a three-foot-long tufted tail in an open field in Showker's Flats. The man who saw it was driving at the time, and slowed down to twenty-five mph to get a better view of the cat. He told the paper, "I'm pretty sure I saw a cougar. It was huge."

But a wildlife biologist with Virginia Game doubted that the animal was either an African lion, as some had guessed, or a mountain lion. Al Bourgueouis told the *News Leader*, "To a lot of people in that area it could look like an African lion (in the photo), but when you start putting things together like the height of the grass, etc., it points to a smaller animal." In the Rowland photo the grass is brushing the cat's belly. Game officials who investigated found the grass in the area in which the photo was taken to be just six to eight inches high.

Some of the most recent reports chronicled by Cougar Quest include "credible" but unconfirmed sightings in Winchester and Alexandria in early 2006. During the summer of 2006, a photograph of a mystery cat taken by Richard Gaya near Crozet, in western Albemarle County, created much excitement among researchers. The cat in the picture appears to be a young adult puma.

So many sightings are interesting for a state in which the mountain lion has not officially been seen since the early 1900s.

Demon Cat of Capitol Hill

From mysterious cats in the wild, we move to an even more mysterious cat in a rather unexpected place. In the District of Columbia, reports of a phantom panther, perhaps one that is more phantom than panther, have been collected under the umbrella term Demon Cat. This large felid makes its home in the Capitol Building, and is even said to be a feline portent of doom!

The story of this mysterious cat has its beginnings during the early days of the Capitol. At the time, staff members, lawmakers, and workmen often brought food into the building with them. It was said that one might find anything from live chickens to cold cuts of pork in an office, so it was no surprise that the Capitol began to experience a rat problem. Some of the workmen began bringing cats to the building to act as mousers, and the felines soon became a daily part of the Capitol's activities. As they killed off the rats, the cats were needed less and less. Many of them were taken home to become household pets, while others simply wandered off into the nearby neighborhoods. As the years passed, the cat population dwindled to nothing, except for one unusual cat that stayed around—for nearly two hundred years now!

Since the 1800s, this phantom cat has reportedly been prowling the darkened corridors of the Capitol Building, carefully choosing when to appear and whom it wants to harass. The Demon Cat, as it has been dubbed, always waits until its victim is alone and the hour is late. Some members of the security service that patrols the Capitol shudder when they think of encountering the cat, having heard the tales of previous instances when the cat has appeared. Such encounters, say the victims, can be traumatizing.

One victim, a security guard, recounted an experience that he had on a cold January night. He was walking down a dark hallway and saw a shadowy cat come gliding toward him in the gloom. As the animal came closer, it seemed to grow bigger and bigger. The man rubbed at his eyes, sure that he was seeing an optical illusion and then realized it was true—the cat really was getting bigger! He froze in place, paralyzed as he gazed into the creature's glowing eyes. The cat came closer to him, still growing, until it was nearly the size of a tiger, the man later claimed. Then, suddenly, it let out a tremendous roar and jumped toward him with its claws extended! The guard tried to scream, but he couldn't move. He covered his face with his arms and waited for the monster's body to collide with his own. He finally let out a scream and then . . . nothing happened. The Demon Cat had vanished into thin air.

The trembling guard was once again alone in the corridor. His body was covered with sweat, and he forced himself to breathe normally again. Finally, when he had pulled himself together, he went back to his desk for the night. He never finished making his rounds that evening.

Over the years, there have been many reactions reported by those who encounter the Demon Cat. Some have fainted and some have run screaming from the building. Others, like the security guard, claim to have been simply paralyzed with fear. Rumor has it that many years ago, an appearance by the Demon Cat actually caused an elderly guard's fatal heart attack.

As scary as the cat may be, though, its mere appearance is not the reason that so many dread encountering it in the dark halls of the Capitol. They

Since the 1800s, this phantom cat has reportedly been prowling the darkened corridors of the Capitol Building, carefully choosing when to appear and whom it wants to harass.

fear the cat because of its accuracy as a harbinger of doom. This phantom feline always appears just before a national tragedy . . . or on the eve of the changing of an administration.

Many who work here will joke about the cat or scoff at the reality of the legend, but no matter what they might say, congressmen, staff workers, maintenance personnel, and security guards alike all walk the corridors of the Capitol in fear of encountering the horrific Demon Cat. It is a meeting that none of them want to have because it can only mean that worse things are still to come.–*Troy Taylor*

Chessie

Sea serpents—large reptilian creatures that surface briefly then disappear back into the deep—have been reported off the coast of Virginia for centuries. However, of late, attention has been focused on a serpentlike creature in the Chesapeake Bay named Chessie.

Reports of a large snakelike animal seen in the Chesapeake Bay and its tributaries made the news in the late 1960s. Then in 1978, a retired CIA employee, Donald Kyker, reported seeing four Chessies about seventy-five yards offshore. His neighbors, the Smoots, also saw the creatures. In 1980, no fewer than four charter boats—carrying twenty-five people—observed Chessie. All witnesses generally agree that the creature appears to be twenty-five to forty feet long, a little less than a foot across, dark, with no limbs, fins, or distinguishing details on its oval head.

Chessie, whatever it is, seems to get around. In March 1980, a Richmond resident saw it in the Appomattox River near Hopewell, which is farther inland than previously reported. The woman had gone to Hopewell with her husband for dinner at the Harbor Light Restaurant, beside the river.

In a letter to a Richmond newspaper she wrote, "I got out of my car and looked up the Appomattox River. . . . Something caught my eye. . . . We watched as it got nearer. . . . It had a . . . long, undulating body." She added that she had not said anything, "for fear of being ridiculed."

She said the creature was "the most fascinating thing I ever saw." It had a dark, snakelike body with a reptilian head that matched those from sightings near the bay.

On May 31, 1982, an opportunity came to document these strange sightings. Around 7:30 p.m. that night, Robert and Karen Frew saw one of the animals in a bay at Love Point, near the mouth of the Chester River. Grabbing his videotape camera, Frew taped the long, dark serpentine form swimming just a hundred feet away. The creature was seen cruising along toward a group of swimmers, before diving beneath them and reappearing on the other side of the swimmers. The two minutes of videotape clearly showed an animate object.

Soon after, Michael Frizzell and the Enigma Project became involved in investigating and documenting reports of the Chesapeake Bay sightings of Chessie. On August 20, 1982, the Enigma Project was able to get the Frew videotape for an audience with George Zug and other scientists at the Smithsonian Institution's Museum of Natural History.

"After thoroughly examining the tape," Frizzell reported, "the scientists, although intrigued by what it apparently depicted, were unable to reach any conclusions about the 'animate' object shown. The videotape's quality was simply not good enough to allow such a determination."

Then in 1994 and 1995, to totally confuse the picture, a male manatee that had wandered far from Florida was positively identified as it traversed the waters of the Chesapeake Bay. What did the authorities decide to name it? Chessie, unfortunately. The manatee was outfitted with a tracking device, and as its seasonal movements into northern waters were confirmed, reports of the bay's mysterious serpent—the original Chessie—dramatically diminished in frequency.

Could some of the original Chessie cryptid sightings be of out-of-place manatees? Of course they could; but the manatee, a gentle, aquatic mammal eight to fourteen feet long, looks like an overweight seal, not a thin, serpentine creature.

Bigfoot

He's called Sasquatch, Skunk Ape, and most familiarly, Bigfoot. Whatever the name, the description is the same. He, or sometimes she, is a big, ape/man creature who's been seen slipping through the forests and mountains of North America since Indian times. Bigfoot's habitat is primarily the Pacific Northwest, but he has been known to turn up in Virginia too, especially in the mountains of the western part of the state. When he does, he shows all the characteristics of the legendary beast: He is hairy, walks upright, and for all his bulk, he is shy and skittish, seemingly as anxious to avoid us as we are to stay out of his way.

One of the most discussed series of encounters occurred in the 1970s.

On June 29, 1972, three people walking up a mountainside scattered when they saw a seven-to-eight-foot-tall Bigfoot. The creature was running on two legs and perhaps was more scared than they were, for it passed them on its way down the mountain!

A number of other sightings occurred in 1977. Two marines saw a giant brown Bigfoot at the Quantico Marine Base on January 17 of that year. In May, a Pittsylvania County woman reported a seven-foot-tall Bigfoot, and a similar sighting followed that summer.

Though the reports from the 1970s were the most concentrated in time, Bigfoot had actually been seen in the state for at least forty years before that, and perhaps longer.

Devil Monkeys

Encountering a huge hairy creature as you're on a peaceful hike in the woods can be unnerving. But what frightens Virginians more may be the giant primates known as Devil Monkeys. Red-eyed, cave dwelling, and aggressive to dogs and possibly to man, these creatures are nothing like the rather shy Bigfoot.

Witnesses say that the beasts that have come to be called Devil Monkeys are baboon- or doglike, with dark, "mean" eyes and pointed ears. They have short to shaggy hair, varying in color from gray to red to black. Their large flat feet tend to narrow somewhat as they lengthen in adulthood. Footprints are usually about twelve inches long, but tracks up to fifteen inches have been found. Each foot bears three rounded toes, usually of the same size and length, with regular spacing between each one.

Their leaping mode of locomotion is one of the major reasons that some observers have confused Devil Monkeys with kangaroos. In Virginia, as well as some other southern states, it appears we may be dealing with a kind of giant baboon, but one that leaps as kangaroos do. Thus the files of cryptozoologists—researchers who specialize in the study of animals unknown to mainstream science—have been filled with reports of "mystery kangaroos" that may in fact be the Devil Monkey.

Many eyewitnesses have commented on the creatures' aggression; they don't back down when confronted by dogs and humans. Though generally thought to be vegetarians, they may kill livestock and small game. To add to the hair-raising picture, they exhibit a wide range of primate hoots, calls, screeches, whistles, and "blood-chilling screams." And to top things off, they smell bad, very bad. So bad that some people call them Skunk Apes.

In 2000, cryptozoologist Chad Arment examined the sightings of creatures that may have been Devil Monkeys experienced by one Virginia family, the Boyds, and their friends. The sightings stretched over a long period, from 1959 to the 1990s, in the mountains around Saltville. It started when the parents of ghost investigators Pauline Boyd and James Boyd experienced a 1959

injury, though they were badly shaken.

Two friends of Pauline's recorded a recent encounter, also from a car, of a similar creature near Saltville. The beast crossed the road in front of them, jumped a ditch line, went over a fence, and then moved through high weeds lining the road, only to disappear into ground cover.

Pauline Boyd said, "According to all witnesses, this animal was unlike any they had seen before. Walking on all four legs, it stood around three feet high. Covered in shaggy, rough, graying brown fur, it had a long muzzle and small pointed ears. The legs of the creature were short, with the hind legs much larger than the front and sporting long, kangaroo-like rear feet. Claws were evident on both the hind and smaller front feet. If this creature had stood on these powerful-looking hind legs, they stated, it would have been at least five and a half to six feet tall. It also sported a long, hairless (opossum-like was the term they used) tail. Though moving quickly, it gave the appearance in its gait and gray mottled fur of being an older animal. They watched in amazement as it quickly disappeared from sight."

Virginia's Devil Monkeys have never been identified as any known creature. But though their origins elude researchers, the creatures themselves haunt the state to this day.

attack on their automobile by a creature that had "light, taffy colored hair, with a white blaze down its neck and underbelly. . . . It stood on two large well-muscled back legs, and had shorter front legs or arms." It left three scratch marks on the car, apparently put there by its front limbs.

Arment quotes Pauline as saying, "Several days after this incident, two nurses in the Saltville area were driving home from work early one morning, and were attacked by an unknown creature who ripped the convertible top from their car." The nurses managed to escape without

Mothman in the Night

Six feet tall, with an insectlike head and wings where its arms should be, the creature called Mothman has been seen frequently in West Virginia. But Virginia has at least one Mothman story of its own.

This account comes from an Arlington businessman who saw something very strange while in the company of three friends in the winter of 1968–69. They were in Prince William County, on a farm near Haymarket, when they went to investigate an unusual whoozing noise. They came upon a dark figure over eight feet tall standing by a tree. Not knowing what the figure was, the group retreated to their car and turned on its lights. "All we saw was this huge thing with large red-orange eyeballs and winglike arms. We couldn't get out of there fast enough."

Giant Thunderbird Roosts in Louisa County

In Indian legend, the thunderbird was a giant creature so large that when its wings flapped it created the boom we call thunder. Its eyes shot bolts of lightning, and it created fear wherever it went. If our correspondent below is right, one of the places it still goes is Virginia.

Back in 1999 or 2000, I believe I saw a thunderbird. I was growing up in Louisa County, Virginia, and the spring of that year we had a tropical storm. I was standing in my backyard watching the birds ride the wind and thermals when I noticed an extremely large bird flying towards our tree line. I had never seen a bird that big before. Turkey vultures that had been flying around quickly flew off, so I could see this animal's size in relation to the vultures. The tree it first attempted to land on snapped from its weight, so for about a minute it went from tree to tree until it found one sturdy enough.

After watching this animal for close to an hour, it hadn't moved from the tree. It had just been resting and preening itself. So after a while I decided to see how close to it I could get. A few minutes later I was well within a hundred feet from the creature and I could clearly see it was not a vulture. I've hunted and have been in the outdoors almost all my life and I've never seen anything like it. Instead of being dull black like a vulture, it was this beautiful jet black, almost like a grackel. Its head was way different too. It was shaped more like an eagle's and it had a big curved beak. Also, around the neck there was a silver "collar," and it had huge grasping feet and the talons to match.

The entire time I was sneaking up to it, the creature knew I was there and it kept its head focused on me. As I got closer, I noticed it was making a loud hissing sound, very similar to a goose. I imagine it did not like me getting so close to it. After a few minutes the creature took off. Initially it needed a few flaps, but after that it soared out of sight.

Once back inside I drew a picture of exactly what it looked like and dated it. But as the years went by, I kinda forgot about it until in the last few years I began to hear people's accounts of a giant bird that matched what I saw. I'm not out to get in the news or be on TV, but I figure if my story can help the mystery in any shape or form, then it is my responsibility to do so. Thank you for your time and consideration. — *Cary Woodruff*

Bunnyman

Thunderbirds. Mothman. Giant Birds. All kinds of flying things seem to enjoy the skies over Virginia. But the weirdest creature of all must be Bunnyman. This rascally rabbit may be a cryptid, a prank, and/or an urban legend—take your pick. Whichever it is, the critter is most often reported in Fairfax County.

Tales of the Bunnyman have been reported in the area since at least 1970. The thing's infrequent and widely scattered appearances tend to occur in secluded locations. Sightings usually tell of a figure clad in a white bunny suit and armed with an ax who threatens children or vandalizes property. By 1973, Bunnyman reports had spilled over into neighboring Maryland and the District of Columbia. And by the 1980s, the Bunnyman had become a more sinister figure, with several gruesome murders attributed to him. Although he has been reported as far south as Culpeper, his main haunt has always been the area surrounding the bridge along the W&OD Railroad tracks and Colchester Road in Clifton, the now infamous "Bunnyman Bridge."

In one important piece of research on folklore, University of Maryland student Patricia Johnson wrote a paper in 1973 entitled "The Bunny Man." She interviewed thirty-three teenage students from Prince Georges County, Maryland, about the stories and legends they had heard of the disturbing rabbit-creature. Brian A. Conley, historian-archivist at Fairfax County Public Library, created the following summary of her findings for his own research on the topic.

a. Fourteen different geographic locations (mostly in Virginia) are mentioned

b. Eighteen involve the Bunny Man chasing or frightening people, usually children, with a hatchet or ax

c. Fourteen tell of attacks on cars

d. Nine claim he attacked a couple parked in a car

e. Five accuse him of vandalism on homes or buildings

f. Only three mention a murder

Conley also tracked down the following article that many had seen but forgotten in recent years, which shows that one of the first encounters with the Bunnyman was published in the *Washington Post* of October 22, 1970.

MAN IN BUNNY SUIT SOUGHT IN FAIRFAX

Fairfax County police said yesterday they are looking for a man who likes to wear a "white bunny rabbit costume" and throw hatchets through car windows. Honest.

Air Force Academy Cadet Robert Bennett told police that shortly after midnight last Sunday he and his fiancée were sitting in a car in the 5400 block of Guinea Road when a man "dressed in a white suit with long bunny ears" ran from the nearby bushes and shouted: "You're on private property and I have your tag number."

The "rabbit" threw a wooden-handled hatchet through the right front car window, the first-year cadet told police. As soon as he threw the hatchet, the "rabbit" skipped off into the night, police said. Bennett and his fiancée were not injured.

Police say they have the hatchet, but no other clues in the case. They say Bennett was visiting an uncle, who lives across the street from the spot where the car was parked. The cadet was in the area to attend last weekend's Air Force-Navy football game.

Is the Bunnyman real? Perhaps, perhaps not, but one thing is certainly true—he has become a permanent part of weird Virginia, as these accounts from our readers confirm.

White Light
The way I heard it, the man who became Bunnyman escaped from the Lorton Prison in the 1920s or 1930s and posted himself out there near the Clifton Bridge. It was mostly only on Halloween that he actually killed and scared kids.

In one case, four kids went to Bunnyman Bridge one Halloween night. Three of the kids dared the other to walk under the bridge to the end which isn't very far, but the Bunnyman was on each of their minds. The kid got to about the middle of the bridge when a bright white light appeared above it. The other kids backed away slowly, but the kid in the tunnel became paralyzed and couldn't leave.

There was a big crashing sound of the train going by above the bridge, and when the kids looked up after it went by, they saw their friend hanging dead from the bridge's entrance. This all happened in just ten to fifteen seconds. One of the kids who witnessed this was marked with a white streak of hair on his head, which is there to this day.—*Sean Anderson*

Bunnyman's in the Window
I grew up in D.C. and found out about Bunnyman in the third grade, when my father told me that when he was a little boy, he saw the Bunnyman peeping through someone's window looking to kill somebody (in D.C., Bunnyman was known to be a killer). So basically, my father ran for his life, told his mother, and they called the police. I was hysterical with fright when he told me this and a few years later, just out of curiosity, I searched online for info on the Bunnyman only [to] find that he was real. Even though I'm now 22, the Bunnyman still scares me.—*Baker*

Rabbit with a Flat Tire
I lived in Fairfax, Virginia, in the early 1970s, and I remember the Bunnyman. I heard that he hacked up his family with an axe or chainsaw and would wait by the roadside to do the same to people who reminded him of his family. It was suggested he would strike every year on Halloween, and one year, it seemed to be true. There was a report of a man standing on the side of a road, dressed as a giant rabbit. Not wanting to take chances, the police closed the road down and surrounded the big bunny, which turned out to be a guy who was just changing a flat tire on his way to a costume party.—*Bird Waring*

Bunnyman: From Birth to Bye-Bye
Back in the late 1800s, the residents of a Northern Virginia town disliked having a mental institution so close to their homes, and they protested to the state, which gave in and decided to move the institution elsewhere. During the move, two patients escaped and took refuge at a nearby bridge.

One of the men was found hung from a tree a few days later, the other man was coined "Bunnyman" after numerous bunny carcasses were found near the bridge. I have heard that the man either ate the rabbits or used the rabbit skin for clothing.

The legend gets a little unclear once again with respect to the fate of Bunnyman. Some say that when police finally tracked him down, he ran onto the tracks of an oncoming train, killing himself. Others say he just vanished into the woods, never to be seen (alive) again. The Bunnyman's body has never been found.—*Dave Wandin*

Bet Your Carrot This Is the Original Article
The bridge most people think of as the infamous Bunnyman Bridge is on Colchester Road, but it is not the bridge by Route 1, across from the Lazy Susan. That bridge is now part of a new condominium development and it is definitely no longer "creepy." The real bridge is near the town of Clifton, on an abandoned right-of-way far back in the woods where the "old" Old Colchester Road turns to dirt and dead ends. Most of the kids nowadays know the wrong bridge. Back there, hidden in the middle of the forest, is the original article.—*Armand*

It's *not bravado* to say that Virginia has produced more heroes than most states. From American Presidents to the generals and admirals who are part of the state's proud military heritage, from valiant early settlers to modern miracle makers, Virginia has had more than its share of worthy residents.

It's no surprise, though, that with such a long history many Virginians have become famous, and infamous, more for weird qualities than heroic ones. These are the heroes and villains we aim to honor in this chapter—those who are strange, murderous, or just plain odd. This chapter is for those people who are remembered in local history, but not necessarily in the history books.

Local Heroes and Villains

P. D. Gwaltney and His Century-Old "Pet" Ham

Navigating the weird world, one can easily become jaded. All manner of strangeness passes our eyes each and every day, so it takes an odd item indeed to seize our attention. We've seen pet rocks, gazed upon people "walking" invisible, stiff-leashed dogs, and even witnessed a hissing pet cockroach. But never have we come across an old pet ham. Sound just a bit gamy to you? Fear not. As we've now learned, proper curing can drastically reduce the stench of departed pork thereby ensuring many, many happy decades of close friendship. Here's the thoroughly bizarre backstory to the Smithfield "ham man" and his century-old "pet" ham.

Pork purveyor and originator of the famous Smithfield ham, P. D. Gwaltney, Jr., found his best friend completely by accident. As he was looking through his warehouse in 1922, he came across a twenty-year-old ham that had miraculously escaped shipping. As a testament to the curing process his company used, the ham appeared remarkably appetizing, even if it had lost some sixty-five percent

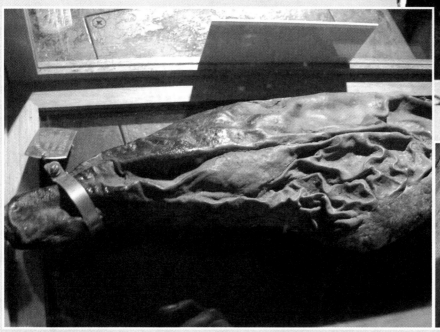

of its original weight over the years. Realizing the potential meatiness of the situation, the pork huckster bolted into action. With the instincts of a showman, Gwaltney took out a $1,000 insurance policy on his newfound friend and set his sights on the future. How long might his pet ham last, he wondered?

By most accounts, the unlikely duo was inseparable from then on. Like a proud parent, Gwaltney would drag his ham to exhibitions, food fairs, get-togethers, anywhere ham-loving (buying?) people might gather. But even with this extra burden, Gwaltney never felt hamstrung. Far from it. In fact, this friendly pairing was only getting started. In 1932, *Ripley's Believe It Or Not!* would feature Gwaltney's pal as the world's oldest ham, an honor that would bring with it national recognition.

For fourteen long years, the two bosom buddies moved happily about in gastronomic circles, until one awful day in 1936 when Gwaltney headed off to that big curing center in the sky. Would this tragic event signal the end of his beloved porker as well? "Not a *ham chance!*" fans seemed to say.

Happily rescued by the residents of Smithfield, Gwaltney's pride and joy would indeed carry on. In 2002, the ham celebrated its 100th anniversary. Today, the porker seems none the worse for wear as it begs for notice at Smithfield's quaint Isle of Wight Museum. There, stored safely beneath protective glass, the legendary mascot rests beside a life-size cardboard cutout of its one-time beloved master. Occasionally, visitors sight wistful glances between Gwaltney and the ham as they together ride out eternity, side by shank. For the sake of all that's strange, we can only hope these folks aren't lying. A man and his meat, such as it were, should never be trifled with.

Let's Get Happy in Richmond

Many artists are remembered as moody, angry, dissatisfied people, having the so-called artistic temperament. There are not many who are remembered for being Happy. In Richmond, one artist is known for both his work and his sunny mood. He is Happy the Artist.

Happy Kuhn is a local celebrity who spreads joy to the streets and galleries of Richmond through his fantastic and often psychedelic-esque artwork. He is known not just for the art he does on canvas. He can be seen even from a distance in what is perhaps his most visible piece of art, his infamous car.

Happy drives a station wagon splashed with colors and adorned with what the untrained eye might call junk, but which Happy fans know is art. From balloons to plastic to anything he might be inclined to glue on that week, Happy's car has become an emblem for the artist.

His personal style extends from his car to his outfits. Happy is usually seen about town in an outlandish hat and an outfit reminiscent of a clown's. He is Happy himself, and for many years has been spreading that happiness to the people of Richmond, as well as the rest of the world, through his bizarre artistic endeavors. Happy primarily paints murals, spreading good cheer in private residences, usually in children's bedrooms, as well as in nursery schools and in hospital pediatric wards.

We had a chance to talk to Happy in early June of 2006, while he was stuck in traffic on his way to painting a mural in Washington, DC.

Weird Virginia: How did you isolate Happiness as your muse and your public image? So many artists are doom and gloom, like the public perception is Vincent Van Gogh cutting his ear off and what not.

Happy Kuhn: That was just merchandising. Vincent wrote his mother every day. This was before cable TV and NFL football, so people were interested in it. . . .

I've raised eight children. I won the Mickey Mouse Club talent roundup in 1956. My father was an artist, although I didn't want to go in that vein. My father was an ornery and unpredictable man, so I associated that with art and it took me a while to overcome that.

I used to get out of school to do posters and special projects. It became a way to set me apart from the other kids. The popularity that came with being slightly different became an addiction. I finished high school in '60. This was the time of Vietnam, confusion, rock and roll; there was a lot of excitement then. The terror of the war—I was involved in that aspect, the meanness of politics and government rule.

I had two young children then. And you can't make a living selling hate and fear. So I stayed with the things that are upbeat. Popular iconography, but stories with peace and growth, my own style. . . . It's always what can we possibly do with our consciousness that will benefit the entire planet?" That's the theme of my lifework.

WVA: At what point did you start wearing your distinctive outfits and driving your car?

HK: It started out as a joke. You're known by your clothes. I've always worn two different kinds of shoes. I started painting the wheels of my car back in high school.

We're known by our vehicles, by our clothes, by where we live. I drove close to 30,000 miles last year cross-country. You're being seen.

I had a '69 Rambler station wagon. I kept adding stuff to the roof. One side said, "Are we having a great day yet?" The other said, "There goes that car again." The back said, "You're number two in my parade."

It was always changing. An advertising agency called

me up and asked if I wanted to be in a McDonald's ad. I held up a sign that said buy two and give one away, it was a deal for three cheeseburgers or something. . . . That ad put me on the map. I was giving out autographs. It was a boon. It didn't mean any money to me, but it raised my visibility level considerably.

WVA: Do you consider yourself an outsider artist?

HK: I've been following art my whole life. I just got back six days ago from Europe. It was my Mecca. I was at the Louvre, Barcelona, Florence, Rome.

I was looking around for contemporary art to find out where I fit in. Three of my boys are into tattooing and stencil making. I get influenced by MTV, cable — what's the difference between video imagery and what's painted on the wall? . . .

I'm working contemporary thoughts into my mural painting, hiding them in there, not preaching. There's so much anger and confusion. I was for many years angry and confused. I'm getting a handle on that. It goes along with getting older.

I'm reading Pat Conroy. *The Great Santini, . . . Our Losing Season*, when he played basketball for the Citadel. He wraps words around thoughts we all had during the Vietnam era. It spoke so loudly to me. I could just weep. That's what art is all about. How can you effect changes in people and give them a voice they don't have?

WVA: How does it feel being such a local legend? You're known for your art, but also for your car, and your clothes, and just for being Happy. How do you feel about being embraced so hard in the Richmond region, what does it mean to you?

HK: That's a great question. After getting back from Rome and Spain and France, I looked at Richmond again. They always say that it's a town, and it *is* a town. Really, if you know of fifty people just by word of mouth, you're a community member. There're 248,000 people in the city of Richmond. Within ten miles out there's three quarters of a million. People see the car. I get thumbs up and waves and honks all the time. I don't know them. But I feel warm.

Terror on the Highways

Most of us think of the 1950s as an idyllic time, all sock hops, rock 'n' roll, and malted milks down at the soda fountain. In reality, the '50s had a dark side and evil people just as any other era in human history. In Virginia, there was one man who proved that many times over. His name was Melvin Rees, but most Virginians who remember him know him better as the Sex Beast.

The most famous victims of the Sex Beast were the Jackson family. On January 11, 1959, their car was discovered abandoned along the roadside not far from Apple Grove. Mr. Carroll Jackson, his wife Mildred, as well as their daughters, aged eighteen months and five years, had vanished.

It wasn't until March 4 that their fate became known. While gathering brush near Fredericksburg, two men made a grisly discovery—the decomposing body of Carroll Jackson, his hands tied together. He had been shot in the back of the head. But the worst of that day was yet to come. As police extracted the body from the ditch it lay in, they were even more shocked to find the body of eighteen-month-old Janet Jackson, tossed into the ditch before her father. She had been alive when thrown in, and had suffocated from the weight of her deceased father.

Two weeks later, on March 21, the bodies of five-year-old Susan Jackson and her mother, Mildred, were also found in the woods. Their corpses made police realize they were dealing with not just a killer, but a truly deviant maniac. Both mother and child had been raped, then killed. Even scarier was the connection police made between the location of the bodies and the strange building that stood nearby.

In searching the area for evidence, the police stumbled upon a shack they realized they had dealt with before. Two years previously, they were tipped off to the existence of the strange building and had investigated it. Inside, they found the walls covered in bizarre pornographic images. Even more disturbing were the thousands of photos taken at and possibly stolen from a morgue, showing hundreds of dead female bodies.

Now, there were fresh tire prints near the shack. It was clear to police that they were dealing with someone who knew the Fredericksburg area, knew about the shack, had possibly been responsible for the bizarre photos, and who was a definite sexual predator on the loose.

The police interrogated dozens of people before finally getting a lead that seemed promising. A Norfolk man wrote to them, telling of a conversation he had had with a friend. The friend, high on methamphetamines, began ranting that he wanted to experience every aspect of human experience. He claimed that murder was not wrong, that it was just another human experience that he wanted to partake in. This man had had previous run-ins with the law, once for assaulting a woman.

The man described in the letter was a twenty-six-year-old jazz musician named Melvin David Rees. The police immediately tried to locate him, but were not successful. However, as they did a background search on him, they found a link to the death of another woman, which had occurred while Rees was a student nearby at the University of Maryland. A soldier and his girlfriend had been forced off the road by a man claiming to own the property they were driving through. He demanded money from the couple and they refused. He then shot the female passenger in the face, killing her. The soldier managed to flee to a house some miles away, where he called police. By the time they got to the crime scene, the killer had vanished. However, he had left behind the corpse of the young woman, Margaret Harold, which he

had sexually abused. The police soon located a nearby basement littered with pornography and morgue photos. In the letter the police had received, Rees's friend had mentioned Margaret Harold.

The cops were now convinced they had their man. They simply couldn't find him. None of his friends had seen him, and no one at the clubs he hung out at knew where he was. Police even called in psychics for help; but eventually, it was Rees himself who led to his own downfall.

He sent a letter to the friend who had written the police. In it, Rees said that he was living in Arkansas. The friend again went to the police, who called in the FBI. The Feds managed to hunt down Rees, and he was quickly identified by the soldier from the Maryland killing as the man who shot his girlfriend.

Once Rees was apprehended, investigators searched his home, where they found a .38-caliber pistol and a series of notes and journals in which Rees admitted his involvement in the murders. He had saved newspaper articles about the crimes, as well as the weapon with which he had committed the murders.

Journalists pounced on the story and quickly dubbed Rees with the name that he is most remembered by, the Sex Beast. He was convicted for the murder in Maryland and, shortly after, for the murders of the Jackson family as well. He eventually admitted to committing two other murders, and police suspect he committed two more on top of that—all simply for the "experience" of it.

Is Jack the Ripper from Virginia?

The story of Jack the Ripper was tabloid news when the infamous serial killer went on his murderous rampage in 1888. Speculation as to the identity of the Ripper continues even today, with books and films still appearing on a regular basis. The world remains fascinated by the identity of the menacing murderer of five young ladies of the night over a century ago in London.

Many have guessed that the killer was a resident of the Whitechapel section of London's east side, surmising that only a local could know the streets and culture well enough to get away with murder after murder. Others have guessed that the killer came from a more affluent section of London and used his wealth, political clout, and social connections to stay above the law. Still others think that the Ripper did not come from London at all, but from, of all places, Norfolk, Virginia!

The Virginia suspect for Jack the Ripper-hood is a merchant named James Maybrick. In reality, he was not a Norfolk native. He was born in Liverpool before moving to Norfolk in 1871. There, a bout with disease left him with a lifelong arsenic addiction. This addiction led to his sensational death well before he was ever considered a Ripper candidate.

In 1889, Maybrick died suddenly, due to what was deemed an overdose of arsenic. It seemed a self-inflicted death, but his wife Florence was eventually accused of murdering him by intentionally giving him an overdose. Though she was

found guilty of the crime, her conviction was eventually overturned. She lived quietly until dying in 1941.

Over time, most people forgot the story of the Maybricks. But in 1992, his name came flying back to the forefront when a diary surfaced that was supposedly his and allegedly outed him as the one true Jack the Ripper.

A Liverpool metalworker named Michael Barrett claimed that he was given the diary by a friend in 1992. It is detailed enough to be identified as James Maybrick's, and it is incredibly specific about the Jack the Ripper crimes. On top of this, the diary also outlines Maybrick's participation in two other murders of the time not usually attributed to Jack the Ripper.

When the diary was discovered, a stopwatch was also found. Etched onto it were the initials "JM" as well as the initials of the five women who were slain by Jack the Ripper.

Most people have written off the Maybrick diary as a hoax. They say it was created well into the 20th century, and the watch was altered, in an effort to cash in on the public fascination with "Ripperology."

Others, including the diary's current owner, stand by it. The only certain truth is that the identity of the Ripper still remains unknown. But it is a fascinating prospect that a man who called Virginia, not London, his home for such a large portion of his life might just be the world's most notorious serial killer.

Jeane Dixon

Famed clairvoyant and seer Jeane Dixon moved within a mysterious landscape of smoke and mirrors. In life, she constructed for herself a reputation as an ultrareliable mainstream psychic. In death and over time, much of that veneer has been stripped away. Does this mean Ms. Dixon was an outright fraud? That her predictions of events yet to be were mere figments of imagination? Not at all. In fact, we believe Jeane Dixon truly thought she possessed the "gift." And so do many of her staunch supporters. In a nod to the latter, a celebratory museum about her life and "astounding" revelations now stands in the unassuming village of Strasburg. How does that old P. T. Barnum saying go again?

Dixon, you may recall, gained national recognition with her widely reported prophecy of John F. Kennedy's assassination. In reality, however, her "dead-on" foretelling contained more holes than Bonnie and Clyde's death car. Dixon herself later admitted that "during the 1960 election, I saw Richard Nixon as the winner." In fact, Dixon could not specify the exact means of Kennedy's death, the precise presidential term, or whether it would come via assassination, an accident, or natural causes. Still, she was credited with this earthshaking prediction.

The Jeane Dixon Museum and Library, to its enormous credit, contains a wealth of Dixon's "misses" as well as many of her "hits." Through books, magazines, tabloids, and artifacts, the visitor is introduced to her bizarre world and left to make final determinations about her "gift of prophecy" on their own. Skeptics, as well, are provided a prominent place in the museum, which is all the better if one looks to gain a balanced view of Jeane Dixon's life and her many predictions.

Also on the plus side, we understand that Ms. Dixon refused to charge for her psychic consultations (Dionne Warwick and Jackie Stallone, please take note), and that she was instrumental in forming a benevolent institution for children. She lived her life firmly within the confines of her religion (Catholicism) and was, by most accounts, a selfless, giving person.

So, then, just where does the weirdness factor exist in all of this? Somehow, some way, this wonderfully savvy and understated woman managed to bamboozle us into believing her more-wrong-than-right predictions were the *final* word on the future. As one debunker put it, "even a broken watch is right two times a day." In our book, that's just about as weird as it gets, so we commend Ms. Dixon for a job well done.

Jeane Dixon sees peace in 2000, defines mystic talent as 'God-given'

by Kathy Streed

Internationally known prophetess Jeane Dixon, in an appearance Sept. 12 at Morris Civic Auditorium, spoke of her extra sensory perceptions, the world's future, and man's purpose on earth.

Mrs. Dixon, a Washington D.C. real estate broker whose prophecies brought her national attention in the '50's, believes peace will come to the world in the year 2000, but will be preceded by "great trouble" in 1998-99. She says, "Peace will be ours by divine intervention."

A deeply religious woman, Mrs. Dixon advises all men to "use the talents given you by God to the best of your life. God and push you the last in mediocrity—God and jority.

Receive

She classifie as "revelation pathy." Revelatio from God, says M are His will, whi changed by man's perienced her fir

when she was seven.

Mrs. Dixon says she has heard the voices of Christ and angels in her revelations. Her foresight of John F. Kennedy's assassination was a revelation.

Telepathy describes the vibration and thoughts Mrs. D receives from men. Thro telepathy, she knew of Ma Luther King's and Robert Kennedy's impending assassi tions.

Through telepathy, Mrs. Dix has decided that the majo Americans consider today' serious concerns to be econ well-being, war, and pol "This talent is not somethi you turn on and off like a wate faucet," says Mrs. Dixon. Sh plains that she cannot always, will, "predict" an event's ome or some future happen-

'A God-given talent'

s. Dixon regards he peareo vic Audit Zehring) Old Hick

Edgar Cayce

Virginia, the saying goes, is for lovers. Not many realize that it's also for psychics, and that one of the most influential psychics the world has known made his home in Virginia Beach. He and his strange abilities became legend in his own lifetime. These days, his legacy lives on through an institute that still stands in the resort town today.

Edgar Cayce was born in Kentucky. He had little schooling, as his family could not afford to pay for his education, but he did read the Bible once a year and started his own business, selling insurance with his father. That business became impossible when he contracted a severe and long-lasting case of laryngitis, which made lengthy sales pitches difficult. While this might seem to be a stroke of bad luck, it actually wound up giving Cayce a life beyond his dreams.

One day a traveling hypnotist and showman came through Kentucky and offered to cure Cayce's condition through hypnosis. The hypnotic treatments worked, but not permanently. Cayce's voice would return to its full timbre while he was in a trance, but once he was awakened, the laryngitis would again take hold. When the hypnotist had to travel on to the next town, Cayce and an associate began their own explorations of healing through hypnosis. Cayce would continuously reenter his hypnotized state and, with the help of his friend, would be able to heal himself for longer and longer periods of time, until his ailment permanently left him.

Amazed at his newfound abilities, Cayce's associate urged him to attempt to use his healing abilities on others. At first he was resistant. He was a devout Christian and he wasn't sure if his abilities could be reconciled with the teachings of the church. He also didn't want to make money by exploiting the weaknesses of others. But in time he agreed. He administered healing to people for free, and word of his powers quickly got out. People from all over the area began visiting Cayce to have their diseases cured. Soon his fame became known well beyond the borders of his small Kentucky town.

At this point, Cayce's life took another strange turn. He realized that he was able to help people who contacted him just through correspondence, provided they described their ailment and its location. He could cure people without ever meeting them personally! As this ability became even more widely known, Cayce was inundated with requests for help from the physically and mentally ill everywhere.

Eventually he realized that to continue his work he would have to ask for donations. This way he could dedicate the necessary amount of time to his healing without having to worry about working for a living.

Not surprisingly, some of these donations came from people who wanted to use Cayce to make a quick buck. Speculators, for instance, offered him money to predict stock outcomes of the day. Cayce tried to do this, but found that his abilities in this area were far from accurate, and the effort was making him physically weaker. He resolved to use his abilities only to serve others.

In 1925, Cayce moved from Kentucky to Virginia Beach, claiming that a clairvoyant voice had instructed him to set up shop there. He hired a staff and established a number of institutions, including a hospital in his name. Funding for that came from one of his wealthier patients.

His work put an immense strain on him, both physically and emotionally. Due to the crushing amount of requests that came to him, Cayce was doing eight readings each day, even though he said that any more than two a day was detrimental to his own health. Still, he continued to push himself. In 1945, he suffered a stroke and died on the third of January.

By the end of his life, Cayce had given readings to over 14,000 of his faithful, who believed absolutely in his powers. Many others insisted that he was a fraud, preying on the sick and using their own hopes against them. The skeptics' voices, though, have not done much to dissuade those who believe in Cayce and his abilities. This is evidenced by the Association for Research and Enlightenment, an organization devoted to Cayce and his teachings, which still exists in Virginia Beach. The group was founded in 1931. From that point until Edgar Cayce's death, those seeking healing were asked to join the A.R.E. After Cayce's death, his son assumed leadership of the organization and has helped guide it. The group still promotes studies of Cayce and further exploration of his abilities. Each summer in the mountains of Virginia, A.R.E. holds a camp for children to explore spirituality.

In his time, Edgar Cayce was embraced as a healer and dismissed as a charlatan. Now, sixty years after his death, he, as well as his powers, are still studied, debated, and marveled at. Cayce helped usher in the New Age movement and opened up a side to spirituality unlike anything the world had seen before.

The Phone Phreak

Freaks abound in the world of the weird, from actual circus freaks to the monstrous freaks of legend. However, there have been other freaks out there over the years, less well known but just as much whispered about. These freaks aren't even freaks, they are phreaks, and for many years they secretly ruled the telephone wires.

One of the most famous and influential phreaks was a Virginia native. He was the linchpin of an underground movement that remains largely overlooked despite the unexpected influence it has had on the world. And his life has taken twists and turns not even his fellow phreaks saw coming.

The man currently known as Joybubbles was born Joe Engressia on May 25, 1949, in Richmond. Blind from birth, Engressia was fascinated by telephones from his earliest childhood. He would dial lines that featured recordings so he could listen to them. While listening, he would often whistle to himself. He realized that when he hit a certain pitch in his whistling, the recordings he was listening to would automatically stop.

Engressia had perfect pitch, so he was able to identify and reproduce the exact tone that stopped the recordings. He was only eight years old at the time. He called the phone company and asked them why the tone produced this result. They told him to forget about it. He did not. Instead, his interest was sparked and he developed what would become a lifelong obsession with figuring out and manipulating the phone system.

Joe Engressia was one of the earliest people to covertly explore the inner workings of the world's phone system. These people would become known as "phone phreaks"; Engressia was one of the kings of their world.

The tone that Engressia isolated was at 2600 Hz. This, he and some others around the country discovered, was the key to controlling the phones. By producing a 2600 Hz tone at a certain point, phone users could trick the phone system into thinking that they were an operator. From that point on, there was a seemingly limitless amount of exploring to be done: free long distance calls, open conference calls, routing calls to specific parts of the world, all by reproducing certain tones.

Joe Engressia had become the hub of the world of phone phreaks when he was caught and arrested. While at college in Florida, he was taken into custody for giving fellow students access to free long distance calls by doing his whistle. An article in a local paper outlining his exploits and his arrest was published. Within days, Engressia was getting calls from other people who had figured out how to mess with phone systems. Joe began chronicling it all.

As more and more people called him, Engressia became the center of a web of phone phreakers. He would pass on new discoveries, give them each other's contact information, and set up times when they could link up in conference calls to discuss their hobby.

The phreakers at the time all pointed to Engressia as one of their earliest influences. Thousands of them were manipulating the world's phone lines each night, including "Captain Crunch" (named after a promotional toy given away in boxes of Cap'n Crunch cereal in the '60s that produced a perfect 2600 Hz tone), Evan Doorbell, and Mike from New York.

In 1971, an *Esquire* magazine article reported on how large a subculture phone phreaking was becoming. The article detailed the government's efforts to curb phreaking, and also told of another Joe Engressia arrest. An undercover agent had coaxed Joe into talking about his telephonic activities and used the information to obtain a search warrant for his home. When police entered, they found all sorts of equipment used to access, manipulate, and travel through the complex world of telephones.

Engressia wound up serving thirty days in prison and pledged not to play on the phones anymore.

Phone phreaking became much less prevalent as phone companies converted to digital systems that could no longer be manipulated by tones. But many in the phone phreak community became innovators in the world of computers.

But what about Joe Engressia? In May of 1988, Engressia legally changed his name to Joybubbles and claimed that he was eternally five years old. He had reverted to childhood, he explained, to overcome some of the trauma dealt to him by sexual abuse in his early years. He lives life as a small child these days, and has listened to every episode of Mister Rogers' Neighborhood. He still deals with phone lines and has created a show called "Stories and Stuff" that callers can listen in on by dialing 206-FEELING. Joybubbles himself tells stories on the show, from his current home base of Minneapolis. He mostly lives off Social Security checks.

From the eight-year-old child exploring on the phone to the eternal five-year-old man obsessed with Mister Rogers, Joybubbles has lived a fascinating life and contributed much to the world around him.

Grand Ascender to the Hierarchy of Weirdness

There is a single man responsible for at least three of the most unusual sites to be seen in Virginia. And to us, that makes him a true local hero. As you will see, though, some Virginians would sooner cast him as one of the state's villains. The sites he has created are Foamhenge (a full-scale replica of Stonehenge rendered in, what else, Styrofoam); Escape from Dinosaur Kingdom (a surreal walk-through park where dinosaurs do battle with Civil War soldiers of the Union persuasion); and the Enchanted Castle (a bizarre hodge-podge of discarded kiddie park remnants and other fiberglass oddities). The man behind all of this madness is Marc Cline.

Cline is the textbook definition of weird, with all of that word's intangibles, twists, and nuances thrown in for good measure. This one-man "imagination factory" has single-handedly brightened the Virginia countryside with his offbeat sculptures and embraced whimsy at a level far above that of most "grown-ups." Let's meet the man behind the magic.

Weird Virginia: Marc, while we were cruising along U.S. Route 11 near the Natural Bridge, we stumbled upon your Enchanted Castle Studios. We were awestruck by its weirdness, but a bit uncertain as to exactly *what* we were standing before. Can you help fill in the blanks?

Marc Cline: Sure! The Enchanted Castle Studio Tour was originally a Willy Wonka sort of place where I would try out new effects on folks before using them in other attractions. People could actually see me at work through two big glass windows as I'd busy myself with the latest sculpture or display. This all came to an abrupt halt on April 9, 2001, when a suspected arsonist burned the castle down. Gone in an instant were my journals, childhood art creations, paintings, movies I'd produced, as well as my comic book collection, interviews, and awards, even early photos of myself sitting on Santa's lap!

WVA: Can you tell us more about the fire? Who would do such a thing?

MC: It went down like this: Just before the fire, someone placed a package in my mailbox. Inside was a one-way "ticket to hell" with my name on it, a photo of me taken from a newspaper, and a handwritten "hellfire and brimstone" letter. Within the text, some fine person wrote that I was "slick upon the face of God" and that I honor and worship Satan. You know, it's funny—all along I've felt as if I've worshiped the Great Spirit and his son by helping people and spreading happiness.

WVA: Despite this setback, you and your strange operations appear to have risen from the ashes. Can you tell us what you have on tap right now?

MC: I thought you'd never ask! A year after the fire, I joined up with the nearby Natural Bridge attraction. We formed a partnership and built two new attractions on their premises: Professor Cline's Haunted Monster Museum and Escape from Dinosaur Kingdom. The Monster Museum was built inside an old Victorian mansion and is "tongue in cheek, not guts and eek." The *Washington Post* called the Haunted Monster Museum "one of the seven weird wonders of VA." Speaking of the *Washington Post*, they just reviewed Escape from Dinosaur Kingdom and declared, "It's amazing, it's brilliant, it's hilarious." I mixed two incongruent

themes together: the Civil War and dinosaurs. . . . Purely for fun, I have my dinosaurs consuming bumbling Yankees.

WVA: Capital stuff, Marc. And now could you tell us about your most mysterious attraction. When we drove down another stretch of U.S. Route 11, we wondered if we had tele-transported and landed in England. How else to explain the fact that Stonehenge was standing right before us? We soon learned that this was in fact *Foamhenge,* your brilliant full-size replica of the ancient monoliths. Do tell us about it!

MC: I envisioned Foamhenge fifteen years ago when I walked into a foam factory and saw sixteen-foot-tall blocks standing straight up. I gave the idea time to gel and waited for an opportunity to present itself. After joining up with Natural Bridge, I spotted a suitable location and shared my vision with my new partner, Lenny. The groovy thing about Lenny is he gives me free rein to create, even as he keeps an eye on the bottom line. In return, I told him not to worry, that I'd pitch the idea to several businesses and try to get everything donated for the construction of Foamhenge. It wasn't a hard sell. Every once in a while an opportunity comes around for folks to become a part

of something bigger than they are. Foamhenge offered just such an opportunity.

WVA: Awesome! Please share with us the nuts and bolts of such a vast and utterly bizarre undertaking.

MC: Foamhenge was prefabricated at the Enchanted Castle and trucked a mile and a half down to its present location on March 30, 2004. The next day it was erected and covered with a huge piece of black plastic. On April Fool's Day, I unveiled Foamhenge by yanking down the plastic to an eager audience of news media, supporters, and friends. To christen this faithful copy of Britain's most famous monoliths, I "phased" through a solid block of foam much as magician David Copperfield passed through the Giant Wall of China. I did this for two reasons. First, I figured going through foam would be easier than stone just in case I lost my nerve halfway through. Second, I did the foam illusion because we couldn't find any virgins around the area to sacrifice. Um, that's just a joke, folks!

WVA: As neat as your replica is, we couldn't help but notice that a few of the stones were lying askew from their original positions. Was this due to a storm or vandalism of some kind?

MC: The trouble is much of Foamhenge is constructed of inferior foam, which was somebody's goof at the foam factory, no doubt. For about five months the whole thing was intact, including the twenty-two-foot-tall interior stones. High winds finally forced this cheaper foam down, and we planned to reerect the larger blocks for

2005 using the good stuff. Unfortunately, the opening of Escape from Dinosaur Kingdom occupied much of my time, so I focused my energies there. Lenny and I kept Foamhenge closed through 2005 until I could give it my full attention. Spectators, however, could still get a great view of it from the pull-off on Route 11.

WVA: Marc, any final thoughts you'd like to share with us?

MC: It's understandable that people fear that which they do not understand. Yet when I began helping schools, churches, and Bible camps, raising money for sick children, donating free tickets to the underprivileged, helping local libraries with programs, dressing up like Santa and delivering flowers to elderly residents in nursing homes, etc., people starting seeing me for who I am: someone who just wants to deliver happiness. Without fantasies and dreams, we may as well die as a race and live amongst heartless and soulless zombies. Oh, but what a wonderful world it would be if everybody's reality was to make others happy. Hey, I can dream, can't I?

Mexican Wrestling Takes Richmond by Storm

Lucha libre is a style of professional wrestling native to Mexico. It's a fast paced, highly stylized, acrobatic sport where most of the competitors wear outlandish masks. Beyond the athletic component, there is a rich and storied culture surrounding lucha libre. Some of Mexico's most beloved folk heroes have grown out of it, such as Santo and the Blue Demon. *Rudos*, the bad guys, are genuinely loathed while *Téchnicos*, the good guys, are embraced and beloved as genuine heroes and icons of the community.

While fascinating as a cultural pastime, lucha libre would seem to have no place in a book about Virginia. Lucha libre is mostly popular in Mexico or areas with high Mexican populations. Traditions transform over time, however. And there is one cadre of young athletes, based in Richmond, who are taking lucha libre and putting their own stamp on it.

These young men are collectively known as Richmond Lucha Libre. They have started a wrestling league unlike anything the world has seen before. With their individual style, their bizarre characters, and their punk-rock attitude and fan base, these brawlers have continued Richmond's rich tradition of pouring forth into the world strange and unique performances.

Weird Virginia had a chance to talk with two of the wrestlers who participate in Richmond Lucha Libre. One was Chris Horrorshow, the league's founder. The other is one of their newest wrestlers, Devil Kimura.

WVA: We were really surprised to hear about a Lucha Libre league on the East Coast. It seems like something that's distinctly Mexican or from southern California.

Chris Horrorshow: It more has to do with the fact that we're all wrestling fans from a long time ago. We grew up watching wrestling and know a lot about wrestling. We decided when we started this thing out that we were gonna stay away from . . . everyone's "World Wide" or "Something and something championship wrestling." We wanted to distinguish ourselves. Plus, as smaller guys, it fits us better to go with the lucha style. It's a little flippier and more showy than your standard American professional wrestling.

WVA: So does your style actually follow the genuine lucha libre style?

CH: It is to an extent the lucha style. It's kind of hard to define to people who don't really follow or study wrestling a lot. It's a faster pace, more acrobatic style of wrestling. We've kind of adopted that. We've modified it to fit the modern times. It's a lot smoother in Mexico. A lot of rolls and throws as opposed to people falling on each other.

WVA: How about the culture of the masks? Do you guys always wear your masks in public like they do in Mexico?

CH: In such a small community like Richmond, it's kind of hard for us to not be recognized without our masks on. I've gone out places not in any

wrestling capacity and people yell "Horrorshow! You!" And I wear a mask that covers my entire face. If I'm making an appearance in a wrestling capacity—we go and intro bands and MC events and stuff like that—I keep my mask on for that. The guys keep their face paint on.

WVA: One thing that does match traditional lucha is the outfits and the characters. You have some really amazing, strange characters. Some favorites are the Amazon and Fighty McIrish. Why do you guys go to such great lengths to go big with the characters?

Devil Kimura: Well, a lot of us are offbeat guys ourselves. And, we're trying to stay as far away from generic wrestling as we can. We want to get heat with the clapping—come on, Richmond. It's easiest for the crowd to get behind us with a definite personality. A lot of our fans aren't big fans of wrestling. Fighty's a drunk. They can get behind that. The Amazon's a monster. He can flip around. For a nonwrestling crowd, that's what's gonna get 'em. Characters they can get behind.

CH: These younger kids come out that don't really know a lot about wrestling. Or they may have watched it in the '80s when [Hulk] Hogan was popular. We're slowly but surely converting them over to like what they're seeing and turning them into a more hard-core wrestling crowd.

WVA: It seems to us that Richmond is kind of a focal point for odd people, especially artistic ones. It seems like what you guys are doing is in a way a part of a pretty long-standing tradition that Richmond produces some off-kilter performance groups. Tell me a little about what the city means to you guys and how important it is that you work out of there.

DK: It's a very rock-and-roll town. There's a big punk scene, lots of metal going on. We do have the art school, which adds to it. It's just that type of atmosphere with creative people. They like new stuff—tattoos, rock and roll, all that stuff. A bunch of girls who have been coming out to the shows are starting their own roller derby thing. Richmond is a great place. If you've got a good product, people will come out.

CH: Richmond being such a small place, it's obviously really important to us to be supportive of the scene. Usually we feature local bands on our shows as well as the wrestling. That kind of thing is very important to me personally. I really feel it should be a far more thriving culture than it actually is. People look at it and think there's not a lot going on and I'm trying to turn that around, at least as much as one guy with a wrestling show can. We want to turn Richmond and Virginia into the new Philly. Then we'll all make a million dollars.

World's Greatest Wrap Artist

Gary Duschl's dentist can't be happy. Duschl, a Virginia Beach resident, has spent more than forty years constructing the world's longest gum wrapper chain—from the wrappers of 1,160,179 pieces of sugary gum.

Duschl began his chain as a teenager in Canada in 1965 with a goal of making it longer than the chains of his classmates. When he met that goal in the blink of an eye, he pushed on—hoping to outdo everyone in his school, then everyone in his town, and yes, eventually, everyone in the world.

He accomplished that goal in 1994, when he beat out Kathy Ushler of Redmond, Washington, to have his chain named "World's Longest" in the *Guinness Book of World Records*. By September 2006, Duschl's stood at 49,578 feet. Making it entirely from the wrappers of Wrigley's brand gums (Doublemint, Spearmint, Winterfresh, Juicy Fruit, and Big Red), Duschl adds an average of seventy-five wrappers (or three feet) a day, which keeps the chain growing at quite a steady pace.

You can track that pace at www.gumwrapper. com, Duschl's Web site. In fact, you can even send him wrappers to help the cause; because as Duschl points out, it would be "crazy" for him to personally chew as much gum as he needs to continue the chain. (He calculates that he would have had to chew one stick every twenty minutes, twenty-four hours a day, for at least the last forty years to get the chain to its current length.) Over the years, family, friends, and even perfect strangers, moved by Duschl's steadfast determination and commitment, have contributed their Wrigley's wrappers to the effort.

Duschl stores the chain in nine Plexiglas bins in his den. Each year on the anniversary of the chain's "birthday" he has it measured, weighed, and counted by a professional surveyor (latest stats: 9.1 miles long, 661 pounds, $67,500 worth of gum). He notes with pride that the chain is as long as 160 football fields and taller than Mount Everest.

Duschl, who has a full-time job and a wife and seems otherwise unweird, is happy to leave his mark on the world one gum wrapper at a time. Now that's something to chew on.

Sasha: Homeless Person or Artistic Visionary?

For many years, a strange, brooding Russian man made the Adams Morgan section of Washington his home. He was known by all who frequented the area, and especially those who visited his favorite bar, Madam's Organ. Born Alexandr Zhdanov, he was known far and wide as Sasha.

Sasha knew few English phrases, and those he did know were often laced with profanity. He sometimes dressed up as Santa Claus, and often looked for mischief. But what he was most legendary for was his art. And even most of those who knew his story didn't realize exactly how legendary he was.

Sasha was known to trade his art for small amounts of money and even, at times, for alcohol directly. These transactions became well known at Madam's Organ, since Sasha was there so frequently, oftentimes from opening until last call. He was regarded almost universally as strange, if not outright crazy.

What most people didn't know was that Sasha was actually an artist of some accomplishment and renown. He was a Soviet dissident, exiled from the Soviet Union because his expressionistic art was deemed dangerous and unacceptable. But throughout his life his art had been displayed far and wide and his work was respected well beyond the bar he called his second home.

For most, this information wasn't revealed until Sasha's death in July of 2006. As more and more tales of his life became revealed, many who saw Sasha on a daily basis were shocked to realize that they had spent time in the company of an internationally known artist.

Compliment Man

Those with low self-esteem should stop spending thousands of dollars on therapy and antidepressants. It's cheaper and easier to swing by the corner of 18th Street and Belmont in the Adams Morgan section of Washington. It's here they can experience the charms of Ron Miller, the Compliment Man.

Miller began his double life as the Compliment Man in 1989. That's when he left his job at a Virginia Chuck E. Cheese restaurant and took up panhandling. While out on the streets, he began complimenting people, and he was given his nickname. It stuck. He has remained at his post since 1989, taking his role in people's lives seriously. There was a brief stretch when he moved to Florida; but after only a few weeks, he returned to Adams Morgan and began complimenting again. These days, he makes a regular loop that takes him to a number of different neighborhoods as well.

Most of the Compliment Man's compliments relate to people's hair, shoes, or clothes. He doesn't ask people for money. A number of imitators have begun offering a similar compliment service, but they ask for money. This makes Miller unhappy, as he feels they are stealing his service and using it dishonestly for profit.

Getting in Shape Backwards

We all know people who have a fanatical devotion to their exercise routines. But there are few who challenge themselves as much as one Washington resident known to all as the Backwards Jogger.

As you might guess, the Backwards Jogger jogs backwards. He makes his way down dangerous city streets and through dangerous intersections all with his back turned to the direction he's moving. He has become a local legend, as he appears seemingly at random and is quickly gone.

While he's always traveling, one unofficial home base for Backwards Jogger sightings is the corner of 13th and H. Locals in that area say the jogger is fond of slowing down at this corner to direct traffic.

Blelvis: Black Elvis Sings Like the King

When we were looking for info on Sasha, Compliment Man, and the Backwards Jogger, all of our informants told us that Madam's Organ was the place to go for info on strange people in the area. We struck up a conversation with a young lady tending bar there, who filled us in on the people we had gone looking for, and then threw a surprise our way.

"It sounds like you'd probably like Blelvis too," she said.

"Blelvis?" we answered.

"The Black Elvis."

This one was a no-brainer. We begged for more information.

"Blelvis is a black man in the neighborhood who likes to dress up as Elvis and walk around. You can walk up to him and give him any topic, and he will pick the Elvis song that somehow addresses it and he'll sing to you right there on the street."

We were flabbergasted. And while we didn't get to see Blelvis for ourselves that day, we figured just his description alone qualified him to join in this pantheon of Local Heroes who call the Adams Morgan section of Washington, DC, home.

Personalized Properties

Some people just won't be confined to a life spent in the ordinary surroundings of your typical private property. Why have just a front lawn when you could instead build a replica of the island of Jamaica? Why settle for a plain brick house when you could build one out of liquor bottles or, better yet, tombstones?

Often the owners of such unique homes and the lawns and garages around them are referred to as folk or outsider artists. They are usually self-taught, self-styled, and rely heavily on their own experiences and vision for inspiration. The things they create are expressions of their own singular personalities, and in them we see a reflection of the homeowner's soul.

Whether places like these are the work of true artists or not may be a topic of debate in some cases. But one thing is for sure. These people have altered the very landscape of our state, and in so doing have made their homes, and ours, a more interesting place to live.

THE BOTTLE HOUSE, HILLSVILLE, VA.

THE HOUSE OF A THOUSAND HEADACHES

Lil' Jamaica

A wonderful by-product of having the country's capital nearby is the multinationalism it brings. From grand embassies and the sometimes colorful ambassadors who inhabit them to the melting pot of ethnicities and cultures on the district's streets, this human hodgepodge now defines an area once noted for its insularism. While technically not a part of Virginia, Washington, DC, often finds itself claimed by this state and neighboring Maryland as well. Since the capital is so close, and since it *does* play host to the little-known yet fascinating "Lil' Jamaica" (a wholly uninspired name of our own coining), we thought it worthy of a mention here. *Okay, mon?*

Immigrants in America, as elsewhere, cling dearly to their past. This is certainly true in northern Washington where homeowner Donald G. Morgan has constructed an enormous relief map of the island of Jamaica on his front lawn. You can almost sniff the scent of jerk pork wafting through the air and feel gentle trade winds kiss your cheek in this place. Ah, there's nothing quite like paradise.

Mr. Morgan, now 77, emigrated to the U.S. from Jamaica in 1961. After living here for a while, he began to feel that most Americans had a poor image of his beloved homeland. This he says was largely due to Jamaica's Prime Minister at the time, Michael Manley, and his ideological sympathies with socialist and communist countries such as the Soviet Union, China, and, worst of all, Cuba. In 1979, with the staunchly anticommunist Ronald Reagan soon to be elected President of the U.S., political turmoil between this country and Jamaica was at an all-time high.

It was then that Donald Morgan took it upon himself to show his DC neighbors what a magnificent place the island really was. He set out to educate the citizens of his adopted country by transforming his property into a giant topographical lesson on Jamaica. It took Morgan only one year to complete his tangible message of peace and harmony. "As a sociologist, I know that you get along much better with people if you know something about where they came from," he told the *Washington Post* in a 1983 interview.

And guess what — the message seems to have actually worked! Political tensions between the U.S. and Jamaica began to ease in 1980 when Manley's opponent, Edward Seaga of the Jamaica Labour Party, was installed as the country's new Prime Minister. Overjoyed by the end of strife between his two homelands, Donald Morgan wrote a letter to President Reagan inviting him to visit his DC home for a mini-tour of the island. Unfortunately, according to the letter he received from the White House in reply, the President's busy schedule would not allow for an island vacation, even if it was right in his own backyard; but he did express his gratitude for the kind offer. "I still have that letter too!" Donald told *Weird Virginia.*

An unscientific guesstimate puts this Jamaica at some fifteen by fifty-five feet in overall size. But don't let its small dimensions fool you. For within these compressed boundaries, nearly everything found on the real island exists. As proof we witnessed plaster renderings of Montego Bay, Bull Bay, Morant Bay; cove upon cove upon cove; even Blue Mountain, Jamaica's tallest chunk, 7,360 feet in reality. In this instance, the peak is represented by a four-foot-tall amorphous lump, with an unspecified species of deranged-looking bird nesting on

top of it. When the display is operating at full bore, real water laps at its many bays, cays, and inlets (courtesy of an electric pump), and permanent outdoor lighting bathes its backstreets at night. A homemade pamphlet that Mr. Morgan hands out to the island's visitors describes it as having a "rugged coastline, majestic mountains, swift flowing rivers, underground lakes, exotic tropical vegetation and white sand beaches dotted with hotels and villas."

Even though the display contains a prominent tribute to reggae musician Bob Marley (quite possibly the most famous Jamaican ever), there were no dreadlocked followers or ganja plants to be found anywhere.

Donald, now retired from his career as a sociology professor at Bowie State College in Maryland, still receives visitors from all over who want to gaze upon his island paradise. "We've had people here just recently from Japan, Holland, and Russia," he told us proudly. If you'd like to plan a little island getaway for yourself there's no need to contact your Liberty Travel agent; just drop by 1201 Kalmia Road NW in Washington, DC. We think you'll find it *ah sey one!*

Walter Flax's Fleet

What old salt hasn't heard the phrase "there's a right way to do things, a wrong way, and then there's the *navy* way"? For one Virginia man, though, there was another option when it came to doing things—the Walter Flax way.

Walter Flax was born in Philadelphia in 1896 and moved to Virginia at a young age. Growing up near the port cities of Norfolk and Newport News, Walter had but one burning ambition in life from very early on: He wanted to be a sailor.

Unfortunately, Walter's fantasies of becoming a seaman were dashed at the local navy recruiting station. In 1975 he was quoted by Elinor Lander Horwitz in her book *Contemporary American Folk Artists* as saying, "When the first war came, I wasn't smart enough. When the second war came, I was too game-legged."

Most other men would likely get their skivvies in a twist over such a crushing disappointment, or go out for a little liquid liberty, but not Walter. Sir, no sir! Instead, he decided to launch his own seafaring fleet, and just to make his armada a bit different from that other seagoing outfit, he used a horizontal flooded refrigerator to float his boats.

Though Flax supported himself as a handyman, scuttlebutt had it that this landlubbing sailor could create dead-ringer replicas of real warships in miniature scale using scrap metal and wood. Flax's fleet eventually amounted to some one hundred vessels, including battleships, steamers, tugs, subs, and cruisers. Since his original refrigerator-going vessels ran out of ocean in fairly short order, Walter started building his ships in larger scale, some as long as twenty-five feet from stem to stern, and launching them into the

Flax's fleet eventually amounted to some one hundred vessels, including battleships, steamers, tugs, subs, and cruisers.

safe harbor of the pinewoods around his two-room Yorktown cabin.

After roughly five decades of shipbuilding, Walter Flax was well into his AARP years when the navy's top brass caught wind of his landlocked navy and finally helped make his lifelong dream come true. In 1978, the commander of the aircraft carrier U.S.S. *Kennedy* invited Walter aboard his vessel for a short cruise.

Master shipbuilder Walter Flax set sail on his final voyage in 1982. After his departure from this life, Walter's floundered flotilla sank into the depths of the Virginia forest. Fortunately, though, the scuttled fleet was salvaged from the abyss when the vessels were rediscovered by the folk-art community and praised for their uncommon craftsmanship. Today, one of Walter's flagships is dry-docked, proudly on display at the Smithsonian American Art Museum.

Sea Kitsch at Chincoteague

If you dig around Chincoteague Island a bit, you're certain to uncover oddness in one form or another. First and foremost, the highly celebrated wild ponies will snare your eye for the weird. Of course, they will also capture the gaze of your aunt Hortense, uncle Waldo, third cousin Clara Belle and everyone else for miles around. Then there is the Giant Viking, shown in the next chapter, who has found his own form of recognition.

Another, perhaps lesser known oddity, comes bundled up in a nautical package and stands just across the street from our beloved Viking. Captain Bob Payne's Sea Treasures, an eclectic assortment of nearly everything and anything relating to the ocean, has become a fixture on this spit of land. For thousands of appreciative fans, a trip to Captain Bob's "store" has become a highly anticipated summer ritual. We can easily see why.

The first thing you might ask yourself when you lay eyes on the captain's mountainous collection of ocean bric-a-brac is "how can the skipper possibly cram so much stuff into such a small space?" Aye, matey, 'tis a

fair question to be sure, but one that will go unanswered. Why? Well, would you have asked Michelangelo why he sometimes worked in a cluttered studio or chastised Thomas Edison for keeping such an untidy desk? Messy or not, these geniuses soared to the top of their respective fields, as has the good skipper. In nautical terms, Captain Bob Payne is the salty king of kitsch!

Starting out in a small hot dog stand, Bob Payne began amassing seaworthy stock to sell, some mainstream, most not, adding sections to his humble shanty as he went. If a person were in the market for a broken wooden pelican, a stylish piece of cracked conch jewelry, a leftover horseshoe crab shell, they knew they could probably count on the captain having it . . . somewhere. Parrotheads—the Jimmy Buffett fans—in particular, must have loved this guy. Heck, he had enough of them to outfit a hundred tropical bars,

at the least. Scuttlebutt has it that Captain "Mr." Bob (his preferred title) would hand out signed photos of himself with each purchase and that he was indeed a joy to behold. Sadly, the landlocked seafarer bid farewell to our world in 2006, leaving his salty enterprise to an uncertain future. Will a worthy swabbie step in and keep this unquestionably weird operation afloat? We have our fingers crossed.

"Airplane" Payne's Flights of Fantasy

As a child, Leslie Payne—no relation to Captain Bob—had a love shared with many boys his age. He was fascinated by planes and the wonder of flight. This might not seem remarkable in itself, but it's what Payne did with this passion that is unique. His love of planes—said to have been inspired by an air show he attended as a child—stayed with him into adulthood; and despite having only a fourth-grade education, Payne managed to construct a fleet of eight sophisticated life-size model airplanes in his Kilmarnock backyard.

In the 1940s, Payne, who had worked now and again around airports, began building what he called "imitations" of planes. But in the 1960s, he must have decided that small models just wouldn't do. That's when Payne started to transform his acre of land into a complete imitation airfield environment. He made certain not to leave anything out. There were nearly full-size replica planes, instrument towers, an airplane machine shop, and of course the planes, though they couldn't fly. Payne used found objects to make his creations—mostly scrap metal, canvas, and old appliances. He painted a variety of colorful patriotic images and faux military insignia on each plane and, taking his imagination one step further, wallpapered the inside of one.

According to the California Science Center,

which held an exhibition of Payne's planes in 2002, one of the craft even had an actual airplane's engine installed in it! The press release for the exhibit says it was "a 75-horsepower engine that propelled the plane around the yard and on the local highways."

By the 1970s, Payne had a veritable airport in his backyard. His fleet was composed primarily of biplanes, along with a replica of Lindbergh's *The Spirit of St. Louis*. It is said that he invited neighborhood girls to sit in his planes and record tales of their imaginary journeys in a logbook. Not surprisingly, he became known as Airplane Payne and reveled in his reputation as chief owner, operator, and mechanic of what he called the Airplane Machine Shop Company.

And he didn't stop at just aircraft. He added model ships, commemorative signs, and whirligigs fashioned

from weathervanes to his fantastical display. Slowly he became renowned as a folk artist.

Unfortunately, Payne's magical world of (non)flight was left to decay when he went to a nursing home in his old age. Some years after he died in 1981, overgrown remnants of the planes were found and eventually restored.

Lately, much has been made of Payne's artistic achievements. His small model planes and other art objects have been exhibited in major folk-art museums and collected by the likes of the Smithsonian Institution and the Corcoran Gallery of Art. All this is kind of strange, since Payne didn't intend to gain fame as an artist of any kind. He was just a man with a love of airplanes and the courage to let his dreams take flight, so to speak—no matter how weird the outcome may have seemed to the neighbors.

The House Made Out of Bottles

At the dawn of World War II, earth-shattering events were unfolding just about as quickly as newsreel cameras could spin. "Doc" Hope's Bottle House in the southern part of the state was, in all honesty, not one of these. Still, for anyone with a playful spirit, this fantasy house was more than worth a notice. We reckon similar appreciation exists today, so join us as we don our Coke-bottle lenses for an up-close look at this definitive shrine to liquid containers.

In 1941, successful pharmacist John "Doc" Hope was looking for a unique way to amuse his daughter. Possessing relatively deep pockets and a penchant for the offbeat, Hope commissioned builder Friel Dalton to construct an elaborate playhouse for this lucky little lass. Tying in with a pharmacy theme, the house would be made almost entirely of bottles. From castor oil to soda pop, nearly every type of glass container would be used in its construction.

At Hope's request, the building would eventually size out at a lavish fifteen by twenty-five feet. For contrast, we can only compare its "playhouse" tag with railroad magnate Cornelius Vanderbilt's insistence on dubbing his Newport, Rhode Island, mansion a cottage. Small this was not to be.

Dubbed the House of a Thousand Headaches for its profusion of wine bottles, the house continues to amuse today.

In a testament to its fine construction, the play space appears uncannily youthful and sturdy. This is not at all bad for a home that recently reached full senior-citizen status.

Unlike other bottle houses (yes, Virginia, there are indeed others) the jugs used in Doc's building are arranged "backward," with mouths pointed toward the exterior of the enclosure. This effectively turns each wall into a giant skylight and greatly enhances what might have otherwise been a rather dim environment. Outside, green bottles forming the shape of an "H" (for Hope's name) adorn one wall, while the inside features such niceties as a blue chandelier made from, what else, bottles! Below this stands a fireplace (just the thing for an unsupervised child and her band of ever curious playmates), and a full complement of cozy furniture that begs one to sit for a spell and just be. Without doubt, this is playhouse living at its finest.

Interestingly, the current owner shuns undue publicity for this worthy treasure that exists just outside her window. To honor her wishes, we shall guard the bottle house's precise location, lest a bottle-peeping riot ensue.

The sheer whimsy of the bottle house will bring a smile to the face of even the most jaded, and the warm muted light that dances so serenely within its walls will warm the innards for good measure. Bottoms up, kiddies!

Banner Blevins: Garden of Prehistory

Little is known about a mysterious site called the Garden of Prehistory. We do know that a man named Banner Blevins ran a country store and filling station in McCall's Gap. In the garden behind his house, this unusual fellow spent his late afternoons and weekends building near-life-size concrete statues of Stone Age people, including one called the Pre-Anderthal Man, and characters from local Appalachian lore. One such legendary figure was the Dagger Woman, a ghost who roamed the hills in search of her victims, as mountaineer parents liked to warn their children in order to keep them from wandering too far from home. Apparently fascinated by the story of the biblical Golgotha, the "Place of the

Skull," Blevins also collected skull-shaped rocks and incorporated them into a miniature Jerusalem built on one side of the site, while behind the scenes a concrete Satan leapt forth from a hole.

— With thanks to Roger Manley's Self-Made Worlds

The Throne of the Third Heaven

By all accounts, James Hampton's life was unremarkable. Born in Elloree, SC, in 1909, he served in the army during World War II, then moved close to his brother in Washington, DC. Shortly thereafter, he took a job as a janitor for the General Services Administration, which he held for the rest of his life. He had few friends, never married, and seemed to have been a quiet, religious man who attended various churches around the city because he didn't believe that any one sect of Christianity had a claim on God.

What few people knew during his life, however, was how Hampton spent his free time. In a rented garage (which no longer stands), near Seventh and N streets NW, Hampton labored for years—fourteen, actually—on what has since become one of this country's most celebrated examples of visionary art: *The Throne of the Third Heaven of the Nations Millennium General Assembly.* When he died in 1964, a tin-foil masterpiece was left behind—much to the surprise of his sister (who discovered the work in the garage) and probably most of the people who knew him.

Clearly, Hampton was ahead of his time, for he obviously saw the utility in recycling. *The Throne of the Third Heaven,* a Last Judgment–setting replete with glittering thrones, altars, pulpits, and much more, is fashioned entirely out of found or reused objects covered in silver and gold foil. Consisting of 177 pieces in all, the panorama is almost 200 square feet in size and stands nine feet tall at its

center. Each minutely detailed piece has been lovingly crafted out of some hodgepodge of construction paper, mirrors, jars, wooden furniture, fruit cans, shards of green desk blotters, lightbulbs, bits of plastic, and so on. It was then covered with tinfoil of the kind found affixed to wine bottle tops. (The story goes that Hampton paid local winos to turn over their foil after uncorking their bottles.) Hampton used glue, nails, tacks, and pins to hold things together, making the finished product, needless to say, a thing of intricate but fragile beauty.

Biblical and religious figures appear in the work—hand labeled as such by Hampton— including the Virgin Mary, a pope or two, and Adam

and Eve. They appear primarily because Hampton also claimed that they appeared to him. In fact, his visions were more than likely the impetus for his work. He even makes note of these visions, on labels with statements such as "this is true that the great Moses, the giver of the 10th commandment, appeared in Washington DC, April 11, 1931" and "it is true that Adam, the first man God created, appeared in person on January 20, 1949 . . . this was on the day of President Truman's inauguration."

Calling himself St. James, Director of Special Projects for the State of Eternity, Hampton also kept a notebook written in a secret, indecipherable language that he said had been given to him by God. It is possible that he considered himself a prophet akin to John, the author of the Book of Revelation, who was the inspiration for *The Throne of the Third Heaven*. Speculation has been made that had Hampton lived, he would have gone on to become a preacher and used his creation as a teaching tool.

Instead, he died and left behind a mysterious, eccentric, and splendid artwork that has taken its place in our weird history. Sold by the owner of the garage to a Washington couple, *The Throne of the Third Heaven* was donated by them anonymously to the Smithsonian in 1970. Now housed in the Smithsonian's American Art Museum, *The Throne of the Third Heaven* has been praised by critics as a prime example of American visionary art and wows tourists on a regular basis. So loved is the piece that for its July 2006 reopening after renovations, the Smithsonian chose *The Throne* as the first work to be reinstalled.

In what seems to us like a strange epilogue to this story, no fewer than two orchestral pieces have been inspired by Hampton's luminous artwork. In 1989, Albert Glinsky's *The Throne of the Third Heaven* premiered at the Erie Philharmonic, commissioned for its 75th anniversary. More recently, Jefferson Friedman's *The Throne of the Third Heaven of the Nations General Assembly* premiered at the Kennedy Center—commissioned by the National Symphony Orchestra and the ASCAP Foundation. Friedman explains that the piece is "the second part of a trilogy of works entitled *In the Realms of the Unreal*, each movement of which is based on the life and work of a different American 'outsider' artist." Both composers describe at length the ways in which their music pays homage to Hampton's visionary process.

One wonders what else Hampton's wonderful work of weirdness might inspire.–*Abby Grayson*

Want to Live in a Wedding Cake?

We can't say for sure why he did it, but in the early 1900s a man named George "Cap'n Til" Lester built a three-tiered house that looks uncannily like a wedding cake, including festive decorations in its faux "icing." Mysteries notwithstanding, the wedding-cake house, located at 308 Starling Avenue in Martinsville, is quite a sight. From a magnificent portico featuring six sumptuous arches (in tasty vanilla, we imagine) all the way up to its trademark diagonally oriented third tier, this architectural tidbit may remind married folk of one of two things: The absolute best day of their lives or, perhaps, the worst decision of their lives.

Closer examination reveals yet more tasty details, not the least of which is three separate patio areas on the first, second, and third levels. Likely intended for the newlywed phase when sweet nothings were buzzing about like bees in a hive, these open spaces could also pull double-duty if the groom wound up in the doghouse and found himself in need of a place to sleep.

These days the Wedding Cake House is without a resident bride and groom. We think that's a darn shame. Let's hope a couple of starry-eyed newlyweds will happen along and adopt the place as their own. If that occurs, this bride in particular should feel indebted to ol' Cap'n Lester. After all, she'll get to have her cake and eat it too.

One Man's Trash, Another's Treasure

We in the Weird world like to think that each offbeat contribution adds to our very existence. It matters little what the item is. In its own deliciously weird way, each entry gives us a reason to wake up smiling each morning. Sometimes, though, some producer of the bizarre stands out for the way he touched the lives of those around him. Robert Nelson Howell, street artiste extraordinaire, was such a man.

To fully appreciate the offbeat sculptures and street art produced by this king of amalgamated improvisation, it helps to know a little something about the artist himself. Born in Powhatan to Charlie and Bessie Howell in 1932, Robert lived to make people smile. Like Hollywood cowboy Will Rogers, he would often declare, "I never met a person I didn't like!" Unlike many of us sadly burdened with a keep-up-with-the-Joneses mentality, Howell found worth and spiritual sustenance in the cheapest and simplest of things. It was the shaping of these "worthless" materials that brought him his greatest joy, not to mention genuine and deserved recognition from an art community that became fascinated by his talent.

When confronted with a surplus of rotting wood, corroded tin, or broken bicycle frames, most of us would simply call the junkman. Not so Robert. Using deft skill that belied his fourth-grade education, the crafty one would fashion these into truly remarkable figures. Whether his weird art culminated in a full-size

horse or a metal whirligig shaped like a duck, it didn't matter; the man was doing what he was meant to do—what he was *born* to do. His generosity led to his creations falling into different hands over the years, even landing in some very chi-chi art galleries. The remainder? Well, these he'd likely store with all the rest of his crazy art; smack dab in the middle of his front lawn.

Which made for some problems. "It was a damn eyesore," barked one decidedly *non*weird man in describing Howell's ramshackle home and cluttered property. "They should've knocked that sumbitch down!" On the opposite side of the coin were those who could not get enough. "Wow, a free art show right out on the street. Imagine that!" said another more in tune with Howell's intended mission.

In the end, Howell's loving deeds and whimsical heart seemed to win most people over. Never was this more apparent than on November 29, 2004, when this uncommonly joyful and simple man passed on to that great sculpting junkyard in the sky.

At his eulogy, an outpouring of affection flowed much like the lines of his precious sculptures. Most spoke of an unassuming man who longed for nothing more than to make himself and others smile. Not all understood his ways, but many did. We like to think that Robert is looking down at us all and saying, "Man, I'm *right*," which was always his way of saying, "I'm fine." Indeed you are, sir, indeed you are.

Elvis in Roanoke

We're all familiar with the many incarnations of Elvis Presley. There was young innocent Elvis, military Elvis, Elvis the Pelvis, heartthrob Elvis, even a bloated Las Vegas–lounge Elvis. But there was another Elvis, known only to a few: Mini-Elvis. That's right, *Weird Virginia* has learned that at a certain stage of his career, this strapping rock 'n' roller somehow slimmed down to a feathery five pounds and six inches in height!

Roanoke doesn't immediately trigger thoughts of the gyration sensation, but it should. At the base of Mill Mountain, the same heap that features the giant Roanoke Star (see "Roadside Oddities"), is a small, nondescript frame house. It is on this near-anonymous piece of land that Mini-Elvis once dwelled. Fittingly, if not too imaginatively, his digs were known as Miniature Graceland.

It is quite easy to overlook Mini-Elvis's old stomping ground. Weeds, fallen trees, and other foliage have conspired to hide much of it from view these days. In fact, if it weren't for a life-size statue of the king himself standing beside the miniature display, we would have driven right on past it.

So what did we find there? Well, just about everything one might expect in a miniature Elvis land. For starters, there was the requisite version of his famed Graceland mansion. Then there was a peaceful little chapel just to the side of it. Also on the premises were a full-size mock-up of Graceland's gate, the king's Tupelo,

MS, birthplace, and a path that meandered to and fro past them all.

Miniature Graceland was created in the 1980s by Don Epperly, a superfan who loved the king so much that he laboriously re-created many of the structures associated with his life. Throughout the years, Elvis fans and curiosity seekers would visit Epperly's yard to examine his skillfully crafted buildings and marvel at the artistry involved in their creation. Unfortunately, Father Time closed in and Epperly's health deteriorated to the point that he could no longer maintain the grounds and buildings.

As a result, today's Miniature Graceland looks like an after photo from some natural disaster. A few of the buildings are standing, but their state of disrepair is undeniable. Even so, there is something to be said for this miniature memorial of the rock 'n' roll king and his court. To appreciate it, though, a visitor must be willing to look beyond Mini-Graceland's missing pillars, its collapsing chapel wall, and its swimming pool filled with rotting leaves. If we do, we can see that the village may actually be a more fitting tribute in its current downtrodden state. Much like sepia-toned photos of a fresh-faced Elvis in his prime, Miniature Graceland reminds one strongly of what once was. That it also reminds fans of what will never again be serves as a sad but necessary counterbalance.

Such bittersweet memories are what legends are made out of. Even minilegends, we reckon.

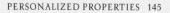

Ain't Nothin' but a Ken Doll

In southeast Roanoke, on Riverland Road, is Miniature Graceland—a small replica of Elvis's home complete with Barbie & Ken dolls attending an Elvis concert. I believe Elvis is also portrayed by an altered Ken doll.—*Peter R. Wells*

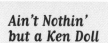

Miller's Castle, Aldie

When people began sending us tales about a bed-and-breakfast in the suburbs of Washington that was built like a castle, we didn't quite know what to make of it. A building with turrets that sold antiques and catered to the B-and-B crowd sounded too Disney to be truly weird. But then we started to hear the details.

This was no Magic Kingdom fairy-tale building. This was a real castle, with thick outer and inner walls, iron bars, gargoyles, and a tube-shaped inner sanctum built of cinder blocks to retreat into in case of invasion. The owner of the B and B was said to be a crotchety old man with a severe military haircut and a wad of chewing tobacco permanently wedged in his cheek. He named the place Bull Run Castle after the first land battle in the Civil War. All kinds of weird seekers from around Washington would drive out there and pay a couple of bucks for a guided tour. When they got there, he would scare children with his aggressive demeanor and tick off women with misogynistic comments.

The way people spoke about this place, it seemed like a medieval-era version of *Fawlty Towers*—a bizarre establishment run by a man so awful you can't help coming back for more. So naturally we called up the owner, John Roswell Miller, and asked if we could stay the night in one of his suites.

"No, you can't," he told us. "I've sold up, and I'm shipping out. Two weeks. That's all you got. You can come up and buy some antiques."

And he hung up on us. This clearly deserved a closer look, so we jumped into the *Weird*-mobile and drove toward Aldie. It wasn't hard to find Bull Run Castle—we just kept our eyes open for anything with turrets and gargoyles, and turned down the drive when we found it. The castle is an impressive building of brick, stone, and cinder block. Even the sturdy doghouses were decorated with gargoyles. The heavy hardwood door with its hideous knocker and dire warnings against letting the door slam was as forbidding as the rest of the place.

Pushing the door open, we discovered a spacious room where a man was throwing paintings on the fire. He looked up, growled, "That one's my mother. Sorry, Mom," and came to greet us. He asked us to pay the fee for the tour—"Two dollars, and if you don't like it, it's ten dollars. If you ask any questions, it's ten dollars." We forked over our money, and then he launched into a well-rehearsed routine, throwing out facts and figures so quickly it hurt to take notes.

He began the project in 1980, moved onto the property in 1986, and finished it in 1998. He had never earned more than $16,000 per year. "Never been on welfare, ate a lot of beans but never gone hungry." The castle has fourteen closets, eighty-nine windows, and an ironclad front door four and three quarters inches thick. "See those beams? Solid oak. That's solid maple right there. There's nothing fake in this castle . . . including me."

Despite being one of the most accomplished outsider artists we've met, Miller has no respect for anything fanciful. This military veteran is far too down-to-earth for that. Bull Run Castle is a real castle "built so it can be defended," as he repeatedly said during his tour. The thin notches in the walls are real shooting ports, designed to repel real invaders. And he regards college graduates, liberals, and whimsical people with equal disdain. In fact, during the trip we got the distinct impression he had us pegged for at least two of those three crimes against humanity.

But somehow, despite his gruff monologue and demeanor, John Miller seemed to be glowing with pleasure. Grown people had told us how scary this man was, but he could barely hide a smile as he spoke. And although he was verbally challenging us, he didn't seem

to have any aggression behind it. It was almost as if whatever had spurred him to build a real castle had evaporated. He was, after all, about to sell the place.

A couple of times, I risked the threat of a ten-dollar fine for asking him a question, but he didn't rise to the bait. Secretly, though, I knew he was dying to tell us something. So after he had played a twenty-minute video

to cap off the tour, he came into the room and explained everything. "I never listened to a female in my life," he said, as if he were trying to bait us into a liberal response so he could throw us in the dungeon. "Eighteen months ago, that all changed."

He went over to a cupboard and brought out a pouch of chewing tobacco. It was only then I realized he didn't have his trademark wad in his cheek. "Haven't opened this in eighteen months. Don't want to. Why? Harriet . . . Hattie. I knew her since third grade. I walked down the road to her house and carried her books. We grew up, we kissed and cuddled, and then I got called to war. And then it was over." This was an unexpected turn to the story. But it explained a lot about this man.

"I spent most of my life unhappy and deserved it. We didn't see each other for fifty-one years. Then eighteen months ago, I met her again. And she took me back. I wore Goodwill all my life. Now it's London Fog here and Bass shoes on my feet. I used to have a flattop. She liked to see a little wave here, so I grew my hair. I even had my nails done one time."

Was this really the aggressive misanthrope we had heard about? Well, his next comment made us realize he's not entirely reformed. "A fellah in town made a comment about

it, and I dragged him up by his arms. Black and blue they were. I told him, 'I'm still the same fellah!' And he believed me."

And with that, our tour was at an end. And even though he suspected we were liberal and college educated, he didn't throw us into the dungeon. In fact, he didn't even charge extra for the questions.

Bull Run Castle is still standing, but John Roswell Miller is gone now. His legacy, though, won't be disappearing anytime soon. This castle was built to last.–*Matt Lake*

Roadside Oddities

Americans harbor a near-insatiable appetite for the offbeat. For oddity hounds, this comes as little surprise. Fact is, we *Weirdos* (an umbrella term used to describe anyone reading this book) live for the giddy thrill of discovering, say, a park made from garbage or a town gone mad for apples. And we would absolutely die to witness a genuine death mask in the, er, flesh.

The highways and byways of the commonwealth are a teeming hotbed for just such rewarding pursuits. From gawky Johnny Appleseed to the sinister-playful cave pixies that stand silent sentry at Shenandoah Caverns, our state has strange stuff in abundance. So hit the asphalt, highwaymen/women—and don't forget to use this section as a primer.

island of the Giant Viking

Chincoteague Island, a sliver of land close to the northern border of the state, has more than its fair share of oddities. Consider the homegrown quirkiness of its free-roaming ponies, and giant Viking. Well, a statue of a giant Viking, that is.

How this seafaring Scandinavian arrived in these parts is really something of a mystery, but most sources seem to agree that the helmeted one originally pulled "see" duty atop a Maryland carpet store, where he resided throughout the 1950s and 1960s. In 2001, he set sail for Chincoteague and came ashore upon an open lot directly across the street from Captain Payne's Sea Treasures.

An Apple Each Way

The town of Winchester and the surrounding area is absolutely nuts for apples!

This town in Frederick County identifies strongly with the crimson bit of nature's candy. Winchester is part of the state's Apple Capital region, where apples, real and reproduced, abound. A fine example of this can be found beside Apple Valley Office Products on North Kent Street. There, standing some eight feet tall and six feet in diameter, is perhaps the largest apple that our apple-loving eyes have uncovered in some time. It is in fact one of twenty such oversized fruits that were scattered about the town of Winchester as part of the Apples on Parade celebration in 2005. The best part about this fiberglass apple (in addition to its immense size) is its awesome shine. Creator Brian Fleming coated his *Bites of Winchester* with a super-high gloss, which would please even the pickiest schoolteacher and tempt anyone who sees it to take a bite. Or a look.

Johnny Appleseed Statue

Not far away, in the town of New Market, just off busy Interstate 81, the apple mania grows as signs for the Apple Blossom Mall and Appleland Miniature Golf vie for a visitor's attention. Then a sign for the Johnny Appleseed Restaurant appears. This Johnny, all fourteen gawky feet of him, stands in front of his namesake restaurant bearing a somewhat mangled smile.

So what does he look like up close? Well, Johnny wears a big pot atop his head, and the apple he's cradling is about ten times the size of your average apple. And the big guy's pants are about five sizes too small. Maybe he's had one too many apples. Even so, his big goofy smile lingers.

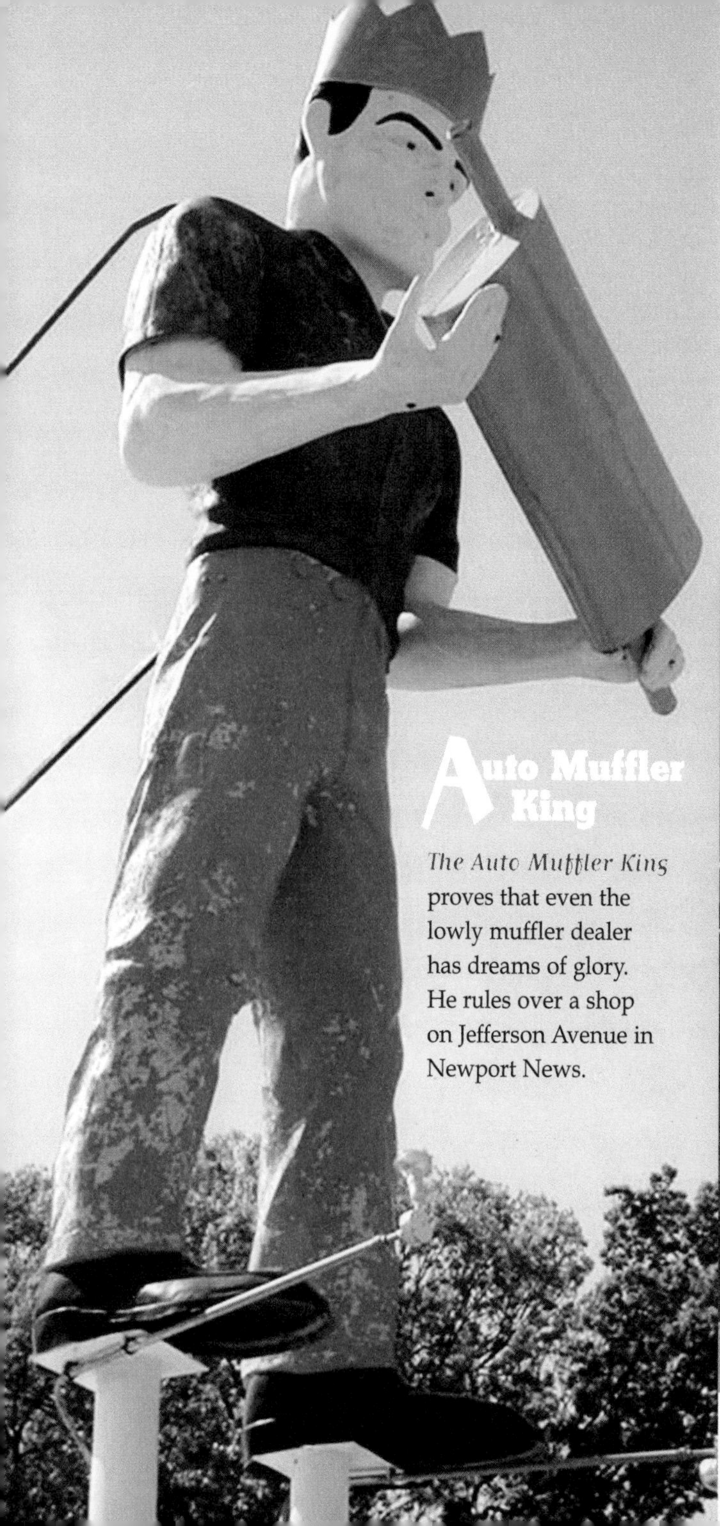

Auto Muffler King

The *Auto Muffler King* proves that even the lowly muffler dealer has dreams of glory. He rules over a shop on Jefferson Avenue in Newport News.

Giant Paint Can

Does anybody have a really big drop cloth? This huge paint can hangs over The Paint Store in Wytheville, near the junction of Interstates 77 and 81.

The Paint Store

DAVIS PAINT

Giant Coffeepot

Savvy weirdness hunters slow down just a click to scan the eastbound side of U.S. Route 60 in Lexington. For it is here that a wonderful example of programmatic architecture—where buildings are designed to resemble the products they feature—stands somewhat unassumingly.

This two-story corrugated metal "pot" opened as a restaurant in 1959 and remained so until the late 1970s. At twenty-two feet tall by twenty-feet in diameter, complete with defining accoutrements such as a generous-sized handle and accompanying spout, it is one of a surviving few in these United States. Today, the giant coffeepot building is looking just a little forlorn, and the building has a FOR RENT sign in front. Any takers?

Monster Milk Bottles

Well, if you have a giant coffeepot, you're going to need a giant bottle of milk, right? That requires a quick dash to Richmond, a mere milk run, really, and an equally quick glance up toward the sky.

The Richmond Dairy must have been some sight when it opened its doors back in 1913. The sturdy four-story brick structure featured a grand gimmick—three giant masonry milk bottles attached at the building's corners. This fun, distinctive edifice became an instant landmark and won the hearts of dairy lovers everywhere with its whimsical playfulness. In 1999, a savvy developer emerged and blew new life into the building, spending eight million dollars gutting the interior and revamping the exterior (including the celebrated bottles) to a better-than-new state.

Giant Pencil

This giant pencil, fashioned from steel, draws attention to itself on West Main Street in Wytheville, where it has pointed out Wytheville Office Supply since the 1960s.

For Really Serious Gardeners

Situated on either side of a concrete railroad bridge in Staunton, where Interstate 64 joins 81, are a couple of six-foot-tall flowerpots and a sprinkler can that reaches at least fifteen feet. Guess they're for people who are big on gardening.

Southland of the Giants

Staunton's Middlebrook Avenue appears interchangeable with thousands of other boulevards across America at first glance. But in mere seconds, *Weird Virginia* would enter another realm altogether, a place we call Southland of the Giants. FERGUSON'S METAL FABRICATION proclaims the sign hanging from the building. Advertising its wares is a size-six pair of ballet slippers (that's six-feet *long*), a dagger as tall as a man, and an open book that has to be four feet across at the very least. Next to these stands an oversized globe, a pile of huge coat hangers, and a ten-foot-tall pair of crutches! A strange combination that made us wonder what kind of companies employ the services of these giant-makers.

Holy Land U.S.A.

Just when you think you've seen it all, an operation like Holy Land U.S.A. pops up. Situated on some 250 acres in the town of Bedford, this Christian-based theme park shows that religious endeavors can sometimes merge with the world of weird.

Anyone expecting death-defying roller coasters and super-twisty thrill rides at this theme park will be sorely disappointed. The reason is simple. Holy Land U.S.A.'s intent is to introduce folks to the life and deeds of Jesus Christ, not to induce retching by tossing them to and fro. It attempts to provide this spiritual lesson via a wealth of displays and dioramas, each depicting a biblical event or lesson. Visitors are invited to walk its three-mile-long nature path at their leisure, a peace-restorative procession. If you'd like to see all of Holy Land without making the pilgrimage on foot, you can take a tour in a vehicle for a cost of three dollars. Praise be: Except for the ride, this divine attraction is blessedly free of admission charges.

HOLY LAND USA PARKING →

JERICHO ROAD
LUKE 19:2-10

← JERUSALEM

Welcome to

BETHLEHEM
OF
JUDEA

CHRISTIAN IS MENTIONED 3 TIMES
IN YOUR BIBLE? May Holy Land U.S.A.
Nature Sanctuary · · · · LEAD YOU
TO BE ONE I PETER-4:16   Acts 11:26
            ACTS - 26:28

HERODIUM

KING HEROD LIVED HERE
IN HIS FORTRESS PALACE →
4 MI. FROM BETHLEHEM

Jesus was born in Bethlehem during
the reign of Herod the great. The wise
men came asking, "Where is he that is
born king of the Jews?" This aroused
Herod's jealous spirit. According to
Matthew's account, Herod tried to
eliminate Jesus by having all the
male infants of the Bethlehem region
put to death. (Matt. 2:13-16). But
this despicable act failed. Joseph
and Mary were warned by God in a
dream to take their child and flee
to Egypt. Here they hid safely until
Herod died. (Matt. 2:13-15).

Of Herod it was said, it is better to be
Herod's hog than to be his son.

Herod murdered his wife and two sons.

Herod died in Jericho - buried in the Herodium
Herod's tomb has not yet been discovered.

The Holy Land Is Really in Virginia

Disneyland is a fun vacation. So is Niagara Falls. But do any of those enrich your soul? Not hardly, friend. For a truly enlightening time, you should head to Bedford, Virginia's, Holy Land U.S.A.

This nature sanctuary covers 250 acres and uses all of that space to teach you about the Old and New Testaments. You will go through Nazareth, see the Dead Sea Scrolls, and view other important Judeo-Christian sites, all presented in kitschy, tourist friendly form.—*Ben Osto*

Roanoke Star

Brilliantly lit stars adorning mountaintops are a somewhat common sight these days. Municipalities with suitable bluffs occasionally feature one of these city stars, if only to help holiday celebrations along. The majority run about ten feet in diameter; a rare few get as big as twenty-five or thirty feet. Big, but not what we'd call *big* big.

Well, the Roanoke Star has these puny entries beat. In fact, it's a behemoth as such things go. At better than eight stories tall, this five-pointer peering down upon Roanoke proper has clearly thrown down the gauntlet in the stellar sweepstakes, and in the process earned itself a place as the world's largest illuminated man-made standing star.

While it's a fact that another, even larger, star exists in El Paso, TX, it's also true that show-off rests *flat* on a mountaintop. So we ask you, who is the real champ—the lackluster star that lounges around all day like some big sloth, or the proud twinkling star that stands tall and proud? Precisely.

Long known as the Star City of the South, Roanoke decided it needed a fitting decoration for its 1949 Christmas season. They chose a star, of course, what else? City planners looked no farther than nearby Mill Mountain, a thousand feet above the city, to find themselves a suitable site to display their new town toy.

But this would not be just any star. At eighty-eight feet tall, this was to be the biggest, baddest star in the entire South. Naturally, it would need a supporting cast, and it found a worthy one: a steel structure some hundred feet tall and a concrete base that weighs in at exactly 500,000 pounds. The neon tubing necessary to fire up the star runs along for two thousand feet, and the electric company must smile contentedly knowing that, during times of illumination, this baby is twinkling away about 17,500 watts of pricey current.

Mermaid Tree of Arlington

Some weird stories are so much fun to contemplate, they very nearly write themselves. The tale of the Mermaid Tree of Arlington is just such an account. Here goes.

Arlington resident Paul Jackson holds a couple of things dear in his life: fishing and women. Knowing full well his appreciation for both, his wife Nancy decided to take action when an opportunity presented itself. What Nancy Jackson did was nothing short of brilliant, as it accomplished not one, not two, but three desirable tasks at once. She had an artist carve a mermaid from a beloved but dying hundred-year-old white ash tree that stood on their property. This combined Paul's two great passions and saved the tree from being bulldozed as well. Sounds like a win, win, and another win, right? Well, not exactly.

When you stare up at the Mermaid Tree's eighteen-foot-tall whimsical form, it's hard to believe that she is not loved by all. But the sad truth is she isn't. In fact, there are some people who don't like her at all.

"That's disgusting!" a senior citizen uttered beneath her breath as she walked past the mermaid. "Wow, are those what I think they are?" asked a smiling, slack-

jawed teenager only an eye blink later. The reason for the discrepancy may be generational and undoubtedly ties in with the carving's state of undress. For whatever reason, the mermaid's "scales" don't quite conceal her formidable attributes. To use a human analogy, let's just say that the mermaid tree channels a va-va-voom Jayne Mansfield in her heyday, front and rear, and leave it at that.

For three hundred dollars per foot, chain-saw sculptor Scott Dustin designed the Mermaid Tree using equal doses of vision and practicality. The latter kicks in mightily when one must design where existing limbs dictate, as was the case here. Bearing this out, the mermaid's bizarrely positioned arms and hands look noticeably oversized and out of place, perhaps even a bit grotesque. Not surprisingly, the artist sees things differently. "If there are mermaids, they need powerful arms to get through the water," he reasons.

Of course, to analyze a sculpture like this is to completely miss the point. This grande dame of the ocean should be judged by the sum of her wooden parts, not by a few anomalies. Looked upon in this fashion, it is hard to deny her overall allure. In fact, we Weirdos declare this mermaid a bona fide Chick of the Sea.

Lighthouse Water Tower

You have to hand it to the citizens of Cape Charles, on the spit of land east of the Chesapeake Bay. When faced with the need to erect a water tower to meet their growing needs, they opted for something altogether different, something wonderfully weird. Since the town is a seaside community that identifies heavily with the nautical life, logic dictated that their water tower be built along those lines. So why not fashion a water tower that looked like a lighthouse? Better yet, why not replicate the already famous Cape Charles lighthouse?

Soaring some 217 feet, the lighthouse/water tower measures twenty-six feet *taller* than the original it apes so faithfully. The 300,000-gallon tower has been triggering double and triple takes since 1992. From a distance, it simply cannot be distinguished as fake. Even up close, it's hard to tell that it's not an authentic lighthouse.

Foot Tree

I recently took a trip to see my father, who lives in Harborton. He showed me this tree that had grown into the shape of a large foot. He spray-painted the "toenails" to finish off the complete look. I just couldn't resist sending it to you guys. –*Rose Johnson*

CLEAR CHANNEL

ESAPEAKE
OPERTIES

CHFRONT

Crusty Old Salt and His Faithful Dog

The water tower masquerading as a lighthouse can be seen from a considerable distance in Cape Charles. But there's another sight of interest just before you reach the tower. A prominent billboard stands on the southern side of the road here. However, it's not the billboard that intrigues. It is what sits *atop* the billboard.

Nobody seems to know how or why a life-size figure of a crusty old salt, clad in a yellow hooded rain slicker and mysterious sunglasses, got here. Ditto for the dog. Since any seaside community depends on tourism as its life's blood, a good mystery can work wonders to promote future visits. Such seems to be the case here.

The creepiest thing about the old salt is his face. From a distance, he looks positively human. Up close, he appears eerily the same. With a cigarette dangling from his mustached mug, one almost expects a puff of smoke to come out at any instant. By day, this all amounts to little more than mild amusement, so by all means drive by and bring the kiddies. At night? Well, let's put it this way: If you choose to walk up to this billboard when the sky is black, then you are one brave soul indeed.

Grand Stalacpipe Organ

Luray Caverns enthusiastically bills itself as "America's largest and most popular caverns." With passageways that descend into grand rooms and a network of paths so intricate they sometimes double and triple back upon themselves, Luray (in operation since 1878) is a major attraction in this part of the world. Teeming hordes hop off tour buses each day to wander through the mazes, and the feds long ago designated the caverns a U.S. Natural Landmark.

But all of this doesn't mean much to us purveyors of the bizarre. Fact is, such mainstream appeal usually sends us packing. Still, this grotto does have *something* strange going for it, and that something is of ungodly size. Ladies and gentlemen, we present for your approval the Grand Stalacpipe Organ.

This melodious device, invented by mathematician and electronic scientist Leland W. Sprinkle, is considered to be the world's largest musical instrument. It has been serenading cave visitors with its ethereal music since 1957, and its appeal continues to the present day.

When you first approach the Grand Stalacpipe Organ, it actually seems somewhat *under*whelming. In fact, it looks much like any organ console found in any church. But this organ lacks the usual array of metal pipes. So what exactly is producing the individual notes?

The organ's music is created by rubber mallets striking stalactites. One amazing bit about this instrument is the trial and error process that accompanied its birth. Sprinkle literally tapped some five thousand stalactites to locate a paltry but key thirty-seven finalists with the perfect pitch he needed. Unfortunately, Sprinkle's top thirty-seven aren't conveniently grouped together, since stalactites don't naturally grow in melodic communities. In fact, the chosen few are spread across three and a half acres. Since the organ network is so

huge, electronic amplification was needed to transport the tones emitted by the stalactites. It is hard to believe that notes heard instantaneously in the organ chamber sometimes originate from parts of the cave system hundreds of feet away.

The organ has also become an integral part of another peculiarity at Luray. Cupid has worked his magic around the enormous instrument, as it has become de rigueur over the years for some Virginians to get married here with the organ "singing" at full wail. This unusual service is still available today, for a fee.

The Elves of Shenandoah Caverns

In the highly competitive world of west-central Virginia caves, it pays to have a gimmick. Shenandoah Caverns realized this fact years ago and took the appropriate measures. If they couldn't outdazzle a few of their larger competitors—most notably superpopular Luray Caverns—with their natural formations, by golly they would ensnare people with man-made enticements. So how did they decide to set themselves apart? It's simple, really. Pixies are at work here.

COME AND SEE, FOLLOW ME.

These five words signaled a new beginning for Shenandoah Caverns in the mid-1960s. Billboards and brochures featured an adorable cave pixie offering this invitation, and people came from far and wide. This cutesy theme continues to this day, as a generous band of elves still stands sentry about the complex and down in the cave. The pixie theme somehow makes the operation instantly likeable, sort of a little-fairy-cave-that-could kind of thing. It's almost as if the little gnomes are smilingly saying to their competitors, "Take that, you big, overblown cavities!"

But the pixies are only part of the Shenandoah Caverns story, as there are other oddities here as well. Luray Caverns may brag about their world-famous Sunny-Side-Up Egg formation, but Shenandoah has zesty bacon strips! Nearby Endless Caverns boasts of their Fairy Land formation, but Shenandoah actually has pixies! Then, of course, there is Shenandoah's premier formation: the Capitol Dome—which looks kind of like the exterior of Washington DC's grand white rotunda. Kind of.

And there is another bizarre secret weapon standing at the ready. A presently unnamed stalagmite pokes up from the floor in one of Shenandoah's subterranean rooms. It is perhaps the most perfectly formed "flipping off" formation ever to be found in a cave. Did nature *really* do this completely unassisted? Bet our ever-playful pixie friends know the answer to this.

Dinosaur Land

As you're driving south of Front Royal along VA Route 340, a giant dinosaur family poised to feast upon all of mankind suddenly appears. This particular dinosaur family has been captivating kids and annoying parents since 1963, eons after these massive creatures were thought to be extinct. Over the years, very little has changed at Dinosaur Land, save for the addition of a frightening new flesh-eater every now and again.

Dinosaur Land is what travelers from another era might have dubbed a "dive."

Now please don't misunderstand. When we at *Weird* say that a joint is a dive, it's akin to bestowing a sort of knighthood. This place is tacky in the most oddly enticing and satisfying way. It has the required "twenty-five years past its prime" look. Hey, what true dive doesn't? It also charges five smackers a head for adults and four for kiddies, which is the ultimate clue. All roadside dives seem to charge about four

or five bucks for whatever it is they're hawking—just enough to turn a profit, but not enough that customers blow a gasket in protest. It has been this way since the beginning of motorized road travel.

But therein lies Dinosaur Land's charm and undeniable weirdness. It seems to be in a time warp. Where else these days can you cozy up beside a full-size Gigantosaurus or ponder a ninety-foot octopus with a goofy mug that's a ringer for Casper the Friendly Ghost? Flanking these ferocious figures are a scary Stegosaurus, a terrifying Triceratops, a giant ground sloth, a twenty-foot-tall Tyrannosaurus, and a sixty-foot shark in full attack mode! In all, there are some fifty-odd figures, including bizarre non-Jurassic specimens like King Kong and an oversized preying mantis that apparently preyed just a bit too close to a nuclear test site. Now that's what we call value!

PREHISTORIC ANIMALS

AUTHENTIC REPRODUCTIONS OF THE PAST

- BRONTOSAURUS
- STEGOSAURUS
- PASITTASAURUS
- DIMETRODON
- HADROSAURUS
- PACHYCEPHALOSAURUS
- PETRANODON
- MAMMOTH
- ORVIROPITOR (King Rex)
- DIATRYMA
- PROTOCERATOPS
- IQUANDON
- PRAYING MANTIS
- TYRANNOSAURUS
- MYLODON (Ground Sloth)
- KING COBRA
- TYLOSAURUS
- SALTOPUS
- TITANOSAURUS
- TRICERATOPS
- MOSCHOPS
- ANKLYOSARUS
- PLATEOSAURUS
- SABRE TOOTH TIGER

Edward Valentine's Death Masks

This may come as a surprise. but generations ago making a cast of a dead person's face with wax or plaster was nearly as commonplace as snapping a photo of a live body is today. Death masks were created for two main reasons. The first is rather obvious, for what heartbroken survivor wouldn't desire such a lasting remembrance of a loved one? The second reason, only slightly less popular, saw masks being used as templates for the creation of highly detailed painted portraits or full-blown sculptures of their subjects.

From the exterior, the Valentine Museum in Richmond, named after its founder, sculptor Edward Valentine, looks pleasant enough. With an airy open courtyard abutting large, sunshine-inviting windows, the workshop appears filled with life, not death. Once inside, however, a different picture quickly emerges. High upon a shelf resides the museum's collection of death masks. One of these casts, the headliner no doubt, was reportedly prepared from the rigid carcass of none other than General Thomas J. "Stonewall" Jackson.

Each of these death masks stands cheek to cheek to the next one like bobbing heads in a movie theater. It's a favorable arrangement that makes viewing all that much easier.

Mount Trashmore, Virginia Beach

This seaside pocket of the offbeat has outdone itself in the strange-but-true category. It has created a newfangled park called Mount Trashmore, aptly named since it's made out of its own refuse pits. This is no small thing. Try to picture for a moment what a heap of decaying garbage piled some sixty feet high and eight hundred feet long might look like after being painstakingly manicured, and you'll have some idea as to the overall "beauty" of the venture. Actually, on second thought . . .

The residents, though, seem to love it. Spread out in the park's 165 acres, visitors will find a basketball court, a playground area, walking trails, volleyball

pits, and even multiple picnic facilities. But with these, Mount Trashmore is only getting warmed up. In addition to these attractions, the park now features a radical skateboard facility, and not just one but two lakes. Lake Windsor, as regal as its name sounds, is really a brackish affair that sits squarely next to a mountain of, well, garbage. Lake Trashmore (yes, the powers that be actually named it this) is a freshwater pond where visitors can fish if they're so inclined.

In the end this bizarre place does indeed deserve your visit. There is much to be learned here about modern sanitation methods, and it provides many entertaining ways to "waste" the hours away.

White's Ferry, Leesburg

Every so often, a weirdness tag comes attached to something not scary, ethereal, or bizarre. White's Ferry, a long-operating car ferry that crosses the mighty Potomac River between Leesburg, VA, and Poolesville, MD, earns this designation not for its "gee-wow" factor, but simply due to the fact that it is, for some reason, still there.

When standing at the edge of the murky brown water of the Potomac, it becomes clear just how uncommonly narrow the river is here. With a proper wind-up, a determined Little League pitcher could probably reach the other side. This relative closeness makes one wonder why some ambitious politico hasn't yet erected a small, ugly bridge here. The driving distance between such crossings is rather long, considering this region's proximity to the greater Washington, DC, area.

Next, there is the ever-present current, which threatens to send this little-ferry-that-could downriver with each crossing, despite the fact that the craft is guided across by a steel cable. At times of unusually high water, ferry service often ceases for this very reason. This unpleasant situation forces motorists to drive some twelve miles to reach the closest available bridge (near Furnace Mountain, VA) and often leads to a good old southern cussing festival while en route.

White's Ferry is named after Confederate Captain Elijah Veirs White, a veteran of the Civil War and original owner of the operation. In the 1930s, Chief Justice Charles Evans Hughes rode the ferry over to the Maryland side. Since his plan involved a round-trip passage, he casually asked the ferry master, "What would you do if I didn't have a dollar?" The ferryman casually replied, "If you don't have a dollar, mister, you don't belong in Maryland!"

A humorous quip? Perhaps. Today, the *Gen. Jubal A. Early* ferryboat can carry some twenty-four cars, where its predecessors once hauled a meager three. It is propelled by a diesel tug named *Early's Aid* and by a back-up tug named the *General's Pusher*.

I Could Die for Some Good Pancakes

The Third Street Diner in Richmond was once a place where you'd go not to stuff your face, but to have it embalmed. During the Civil War era, the building was used as a morgue!

Where Floats Go for the Winter

There is this museum in Shenandoah where they keep the big floats used in parades. The floats are huge, and when you walk in, it doesn't even seem like a real place. The place is kind of in the middle of nowhere. It's weird, because we didn't even know what it was at first—we were really looking for the caverns. When we walked in, it was like a dreamland, with huge eagles and animals. Some move, and some you can get inside of. It's the strangest site I have ever seen in the U.S. Trust me, it's worth the trip to see something this weird.—*Kady Lee*

A Roadside Rising?

The gargantuan *Crux Gloria* (Latin for "Glorious Cross") adjoins St. Francis de Sales Church on Route 7 in Purcellville. Depending upon personal perspective, driving down this rural stretch of Loudoun County can be either joyous or unsettling. Either way, it surely grabs one's attention.

Since 1989, Tomas Fernandez's cross has inspired and perhaps even frightened those who drive by it. The artist says that the magnificent *Crux Gloria* "serves as an icon of hope for western Loudoun [County] and beyond."

At some 17,000 pounds and thirty-three feet in height, the all-metal *Crux Gloria* is a sight to behold, but its outsized dimensions do not represent its only claim to fame. For that, one must look toward the humongous Jesus silhouette stamped out of its steel skin. Standing below this masterpiece-in-metal is quite an experience. Whatever your religious persuasion, one thing is sure: This artist has certainly made a statement.

The World's ONLY Ass Kicking Machine

Prices availible by owner children 5 and under are free Pregant women over 12 months free Others will be charged acording to size and shape if not completly satisfied you will be taken to the wood shed for complete satisfaction → OPEN 30 hours per day owner and operater Bob Boothe.

Bob Boothe's Ass-Kicking Machine

During the course of an average day, we members of this harried, frazzled place called Earth encounter at least one person in need of a good swift kick to the . . . ahem. Fun-limiting assault laws aside, wouldn't it be wonderful if we could deliver such blows repeatedly, like a Gatling gun, and *not* put our fragile feet at risk in the process? Bob Boothe, a seer of sorts, has apparently heard our clarion call and taken action. He has placed his southern Virginia property on the weird map with his "tail kicker" and in the process redefined the term southern hospitality.

After nearly nine decades of taking it on the chin, Bob Boothe, 89, of Burnt Chimney sought retribution. As an ex-navy man, he knew well the principles of water propulsion, so it logically followed that he'd choose this method to deliver his "kicks." Starting with an electric pump and a waterwheel, Boothe attached boards to the spokes of a

second hoop and fitted them with work boots. Presto! The "world's *only* ass-kicking machine" was born.

Actually, the *only* part is an overstatement. Boothe readily admits that his idea emerged after first witnessing a smaller butt booter in North Carolina twenty years earlier. Still, it's nice that our number two man gives due credit to his esteemed predecessor in rump-thumping.

These days, the ass-kicking machine looks none the worse for wear. In fact, when we dropped by for a demonstration, we were cordially invited to plug the beast in and "let 'er rip!" Never the type to decline such a tempting offer, we enlisted (bribed) a willing subject and waited for the waterwheel to build up steam. When the device reached critical mass, we asked our patsy—er, tester—to take the cure. At the precise instant that her cautious smile morphed into a pained grimace, we fully understood the magnitude of Bob Boothe's contribution to the world.

Head Honchos

Entrepreneur Everette H. Newman III had a dream. Bothered by the fact that many Americans couldn't distinguish between a Fillmore and a Buchanan, this successful motel owner wondered if there weren't a way to address such a woeful lack of presidential knowledge. Suddenly, like an epiphany, it came to him. He would commission the building of enormous presidential heads and place them side by side in a park for all to see. All he needed was the proper site and an artist to pull off such an ambitious project. He set out to find them.

Texas sculptor David Adickes fit Newman's requirements for an artist to a tee. He'd already created a number of oversized sculptures, most prominently a seventy-six-foot likeness of Sam Houston, displayed near Huntsville, TX. Utilizing his immense talents and penchant for the oversized, Adickes got busy sculpting figures of each U.S. President. Newman, in turn, worked on a plan to display the giant heads in a suitable setting. It looked like "Presidents Park" would soon become a reality. Of course, as any weird lover can tell you, looks can be deceiving.

To better explain the convoluted journey of the heads, it's helpful to channel famous song lyrics: "What a long strange trip it's been" not only describes the Grateful Dead's drug-fueled odyssey, it approximates the troubled birth and adolescence of Newman's oversized statues. So what happened along our hero's path to patriotism? Let's just say that antivisionaries put up a substantial roadblock, or if you prefer, wrapped his giant heads in a turban of red tape.

After learning that a permit was required to display his initial shipment of six heads, Newman quickly applied, but was forced by county commissioners to put his Presidents Park on hold until such "public display" credentials were obtained. To add insult to injury, it was further ordered that no other heads were to be shipped until the problem was resolved. This effectively placed the entire venture in jeopardy.

To comply with the orders of the powers that be, Newman had his giant heads (some standing as tall as twenty feet) transported via flatbed truck to the parking lot of his Days Inn Motel in Williamsburg. More than a few weirdness enthusiasts took note of the mysterious heads littered across the motel lot and made continuing pilgrimages to this impromptu presidential party. But even this would come to an abrupt halt when Newman was again ordered to move his heads. "It is *still* a public display without a permit," said the unpatriotic dream killers.

The supersize craniums, now nine in total, were split between two sites. Six found a warm nest beside the flora at the Norfolk Botanical Gardens, while the remaining three were perched atop a windy hillside at Buena Vista's Glen Maury Park. At both places, a phenomenon took place as viewers, clearly delighted,

scratched their own heads in awe and wonder.

But this is where our tale takes a strange, or perhaps *un*strange, turn. Somewhere, somehow, the necessary permits were obtained. By virtue of this official act, the statues were released from their illegitimate (and decidedly weird) limbo, and catapulted directly into the mainstream. Soon, Presidents Park would be assembled in all of its glory with all the pomp and circumstance befitting a presidential tribute.

Today, forty-three humongous noggins rest just a stone's throw from Colonial Williamsburg. They are viewable for a small fee, and stand at the ready to clear up any questions we average Joes might have about their respective places in history.

To advance Newman's stamp-out-presidential-stupidity campaign, each president has his own professionally researched bio blurb attached to his statue. This is a far cry from the time they spent in the motel parking lot where folks were overheard to ask, "Which dead guy is this, Henrietta?" or "Why did they make one of *that* bum?"

Washington's Wonderful Palace of Wonders

Hurry hurry hurry! Step right up, ladies and gentlemen. Your friends and neighbors are inside enjoying the show right now.

That's what James Taylor, Palace of Wonders museum director (and owner of its outrageous attractions), wants you to hear whenever you drive through Washington's Atlas Entertainment District, just north of Capitol Hill. The Palace, as Taylor says, is the world's only full-time operating vaudeville revival house, featuring regular live entertainment. The latter is the essential ingredient at the Palace of Wonders. "Without the live entertainment—from regular burlesque and vaudeville shows to magic acts and sideshow entertainers—my museum attractions become as stuffy as some of the other museum collections in this town," Taylor says.

Hardly. The riot of a collection is a showcase for "the weird, the strange, the bizarre, the odd, and the unusual." Of course it features such wonders as the World's Only Unicorn (once exhibited in the Ringling Bros. circus), the mummy of Devil Man (a front cover of the *Weekly World News* a few years back), the Head of the Snake that Killed Sailor Katzy (safely preserved in a jug of formaldehyde; the snake, that is, not Sailor Katzy), Spider Billy (the desiccated corpse of a six-legged kid, um, young goat), a genuine tattooed mummy's arm, the Samoan Sea Wurm (a dried sea serpent that purportedly killed a ship's cat before being dispatched by the angry sailors on board), Fivey the Five-Legged Dog, and Oojeeboo or the Terror of the Sioux (don't ask). It's been called a "world-class collection," and, at over half a thousand attractions, it's a serious sight for wide eyes. As Taylor puts it, "It's a glorious mess."

Taylor's interest in the museum business—and his inspiration for the collection that forms the Palace of

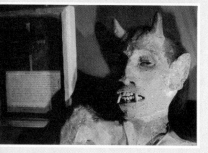

never made me happy that we couldn't have regular performances. Live shows were the heart of the old dime museums." Still, it gave the artifacts some of their first national, even international, attention. And when Taylor left the Dime Museum, it was only logical that he and the "strangest collection in the world" would find another home eventually.

Wonders—started with his *Shocked and Amazed! — On & Off the Midway,* a publication he created in the '90s to shine a light on novelty performers and variety shows, especially sideshows. "Nobody had ever written about the performers as people, gotten behind the stage acts to cover the showfolk and the business itself." Nearly ten volumes later, Taylor sees *Shocked and Amazed!* as more than just a journal devoted to "weirdness as entertainment." As he puts it, "It's more like an encyclopedia devoted to all of the novelty and variety arts, from magic to wax museums, from sideshows to animal acts, thrill shows, mentalism and hypnotism, you name it."

His first experiment in the museum business wasn't the Palace of Wonders, though. That would be the American Dime Museum, which he cofounded in Baltimore and named after the old attractions from the 1800s, which charged a dime for admission. "It was a great place to start, and it featured a small percentage of what I've got here at the Palace," but, he adds, "it

"Eventually" turned out to be just a few months. Soon after Taylor left the Dime, DC club entrepreneur Joe Englert approached him with an idea. Englert at that time was in the midst of "clubbing" the northeast corridor of H Street and wanted to devote one of the clubs to sideshow and variety entertainment. Over the next two years, the building that would eventually house the Palace went from a shell that had once held an assortment of retail establishments

to the full-fledged home for Taylor's museum of oddity attractions, the Palace of Wonders, designed by local burlesque queen Jill Fisher, with Web-site and on-site art by Lee Wheeler. Better,

it became a ready-and-waiting performance space for some of the country's foremost novelty acts. The weekend-long opening celebration included an assortment of Wild West and sideshow acts, a number of burlesque performers, sword swallowers, and even a flea circus. "An old showman told me once, 'You're givin' 'em too much!'" Taylor says. "'They'll come to expect it!' But I don't know any other way to do it."

As the saying goes, though, too much of a good thing is still a pretty good thing. The Palace is chockablock with wacky attractions and odd artifacts on both floors. The first floor is given over to the main bar and the stage, but that still leaves plenty of room for wall cases filled with exotic animal skulls, wax heads, and fortune-telling paraphernalia, as well as the head of King the Two-Faced Bull, which stares balefully across the bar. The eerie amber light that fills the hall glows from a half dozen "monkey faces" or carousel medallions that once graced the hub of a 1920s Dentzel merry-go-round. Upstairs—where the crowd can view the stage over the rail of the mezzanine or on the large-screen TV—there are still more monkey faces staring down at the second-floor bar. Outside is a deck set up as though it were an old circus tent, its privacy fencing painted in red and white strips.

The Palace of Wonders is located at 1210 H Street NE, Washington, DC (www.palaceofwonders.com). Drop by sometime whenever you feel a need to renew your own sense of wonder.

SHRUNKEN HUMAN

Roads Less Traveled

efore we begin this portion of our weird journey, we have to ask: Have you ever run across a road that just seems to be bad? It might be a dark path about which stories linger, or it might simply be a place you stumble across one day that leaves you with the unshakable feeling that "something is wrong here."

We night riders have always been intrigued by those stretches of roadway that give travelers a creeping sensation at the back of the neck. Some may have been the scene of an unusually high number of accidents. Others are haunted by some horrific event from the past, memories that can't quite be forgotten. Or is it just that the road itself remembers these events?

Perhaps these roads are not really scary at all. Perhaps they are merely a means for us to delve into our own innermost fears and the dark corners of our imaginations. Who among us has not, at some time in our life, climbed into a car with a group of friends in search of some haunted bridge or old graveyard? With the tales told along the way, even the most innocent happenings reek of the supernatural by the time we reach our destination.

So are we turning otherwise ordinary roadways into spooky "roads less traveled"? Perhaps we are—or perhaps not. Whatever the answer, it cannot be denied that these roads less traveled have become key ingredients in the weirdness of the state.

Persistent Paranormal Hitchhiker of Walney Road

Is *there anything* more eerie than a lonely figure seen walking a highway on a dark and stormy night? Virginia has several strange roads that are said to be home to such lonely phantom figures, including Walney Road in Chantilly. The story has it that many years ago, before the road was paved, a man was killed while out walking one evening. As he strolled along, he was struck and killed by a passing automobile, the driver of which was never found. Since that time, the ghost of this man has been walking this road, trying to flag down passing cars. It's said that he is searching for the driver who killed him and fled.

Interestingly, according to the story, drivers who see this man are encouraged to pick him up, rather than simply pass him by. The man apparently appears to drivers three times on Walney Road, at three different locations. Those who tell this tale claim that if you do not pick him up after the third time, he will appear in the passenger seat of the car and force you off the road. There are those who can point to a number of accidents that have occurred on this windswept roadway and say, without hesitation, that they happened because a driver passed by the Walney Road Hitchhiker one too many times!

A Visit to Walney Road

Try explaining yourself to a startled woman when she finds you bent over in a corner very late in the evening seemingly taking photos of nothing in the pitch black. That is what happened to me when I was investigating Walney Road. The road lived up to my expectations, especially at night. It was extremely dark and rolled up and down through dense woods that seemed to choke at it from each side. I was on foot photographing the road sign when a woman appeared out of the shadows, walking her dog. She was kind and seemed to grow more at ease after I told her what my purpose was there (absurd as it sounded). She seemed to have vaguely heard about the ghostly hitchhiker but told me a more current and extremely sad story of Walney Road. Apparently, only a few weeks before my visit, a young guy was traveling home very late at night down the road. He could not have known there would be a woman making a turn in the middle of that unlit road and he drove straight into her car and, tragically, was killed. I could easily imagine how startled he would have been when his headlights caught the car at that last moment, painting it into view. The worst part, the woman told me, was that his mother was following behind the young man in her car to make sure he got home okay. She had witnessed the entire accident. The woman with the dog walked on after her tale and I was left feeling horrible for that family and very much wanting to leave the darkness of Walney Road.—*Ryan Doan*

Dead Engines Come Alive in Bassett

The small town of Bassett has for many years been home to a weird legend about a local junkyard, or rather about the road that runs past this old salvage yard. It is a place that is said to be haunted by the ghosts of those who were killed in auto accidents and whose wrecked vehicles ended up here at the yard.

According to the stories, those who drive along the old road at night will actually see the headlights of the abandoned cars in the field flashing on and off. The lights will suddenly appear and then fade away a few moments later, as if their batteries had died. Of course, these batteries have been dead, in some cases, for decades.

Travelers are told that should they park their cars along the road, they will hear the sounds of car doors opening and slamming and radios playing, as if the vehicles—and their long-dead drivers—have somehow come to life. At the bottom of the field, some claim, they have even heard the sounds of engines racing and cars driving back and forth. To the visible eye though, the field is still and deserted, and if there are automobiles racing here, they are from another dimension.

Foul-Weather Phantom of Coast Artillery Road

Another mournful figure is said to walk along Coast Artillery Road near Fort Story in Virginia Beach. He seems to appear on the wettest, most chilling nights of the year. During the winter, he appears so frequently that he has been sighted many times by soldiers who patrol this area near the base. And while the sightings of the grim specter are unnerving enough, what makes things even worse is that some of the soldiers recognize the man. They actually served with him several years ago!

In this life, the man was a soldier who was stationed at Fort Story in the mid-1990s. For reasons that have never been discovered, he grew depressed and withdrawn, and one night committed suicide. Two of his friends found his body hanging in his quarters the following morning.

But even though this young soldier is dead, he still makes his appearances along Coast Artillery Road, an area that he often patrolled during his normal duties. No one knows what he wants here, or why he appears, but many drivers have spotted him as they travel along this secluded road. Both soldiers and civilians alike have slowed to see if he wants, or needs, a ride; but he angrily motions for them to go on past, to keep driving. When the drivers look into the rearview mirror, however, the figure has vanished.

Indian War Party of Pocahontas Parkway

It was nearly midnight on July 15, 2002, as a delivery truck sped along the highway, traveling quickly along the recently opened Pocahontas Parkway, near Richmond. As the driver motored across the road's long bridge, his eyes widened at the sight of three flickering lights that appeared up ahead to his left.

"The truck driver came through and said he seen [three] Indians in the middle of the highway, lined up by the woods, each of them holding a torch," said a report filed by the parkway toll taker to whom the driver related the incident. The warriors, clad in breechcloths and heavily armed, were clearly illuminated against the tree line by the light from the torches they carried. The stunned truck driver turned his attention back to the road and suddenly had to let loose a blast from his horn to warn away two more Indians, who were standing in the road ahead of him. These men also carried burning torches, and the driver saw them clearly in the light from his headlights as well.

Was the story a result of too many hours spent on the road? Not to the truck driver who saw the figures or the woman who staffed the tollbooth where he stopped to tell of his eerie encounter. As he leaned out to her and told her his story, he described what he thought was some sort of angry protest by local Native Americans, upset that the new roadway had been paved over a forgotten burial ground or some such sacred site.

But the woman in the tollbooth did not share this opinion. She had seen and heard too much since the new highway had opened. She knew the driver had not seen angry modern-day Indians along the road. He had seen ghosts. At the end of her shift, she filed her report. It was now on record—the new Pocahontas Parkway was officially haunted.

Virginia State Highway 895, more commonly known as Pocahontas Parkway, is a toll road, and therein lie some of its problems. Less than nine miles long, it connects Interstate 95 and Virginia State Highway 150 in Chesterfield County with Interstate 295 near the Richmond International Airport. Two workers died during its construction, and whether this had anything to do with the later strange reports is unknown. However, it certainly did not add anything to the good reputation of the new highway.

In addition to the deaths, trouble began to arise almost immediately during the building of the road. First came cost overruns, mostly connected to soil conditions that made it necessary to use much deeper foundations than had originally been planned. Then there was the last-minute addition of an exit ramp for traffic headed toward Richmond. (But not one for return traffic. Once you entered Richmond by way of the new highway, you would find it impossible to leave by the same route!) One of the biggest problems was the loss of the

Interstate designation. Because of an anti–toll-road quirk in government funding statutes, the project lost the right to bear the Interstate shield.

Despite all the problems, however, the highway opened more or less on schedule and seemed to be running smoothly, at first. And then came the ghosts.

The strange stories surfaced in the summer of 2002. Truck drivers and motorists began calling the police to report being harassed on the roadway by what appeared to be people in Native American costumes, waving torches. The Virginia state police were called to investigate, but they found nothing—no Indians and no burning torches. Two of the calls were documented in state police incident reports.

The first was on July 1 at 3:11 a.m. and then two days later, at 1:44 a.m. Workers at the toll plaza reported "see[ing] a subject running back and forth around the loading dock." State troopers responded in both cases but found no sign of the phantom trespassers. At both times, the specters were described as having cloudy but

fully formed legs, arms, and torsos, with only the vaguest outlines of heads. Both the workers at the toll plaza and the troopers claimed to hear the pounding of drums in the darkness.

There were also reports of what seem to be war whoops, shouts, and the cries of seemingly dozens of voices. The frenzied chants and screams usually came long after midnight, and throughout that summer were heard on an almost nightly basis. Many skeptics dismissed the sounds as coming from an illegal dog kennel that was rumored to be in the area, or even ducks and geese from the nearby James River. But those who actually heard the sounds knew they were something else entirely. One witness was a Virginia state trooper who spoke to a newspaper

reporter: "I know what a bunch of hunting dogs sounds like, and it doesn't sound anything like that," the trooper said.

Corinne Geller, a state police spokesperson, confirmed the noises were real. Geller visited the toll plaza late one night in the summer of 2002 and heard the eerie sounds. "Three separate times during our watch, I heard high-pitched howls and screams," she said. "Not the kind

of screams of a person in trouble, but whooping. There were at least a dozen to fifteen [voices]. I would say every hair on my body was standing up when we heard those noises."

Officials were assured that the figures being reported on the roadway were not part of some Native American protest. Deanna Beacham of the Nansemond tribe was positive about this. "We are anxiously awaiting our federal

recognition," she said, speculating that any such activity would harm chances that the U.S. government would officially recognize Virginia's Indian tribes.

Beacham wouldn't commit to the idea of Virginia Indian spirits wandering around the area. But it's not impossible, she added. "We're still here as place names," she said. "We became rivers and streets and roads and communities. Why shouldn't people see physical manifestations of that?"

Some researchers looked to history for answers. There was evidence of Native American habitation in the area of the highway, dating from the 1600s to as far back as 3500 B.C. Archaeologists, like Dennis Blanton from the College of William and Mary, launched a dig at the site in advance of the bridge's construction and found that Indian artifacts were plentiful. "There were artifacts scattered all over, dating back five or six thousand years," Blanton said.

Edward Haile, an area historian who had used modern scientific evidence to corroborate Captain John Smith's 1608 map of the James River, agreed that the location of the Pocahontas Parkway was home to Indians for a very long time. "There are two [villages] that are dead hits—right there," Haile said.

As the tales made the rounds, people began coming to the highway and bridge in droves, all hoping to see the Indian spirits. Since they were usually reported well after midnight, many came to the area prepared to spend the night and some brought along plenty of "spirits" of their own. The nightly revelers were disturbing not only to the toll plaza workers and the people who lived in the area but also to local ghost hunters who wanted to investigate the documented sightings seriously. "Unfortunately, the crowds of rowdy spirit spotters singing and shouting in the woods are not likely to encourage the ghosts to appear," said Ben Keys, a local paranormal researcher who had investigated other Virginia hauntings. "It's a very spiritual place, a holy place to the Indians, and these people are just making a party of it. Quiet and reverence is what you need."

The constant problems with those parking along the highway eventually pushed the Virginia Department of Transportation into placing "no parking" signs along the shoulder and the median of the road. Today it is no longer feasible to visit the lands adjoining the Pocahontas Parkway. But that doesn't mean the spirits are no longer active. There are those who maintain that occasional happenings still occur, although on a less frequent basis. According to Ben Keys, a toll plaza worker was enjoying her dinner break one night and suddenly lost interest in her food when her drink began moving all over the table! She just assumed that the spirits wanted her drink more than she did, and she hurried back to work.

So if you happen to be driving along the Pocahontas Parkway some night and happen to see what looks like a burning torch in the woods alongside the highway, slow down—but don't stop—and offer a gesture of respect to those who came before us here in the wilds of Virginia. May they rest in peace.

Victims Haunt Elbow Road

One of the darkest and most dreaded roadways in Virginia is an isolated spot called Elbow Road, located just east of Chesapeake. The old road snakes through a heavily wooded area with no streetlights. Its dangerous curves have claimed the lives of at least two people over the years. Not surprisingly, many ghosts are said to haunt this road, making it an attractive journey for late-night riders in the region. But do these eerie tales have any connection to the truth? Do strange things really take place along Elbow Road?

The weird stories of this narrow drive date back many years and involve a number of different ghosts. One of the most famous specters is that of Mrs. Woble, who once lived here. One night, she vanished from her home and was never seen again.

Mrs. Woble's friends and neighbors became concerned when they had not heard from her in a while, so they contacted the authorities. At first, police thought she had simply left the area without telling anyone, but they went to investigate anyway. When they arrived at her house, they found that the back door had been broken open and glass was left on the floor. All of the lights in the house were still burning and the television was on in the living room. They called out, but no one answered.

As they began searching the premises, they found a number of odd things. Mrs. Woble had apparently left her dinner untouched when she left the house. A plate was still sitting on the dining room table, but the food on it was now cold and congealed. Her car keys were still resting on a small entry table just inside the front door. Everything in the house seemed to be just as she had left it. Only the broken glass at the back door seemed out of the ordinary—but then the police officers went upstairs.

In Mrs. Woble's bedroom, they found a horrific scene of butchery and bloodshed. The walls had literally been sprayed with blood and gore; it looked as though someone had been torn apart in the room. However, Mrs. Woble, or her dead body, was nowhere in sight!

The mystery of her disappearance was never solved, and eventually the case was filed away with others that had long ago gone cold. Realtors tried to sell her house for years; but as soon as prospective buyers heard what had happened there, they started looking elsewhere. Finally the house was torn down. Mrs. Woble was gone, but she certainly has not been forgotten. . . .

To this day, it has been said that her ghost haunts Elbow Road. She is often seen walking near the curve where her house once stood. She is a shocking sight when glimpsed in the headlights of passing cars. She has been reported wearing a pale-colored housedress that is streaked with blood. As the woman walks along, she stumbles in the direction of the curve in the road, where many have reported seeing the flickering lights of a house at the edge of the woods. Mrs. Woble vanishes as she reaches the front porch of the house, and then the entire scene goes dark. Those who investigate later discover that no house stands here—only the crumbling foundation of the house that once was.

If the ghost of Mrs. Woble still haunts this road less traveled, she does not do so alone.

One of the other phantoms here is said to be a man in shorts who died one night while running with his dog. No one knows the identity of this man but the legend has it that he was out on the roadway one night, near dark, and that he was struck by a truck that was coming from the opposite direction. The truck slammed into the jogger, then shuddered to a stop. Its brake lights flashed for a moment, and then it sped off as quickly as possible. Another motorist, who saw the accident occur, called

the police and an ambulance. The driver of the truck was never caught, and the jogger tragically died before making it to the hospital. His dog was never found.

But the man's ghost still runs on Elbow Road, his spectral hand still gripping the empty leash of his small dog. Most who have spotted him first think that he is a real person—until he vanishes before their eyes!

Another Elbow Road spirit is one that is never seen but does leave evidence of itself behind. The stories say that if you park your car along the sharpest curve on the road, near Stumpy Lake, the ghost will leave a little something behind for you. You have to be very quiet and patient for this to occur; but right around midnight, the small footprints of a child will appear and start to walk toward your car. The footprints have been reported in the dust alongside the road and sometimes, on rare occasions, they appear as wet footprints on the pavement of the road itself. According to legend, the phantom footprints belong to a little girl who drowned in the nearby lake one day when she and her father were fishing.

While *Weird Virginia* was unable to find any record of a drowning that occurred nearby, we did find a report of an accident that occurred at this very curve—which claimed the lives of two young girls. Could one of them be the source of the phantom footprints?

The accident occurred one night in the early 1990s. The automobile involved was traveling along Elbow Road just after midnight when the driver misjudged the curve and slammed into the ditch. The car then became airborne and landed on the opposite side of the road. No one knows how long the victims in the car waited for help that night, along this dark and sparsely populated road. Eventually, though, another motorist passed by and stopped at the scene. When he saw the carnage inside the car, he hurried to a nearby home to alert the sleeping residents.

Two of those in the car died at the scene. One of them was an infant, who had been sleeping on her mother's lap in the front seat during the crash. The little girl had been thrown through the windshield and died instantly. The other person who met the grim reaper that night was a fifteen-year-old girl who had been riding in the backseat.

Could someone from this real-life accident be the spirit haunting the curve on Elbow Road? That remains a mystery. One thing is for certain, though. Elbow Road is a strange and haunted place and one of the weirdest roadways that Virginia has to offer!

Witnessed the Elbow Road Jogger

My friends and I always heard stories about this road called Elbow Road, how it's a drive through darkness with no streetlights and the road is narrow with various sharp turns.

So one night my friend and her boyfriend decided to take a little trip to Elbow Road. She asked my boyfriend and I to come along. So we agreed. We wanted to see it for ourselves. As we got closer to the road, I began to get a bad feeling, like something was going to go wrong. I told my boyfriend and he said not to worry, nothing is going to happen.

We finally came to the road. As we were told, there were no streetlights and the road was narrow. As we came around the corner, the tire on the car blew, which caused us to have to pull over. We didn't worry about it too much since we all had cell phones. When my friend tried to call someone on her phone, she couldn't get any service. All of the phones were the same. We were stuck.

We all got out of the car just to watch and make sure nothing would happen to her boyfriend as he changed the tire. We were surrounded by woods, which made it more intense. My friend, who was standing near the back of the car, made a gasping noise and was pointing off into the distance. We all turned to see what she was pointing at. Shocked and scared, we saw a man jogging toward us! We couldn't move. We all watched him jog by, calling for his dog. Her boyfriend then got it together to hurry and finish changing the tire. We all could still see him [the jogger]. Then suddenly he vanished into the night. We all got into the car and drove away, looking to see if we could see him along the road again and no, we didn't.

Finally we reached a friend's house and told them about it. They didn't believe us. No one believes us. But we all knew what we saw and heard, and no one could ever tell us that we didn't!!!–*Letter via e-mail*

Ghostly Jump on Crafford Road

Weird Virginia received a letter recently from someone who outlined the "ways to know you are from York County, Virginia." Interestingly, the third item on this list was: "You've been taken down Crafford Road ONLY ONCE and have sworn to never go back."

Needless to say, we at *Weird Virginia* are always up for a dare, so we decided to see what we could find out about this apparently legendary spot. Many people had come forward with strange tales of Crafford Road near Yorktown, but did the reality of the place live up to the hype?

The source of most of the strangeness seems to be a section of the roadway where Tour Road crosses over Crafford. There is a bridge here that stories say was once used to lynch African Americans in this area. No one seems to know if there is any truth to this story; but if there is, it just might explain what generations of people have experienced along Crafford Road at night.

The stories state that a black woman in a white dress has been seen many times standing on the edge of the bridge that crosses over Crafford Road. Those who have seen her say that she teeters there on the edge of the bridge for a few moments and then plunges toward the road below. As she falls to the ground, she vanishes before she ever reaches the pavement. Whoever she was, she is gone!

In addition to the ghostly woman, other strange happenings have been reported around the bridge. Some people claim that their cars have stopped running as they approach the bridge, only to start up again after they have been pushed past the affected area. Some have claimed to turn off their engines under the bridge, only to have the impossible occur. In one report we collected, a driver claimed that she and a friend had stopped under the bridge, with their car shifted into neutral. They'd been there about ten minutes when, without warning, the car suddenly began to move and actually rolled uphill for some distance!

Frightened, they drove off and stopped at a nearby convenience store to examine the car. When they climbed out and looked at the trunk, they found smeared handprints all over it, as if someone had been pushing the car. They also found footprints on the roof and fingerprints on the side windows—as if someone was trying to get in. They had seen no one around while they had been sitting under the bridge. Where had the prints come from?

With all of the tales that have been told about Crafford Road, we were anxious to see it for ourselves. The weird and "haunted" roadway certainly looked the part. At the time of our visit, the leaves were off the trees, and branches stretched out menacingly across the narrow roadway. We could certainly understand why many people only ventured here one time and never came back. As our car curved around numerous potholes and standing water, we watched nervously as the headlights illuminated the shadowy woods and then pointed to the legendary bridge in front of us.

We parked under the bridge and got out and hung around in the darkness for an hour or so to see what might happen. Unfortunately (or fortunately, depending on how you look at it), nothing occurred, and we decided to get back into the car and call it a night. We were a little disappointed; but even so, we were not surprised that so many of Virginia's night riders had encountered things here they could not easily explain away.

Then, as we opened the car doors and started to climb in, a new, strange sound could be heard in the darkness. Was that whistling? We weren't sure—and we didn't stick around to find out. We may not be from York County but we had braved Crafford Road one time and didn't plan on coming back!

Pedal to the Metal on Crafford Road

I had heard from a friend the story of this road, that if you drove down it at night you could see someone hanging from the bridge where someone was hung years ago and that cars have shut off underneath the bridge. Well, I decided one night to check the story out. I started down the road and as I approached the bridge, my car started to speed up. At first I thought maybe I was on an incline, but then I noticed that was not so. I put my brakes on and my car continued to speed up; I even had my brake pedal mashed on the floor but was still speeding up.

As I got further down the road, something flew and hit my car, making a very loud noise. Another car seemed to appear in front of me out of nowhere. At one point, I thought I was going to hit it, but then it was gone. As I got to the end of the road, my car finally slowed down. After leaving the area, I decided to stop and check to see what had hit my car, at which point I found five of what appeared to be A's marked over the car. . . .

I can't explain what happened on Crafford Road, but I do know that something is definitely going on there.—*Letter via e-mail*

Witch Pulls You Toward Her House

There's a gravity hill in Danville—a road called Oak Hill Road. If you stop on this road, it's supposed to pull you uphill.

There used to be a witch who lived there way back when witches were around. There was also a church, and a lot of religious people lived on the road. The witch moved there to torment the religious people. So the religious people ended up killing her by hanging her and just leaving her there for everyone to see. They put crosses up around the road to make the land holy. Now the witch haunts the place and tries to pull you to where her house used to be so she can kill you for what the religious people did to her.

I went to this road with my stepbrother on Halloween around midnight, and there was nothing but fog around us, which made it look scarier. My stepbrother put his car in neutral and turned it off and we started to roll up the hill. It took us all the way up to the witch's driveway, around a curve, and pulled us right toward her house. There used to be gates there at one time, but they got torn down. Now the hill only pulls you that far, and I don't know what's supposed to happen when you get to the gates. I didn't wait around to find out. . . . *–One Twisted Chick*

Feeling Gravity's Pull

For some reason, Oak Hill Road is hard to find on Mapquest. This rural route winds through farmland speckled with quaint homes. I was on the hunt for Virginia's Gravity Hill and was looking, obviously, for a spot with a decent downgrade. The problem was there were too many spots that could be "the spot." I tried putting my car in neutral in a few areas but nothing happened. Plus it was dangerous, as the local truckers seem to find these country roads great places to let off some aggression through their gas pedal.

Eventually I noticed a large church, a United Methodist Church, and several teenage girls getting out of a van driven by one of the girls' mothers. I figured one of them would have an idea of where Gravity Road was. I wasn't expecting all of them, including the mother, to know of it and its peculiar nature. They all swore it was real.

Leaving the goodly church people behind me, I followed their directions to the nearby stop sign that marked the end of the road and the spot where the effects of Gravity Hill would work. And it did. It did all too well. My rental car, in neutral, rolled back *up* the hill. That wasn't as frightening as the random mileage I noticed on my speedometer as I sped away. The digital indicator showed the numbers 666.1. I noticed this as I was photographing what I suspected to be the "witch's" house that is part of the legend, exactly 0.1 miles from Gravity Hill. That is some devilish irony.*–Ryan Doan*

The Lost City off Portugee Road

I live in the Richmond area and know many stories of the strange and spooky. The strangest has to be Lost City, which has become something of a myth in the area. In school I had heard stories of a city in the woods near Richmond International Airport. The stories involved government agencies, Satan worshipers, Bigfoot, families of cannibal crazies (offspring of escaped former asylum inmates), and even a creature known as Stickman.

When I was young, some friends and I finally took a trip there on bicycles. There were six of us, and the ride took over an hour. On the way, the woods along Portugee Road became thicker and darker. And before we arrived at the path leading to the City, we discovered the carcass of a freshly deceased goat!

Taking the path into the site, we found the forest was riddled with gravel roads that meandered and diverged throughout. The roads were curbed, with sidewalks, fireplugs, streetlights, and brick-lined storm drains. There was also a large water tower. One area held a half-flooded pump house, a paneless greenhouse, a water-treatment area, and several hangars. The pump house was being used as some form of Forestry Department building. There, we found several Forestry documents from the '50s relating to the area, then known as Elko Tract.

I continued to visit the Lost City thereafter and acted as a guide for friends (usually at night, for the adrenaline rush). Since then, parts of the area have been developed, but I've noticed that some of the paths off of Portugee Road still exist.

—*Chris Whiteowl*

Washington's Weird Bridges

The city of Georgetown has long been known as a historic and bustling port. It is bordered on the east by Rock Creek and on the south by the Potomac River. Several bridges provide access to Georgetown from the Washington area and from Virginia. Strangely, these bridges have been the scene of a number of weird happenings over the years.

One of the bridges that once spanned Rock Creek was a long wooden structure that no longer stands today. It caused many local residents to shudder over the stories of two accidents that were set around it.

One story took place in the years just after the American Revolution. It involved a young drummer boy who hailed from nearby Falls Church. He was crossing the bridge one windy afternoon and, according to the legend, he was nearly knocked down by a great gust of wind that sent him teetering to the bridge's edge. He struggled for a moment to regain his balance, but since he was carrying his drum at the time, he was clumsy and a little top-heavy. He pinwheeled his arms and straightened for a moment, but then suddenly he pitched over the bridge and fell into the river below. He clawed for the surface but the current was too strong, and he sank into the darkness. His body was never found.

In the years that followed, there came reports of muffled drumbeats that could be heard on the sounds of the wind. One newspaper article stated, "There are residents who insist that when the nights are quiet and Rock Creek is but a babble, one may hear the roll of a drum trembling in the air." The sound supposedly began faintly, as if far away, but would grow louder as it reached the spot on the bridge where the drummer boy had fallen over the side. Moments later, there was silence.

The other incident involving the same Rock Creek bridge occurred many years later. By this time, the wooden span had grown rickety and dangerous with age, but it was still in use. One night, during a fierce thunderstorm, it collapsed just as a carriage was hurrying across it. The driver and the horses fell to their deaths in the river below.

For years after this accident, local residents whispered of a ghostly reenactment of these tragic events. Those who lived in the vicinity of where the old bridge had once stood often recalled what they had seen on stormy nights. They told of a phantom carriage, with a driver who seemed to whip the horses in a panic as he tried to cross a bridge that was no longer there. Each time this apparition was seen, it would vanish in a flash of lightning as it neared what should have been the middle of the bridge.

These stories continued to be told for many years and then faded away, just as the memory of the old bridge also faded with time. But locals still tell tales of another bridge—tales that are even more terrifying.

For years, travelers going from Georgetown

into the District of Columbia usually used the old K Street Bridge that crossed Rock Creek. The bridge became the source of a legend that persisted for many years, although the stories started to lose their impact once electric lights were installed and when homes and businesses started to replace the surrounding dark woods. It was on the once shadowy roadway that locals feared encountering the "headless man of the K Street Bridge."

The stories of this macabre apparition began in the latter part of the 1800s, and it was rare when anyone who encountered him ever dared to cross the bridge again. No one knows how the ghost of the bridge came to be or how he managed to lose his head. One old newspaper account surmised that perhaps he was the victim of some vile crime, but no one really knew for sure. What they did know was that when he came lurching toward them from out of the shadows of the bridge, he was a horrifying sight—and one not to be seen for long. Anyone with the misfortune of meeting up with him seldom took the time to wonder where his head had gone, and why. They only wanted to make sure he didn't take theirs away with him before they could make their escape!

It was on the once shadowy roadway that locals feared encountering the "headless man of the K Street Bridge."

The Exorcist Steps

Ask anyone with a penchant for the Weird about an interesting place to visit in Georgetown and locals will almost always suggest a trip down "the Steps." Even those who have not seen the movie know them: those ninety-seven stone steps that lead from Prospect Street down to M Street. Before 1973, they were known as the Hitchcock Steps, named for the director of countless screen thrillers. But more than 30 years ago, a movie filmed in Georgetown changed the face of horror films forever and the steps were rechristened—*The Exorcist* Steps.

As it would happen, the story of *The Exorcist* had its roots in the Washington, DC, area. In January 1949, when future author William Peter Blatty was a junior at Georgetown, a newspaper story broke about a local boy who was allegedly possessed. After scratching and hammering sounds rang throughout his house, and objects flew about accompanied by the boy's sudden rages, the conclusion was that the events were supernatural. The family traveled to St. Louis, where the boy was placed under the care of a priest and permission was granted for an exorcism. The exorcism was carried out, and the boy was believed to be released from his paranormal problems. He grew up to lead a normal life and to this day has no recollection of the incident.

Blatty was enthralled by the story, one he never completely forgot. After receiving his degree in English, he moved to Hollywood to become a comic screenwriter. The story of *The*

Exorcist stayed in the back of his mind for twenty years, but he didn't write it until he had to—when he was unemployed. Comedy had dried up for him, and he wanted to prove that he could write in another genre. He changed the character of the boy in the real story to a girl and, with a lot of dramatic license on the actual events, created a best-seller.

The time came to turn the book into a film, and director William Friedkin insisted on using Georgetown, where the action in the book takes place. Filming began in October 1972 and lasted for about two months. Many locations on the Georgetown University campus were used, as were street scenes, the exterior of the Prospect Street house, and, of course, the Steps.

It was here that the fictional Burke Denning's body was discovered, after his head had been turned around and he was tossed from an upper-floor window, and where Father Karras ends up after the dramatic climax of the exorcism. These steps remain, to this day, one of the most recognizable sets in American film history; and yes, someone actually took a fall down those dizzying heights during the shooting. Set designer Marcel Vercoutre lined the staircase with dark foam padding and then Jason Miller (Father Karras) rolled down them twice.

So, if you happen to be sightseeing in Georgetown some day and are looking for someplace weird to check out, don't miss taking a walk down the infamous Steps. Just be sure to watch your footing when you do!

Ghostly Hauntings

Who can say for sure that ghosts do not exist? Are you totally convinced that restless spirits do not wander the lonely roads and abandoned battlefields of Virginia? Is that creaking on a staircase just the sound of an old house settling, or is it the passage of a being still treading the boards in another place and time?

If you have to stop and wonder, then perhaps you already realize that ghosts may not be just fanciful tales told by fools and drunks. Our modern world may be so bright, so loud, and moving so fast that it's hard to believe there are still spirits here who linger from the past. But so many weird things happen, things that resist explanation. And many of these stories take place within the borders of Virginia and the District of Columbia. Some spectral shapes have even been seen in the White House and the Capitol.

Haw Branch Hauntings

For more than a century, the hauntings at the Haw Branch Plantation were known all over Virginia — and beyond. Manifestations of the supernatural here were seemingly endless, including phantom footsteps, the apparition of a woman in white, reports of bloodcurdling screams that came only on a certain date, and strangest of all, the odd behavior of a certain portrait in the house.

The Haw Branch Plantation rests quietly outside the town of Amelia. It dates back to before the Revolutionary War, when Colonel Thomas Tabb purchased the land in 1743. The name Haw Branch came from a small stream on the property, the banks of which were lined with hawthorn trees. The white manor house is situated on a low hill and set into a brick-paved depression that resembles an ancient moat.

Haw Branch continues to look just as it did in the days before the Civil War. It is filled with canopied beds, authentic antiques, handmade rugs, and vintage family portraits. One of these portraits, hanging over the fireplace in the library, has a very bizarre history.

It is of a beautiful young woman named Florence Wright who lived in Duxbury, MA, many years ago. The picture shows a woman with fair skin, reddish-brown hair, and bright blue eyes. She is sitting in a dark green chair, and a soft pink rose rests gracefully in a jade-colored vase nearby. It seems to be an ordinary portrait, but anyone who doubts the weirdness of the picture could not be more wrong!

Cary McConnaughey and his wife, Gibson, purchased Haw Branch in 1965. Mrs. McConnaughey could trace her family tree back to Colonel Tabb, but by the time she and her husband bought the old homestead, it was almost in ruins. After an extensive renovation, the family moved into the house that August.

Four years later, a cousin gave Gibson the portrait of Florence Wright, who was apparently a distant relative by marriage. All the cousin knew was that Florence's parents had had a summer home in Massachusetts and that just before the painting was finished, the young woman had unexpectedly died. The cousin also knew that during her lifetime, Florence Wright had never visited Haw Branch.

The cousin told the McConnaugheys that the portrait was a beautifully colored pastel drawing. But after it was uncrated and the glass was cleaned, the painting appeared to be a charcoal rendering in dirty white, gray, and black.

A few days after the portrait was hung over the library fireplace, Gibson was in the basement when she thought

she heard the voices of women talking in the library. But when she went to investigate, no one was there. A quick search of the house revealed that it was empty, and there were no cars parked outside.

A few months later, in February 1970, Cary McConnaughey was seated in the library reading the newspaper. Glancing up, he was shocked to notice that the rose in the portrait was turning pink before his eyes! Taking a closer look, he could also see that the girl's black hair was getting lighter and that her gray skin was starting to take on a fleshy tone. In fact, nearly all of the grays and blacks in the portrait were beginning to take on color. The changes continued slowly each day, as the colors of the pastel became more obvious and then more vibrant. The once drab portrait was transformed into something bright and wondrous. In the meantime, voices of young women talking and laughing were still sometimes heard coming from the empty library.

A nearby clairvoyant heard about the portrait and came to Haw Branch to have a look. After studying it, she told the McConnaugheys that Florence Wright's spirit was forever bound to her picture because she had died before it was completed and that she had the power to remove the color from it if she was unhappy about where it was hung. Her spirit had accompanied the portrait to Haw Branch, a place that she immediately liked. With the help of the spirits of two other young women, she had restored the original color to her portrait. And the medium may have been right. After the color returned, the voices of the young women were no longer heard.

While the events surrounding the portrait were certainly strange, they seemed almost commonplace to the McConnaugheys, who had been dealing with other, and even more terrifying events at Haw Branch since the time they moved in.

Early in the morning on November 23, 1965, the entire family was awakened by the bloodcurdling scream of a woman. Gibson and Cary dashed up the stairs from their first-floor bedroom and found their children gathered at the foot of the staircase leading from the second floor to the attic. This is where the children were sure the scream had come from. Porkchop and Blackie, the family's two dogs, were also huddled nearby, shaking with terror. None of them dared go into the attic until after the sun had come up, and when they did, they found nothing out of the ordinary.

This was the first inkling the McConnaugheys had that something very strange might be occurring in the house.

On May 23, 1966, six months to the day since the family first heard the woman's scream in the night, the anguished cry once again echoed through Haw Branch. As before, no source could be found. Six months later, again on November 23, the chilling shriek was heard again, then again on May 23, 1967.

During the summer of 1967, things took another turn at the plantation. One night, as Gibson was on her way to bed, something in a semidark hallway caught her eye. "I could plainly see the silhouette of a slim girl in a floor-length dress with a full skirt," she remembered. "I could see no features but she was not transparent, just a white silhouette. I saw her for perhaps ten seconds. In the next instant, she was gone. There was no gradual fading away; she simply disappeared from one instant to the next."

Gibson quickly rushed to the bedroom and told her husband what she had seen. He laughed at her and, embarrassed, she didn't tell anyone else about it.

Several days later, one of Gibson's daughters told her of another visitation from the woman in the white dress. At that time, she knew nothing of her mother's encounter a few nights before. The girl said she had been kept awake the night before by Blackie barking on the front porch. It was so annoying that she finally went downstairs and let him in. He scampered past her into the drawing room. When she looked after him, she saw Blackie wagging his tail and looking up at a lady in white who was standing in front of the fireplace. Before the girl could say anything, the woman disappeared in front of her eyes.

The Gibsons eventually decided to try to tape the bloodcurdling screams they'd heard. Knowing they appeared every six months, the family prepared for the coming event with several flashlights and a tape recorder. On November 23, 1967, from midnight to dawn, they took turns staying awake. The two dogs and the cat behaved nervously, but the scream never came.

On May 23, 1968, the McConnaugheys again waited with flashlights and the tape recorder. This time, the entire family heard heavy footsteps walking across the yard—and then the screeching wail of the woman.

"We heard something running heavily," Gibson said, "and in a matter of several seconds, heard the scream coming from behind the barn. The next morning, our son and one daughter reported that they saw a giant bird standing in the yard in the moonlight under their windows. It was standing there with its wings spread out, appearing to have a wingspan of over six feet." The woman's chilling screams were never heard again after that, but the screech of what sounded like a huge bird was heard on a number of occasions, though the bird was never actually seen again.

What has haunted Haw Branch plantation for so many years that the mansion is now regarded as one of the most haunted houses in Virginia? No one knows for sure what mysteries of the past may have created these eerie manifestations. But legends abound and stories continue to be told about this place and its ghostly connections to the past.

Hauntings of the Octagon

One of the most famous haunted houses in the city of Washington is the Octagon. Located at the corner of New York Avenue and 18th Street NW, it is perhaps most famous for being used by President and Mrs. James Madison while the White House was being rebuilt after it was sacked by the British in 1814. Dolley Madison's ghost is one of the many that has been spotted here from time to time, but ghost stories have been recorded about the house for centuries.

Colonel John Tayloe III, the wealthiest man in Virginia at the time, purchased the lot in 1797 to build his townhouse. The lot was odd-shaped, so the building was designed with six sides (although the Tayloe family called it the Octagon), which made for some rather interesting architecture. Some of the rooms are positioned at angles that make for strange corners, and closets open into other closets. A magnificent freestanding oval staircase curves gracefully from the entrance hall to the third floor, dominating the structure. According to period accounts, the Tayloe daughters were known for their grace and beauty — and for their turbulent love affairs. Just before the War of 1812, one of them fell in love with a British officer, a relationship that her father strongly disapproved of. His refusal to allow the officer into the house began a heated argument, and the girl stomped off up the grand staircase. Seconds later, there was a scream and the girl plunged from the staircase to her death. Whether she fell or committed suicide is unknown, but her ghost is said to haunt the staircase today. She is not seen, but the flickering candle she carried as she ascended the steps still manifests itself, glowing in the dark night.

After the war, when President Madison returned to the White House, the Tayloe family moved back into the Octagon — to meet with more tragedy. Apparently

another daughter had eloped and then returned home to ask her father for forgiveness. The father and daughter clashed on the same stairway. The colonel brushed the girl aside as he passed her, and she lost her balance and fell, breaking her neck. It may be that this second daughter also returns to the staircase where she died. People who have never heard this tale are drawn to the exact spot at the bottom of the stairs where the girl fell to her death. It is said that one can feel a strange sensation, or a cold spot, in this area.

And there are other stories at the Octagon. . . .

The Slave Girl and the Nuns

For more than a hundred years, thumping sounds from within the walls of the Octagon plagued occupants of the house. No one was ever able to find the source of the noises until one day when workmen were repairing a damaged wall. Behind the stone, they found the skeleton of a young girl. The fingers of the corpse were clenched tightly, as if she had died while knocking on the wall. When the body was removed and given a proper burial, the sounds were never heard again.

How the body got there is unknown, but there is a tale of a soldier and a slave girl, which dates back to the early 1800s. Apparently, the two had been lovers, but things went awry and the soldier killed the girl in a jealous rage. Somehow, he managed to seal her body in the hollow wall. But was she really dead? Or did she spend centuries knocking at the wall, begging to be released?

The family moved from the Octagon after Mr. and Mrs. Tayloe died, and it changed hands several times. The house began to deteriorate, and according to reports of the time, people often heard screams of agony and sobs of despair coming from its walls. During the Civil War, the Union Army used it as a temporary hospital for wounded and dying men, and it may have been a stop on the Underground Railroad, which guided fleeing slaves to freedom. Because of this, there are conflicting stories that claim the moans, screams, and sobs heard in the house are either the spectral voices of escaped slaves or those of wounded soldiers.

When the Sisters of Charity moved into the house in 1891, they were determined to put an end to the ghost talk once and for all. They "purified" the house from top to bottom with holy water, but it did no good. Soon the sisters were telling ghost stories of their own. They decided that it was time for something to be done, and they recruited a dozen men to spend the night in the house and investigate.

Shortly after midnight, a number of terrifying sounds ripped through the dark house. The investigators heard "female shrieks, the clanking of sabers, and thumping sounds in the walls." The dozen intrepid men abandoned the house in a hurry.

In 1902, the American Institute of Architects purchased the house, renovated it, and still occupies the place today. Over the years, they have had their own ghost stories to relate, of beautiful but ghostly figures on the staircase, phantom soldiers, and disembodied footsteps. The Octagon remains haunted after nearly three centuries.

Spirits of the Shenandoah Valley

No period has left a greater mark on the history—and hauntings—of Virginia than the Civil War era. It was a time of great violence, death, and despair for the region. It should come as no surprise to the Weird reader that many of the state's stories of ghosts and phantoms come from this dark time.

It was in the Shenandoah Valley that a man named Colonel John Singleton Mosby, the "Gray Ghost of the Confederacy," commanded the 43rd Battalion of the Virginia Cavalry, or as they were generally known, Mosby's Rangers. The Rangers carried out a successful guerilla war against the Federal forces in Virginia, using hit-and-run tactics to surprise the enemy, derail trains, cut supply lines, and capture literally tons of Union supplies. Though small in number, they soon became one of the most famous legions of Confederate fighters.

Mosby's Rangers fought with honor, something that could not always be said for other guerilla fighters in the Shenandoah, who would pillage and plunder the local populace and indiscriminately kill any Union soldiers who were separated from their units. In retaliation, a group of Federal cavalry soldiers executed seven of Mosby's Rangers, alleging that they had committed atrocities against Union forces in September 1864. Three of the Rangers were hanged and the other four were shot.

Mosby secured permission to execute an equal number of Union prisoners in reprisal. On November 6, he ordered prisoners to draw slips of paper from a hat. The seven men who drew the marked slips were to be killed,

Colonel John Singleton Mosby

just as the seven Rangers had been. After the drawing, the unlucky seven were escorted to the Valley Pike, where they were to be executed as close to Union general Philip Sheridan's headquarters as possible.

But one of the prisoners managed to escape into the forest near Berryville. With Federal patrols in the area, the Rangers decided to go no farther and contented themselves with hanging the six remaining men at a place called Beemer's Woods, north of Berryville. Before the Rangers left, they pinned a note to the clothing of one of the hanged men that explained why they had been executed: "Measure for measure."

After this event, both sides agreed that neither would harm their prisoners as long as the other side kept to the agreement. Following that, there were no more hangings.

As the years passed, local folk who lived near Beemer's Woods often spoke of the eerie sounds and creaking limbs coming from the place where the men had been hanged. Some also claimed to feel a strange presence near the entrance to the woods, as though something remained behind there—something that would never rest in peace.

It was not the only instance when those executed in the Valley returned from the grave. One young man who lived in the Front Royal area was falsely accused by Federal forces of being a member of the Rangers and was beaten to death by a mob of Union soldiers. The ghost of that young man has reportedly returned to the Valley many times over a span of years from the 1870s until about 1925. Accounts of his appearances spread fear through entire communities.

One eyewitness, in 1912, was Judge Sanford Johnson, who lived near Riverton. He was outside feeding his dogs one cold winter's day and happened to notice a thin, ragged figure near the creek that crossed his property. He saw the form of a young man in a Confederate uniform and with a cap pulled down low over his brow. The judge said that the figure jerked and stumbled from the creek and then shambled down the long road in front of the house. Johnson did not stay around to see where the ragged figure went next. He ran full speed into the house. He was not sure why he had done so but only knew that the figure filled him with fear. He would later notice that although the figure crossed directly in front of the house, it left not a single track in the freshly fallen snow!

The chilling apparition would appear several more times, but strangely, there have been no reports of him since 1925. Did the wrongly executed young man finally find peace?

The Phantom Stage

Perhaps the most famous tale of the Shenandoah Valley is the story of the Phantom Stage of Valley Pike. There is little doubt that this tale falls into the realm of ghostly legend, and yet there are some who stubbornly maintain that it is true.

On May 24, 1862, the eve of the Battle of Winchester, General Thomas "Stonewall" Jackson had his army in New Market and was prepared to move against Union general Nathaniel P. Banks, whose troops were gathered nearby. The road that connected New Market to Winchester was a portion of the eighty-mile-long Valley Turnpike. A wide road paved in crushed limestone, it was ahead of its time for 19th-century construction, and Jackson used it to great advantage. Moving quickly along the paved road, he was able to fight battles at either end of it within days of each other.

The story of the spectral stagecoach actually begins in New Market. It was said that a Federal spy stole the coach and escaped toward Winchester to warn General Banks of Jackson's impending attack. Shortly after he made off with the coach, two Confederate officers discovered his plans and quickly went in pursuit.

Although the spy had a good lead, the heavy coach hampered his journey, and the Confederate pursuers quickly closed the distance. As they grew closer, lightning flickered across the sky and they could see the man hunched over, snapping the reins and urging the horses to go faster. The Confederates were only yards behind when the spy turned and saw their drawn pistols. He reached into his coat and withdrew his own revolver, then unsteadily tried to aim it at the advancing Confederates as the coach rumbled on. Suddenly, a brilliant flash and a thundering roar swept over the stage and the driver. A bolt of lightning streaked down from the dark clouds above and blasted the stagecoach. It literally exploded into flames, and the driver simply vanished from his seat—utterly destroyed.

The pursuing Confederates were stunned by what they had seen and, after calming their horses, returned to New Market to spread the story. The following day, Stonewall Jackson triumphed at Winchester, thanks to the fact that Banks had no warning of his attack.

Time has passed and the war has long since ended, but they say that on certain nights, when lightning dances across the sky, travelers along the Valley Pike (now U.S. Highway 11) still report seeing a ghostly stagecoach rattling silently along the road. Its driver frantically cracks the reins across the back of the horses, urging them on toward Winchester, still trying to complete his final mission.

The Gray Man of Waverly Farm

By the fall of 1864, the Shenandoah Valley had become the most hotly contested piece of ground in Virginia. It was vital to the Confederacy for its location and for the rich stores of food and crops that could be found there. For this same reason, the Federals were intent on destroying it. That season became known as "the time of the burning." During this period, one of the great ghost stories of the Civil War took root at a place called Waverly Farm.

It was there that North Carolina colonel Charles C. Blacknall, commander of the 23rd North Carolina, had been taken after being wounded in the foot on September 19, 1864. At the time, Blacknall and his men had been fighting alongside the Berryville Pike, about three miles east of the town of Winchester. The Union soldiers were advancing, beating back the Confederates, and Blacknall was deeply worried about the fate of his men.

She was surprised to see a man in a gray Confederate uniform walk across the room and stop at the window. It seemed as though the man was watching for someone.

At Waverly Farm, the colonel's condition worsened, except briefly on October 17 when he heard cannon fire in the distance, from the Battle of Cedar Creek. He asked his servant to help him into his uniform, and he hobbled over to the window, hoping to be reunited with his troops. But the guns grew distant and Blacknall realized that the Confederates had lost. Heartbroken, he returned to his bed—and never rose from it again. Even the amputation of his leg at the knee did not stop the spread of infection, and he died at Waverly on November 6. Blacknall was buried in nearby Stonewall Cemetery beside his fallen comrades from the 23rd North Carolina, but the legends say that he does not rest here in peace.

The sightings of the "Gray Man" at Waverly began a short time after the war. The first reports came when a woman named Mrs. Joliffe was visiting the family who owned the farm. She was asleep in the guest room—the same room in which Blacknall died—when the opening of the door awakened her. She was surprised to see a man in a gray Confederate uniform walk across the room and stop at the window. It seemed as though the man was watching for someone.

Mrs. Joliffe was not accustomed to having strange men appear in her room at night, and she demanded to know what the man was doing there. He gave no answer and in fact seemed oblivious to anyone else's being there. After several minutes, he bowed his head as if disappointed and turned away from the window. Then he was gone. The description that she would later provide matched that of Colonel Blacknall, right down to the shape of his face and the color of his hair.

She was not the last to see the depressed colonel take up his post in the guest bedroom. In fact, sightings continue to today. Those who have encountered the apparition report the same things. They tell of the sounds of footsteps entering the room and the ghostly figure, watching and waiting. Sometimes a figure is seen from outside, framed in the room's window. All the reports are of a man in a gray uniform who matches the description of Colonel Charles Blacknall.

Why does his ghost remain here at Waverly? Or does he remain at all? Could the energy of Colonel Blacknall's dying days and his disappointment over the Confederate loss have left a mere impression on the place, one that keeps repeating itself over and over again? Perhaps . . . or maybe Blacknall's spirit has simply never found rest. Perhaps he is still waiting for the return of the Confederate army—a day that will never come.

The Hauntings of Jefferson Davis

Perhaps two of the most tragic figures connected to the Civil War era were the men chosen to lead the opposing sides in the conflict, U.S. President Abraham Lincoln and Confederate President Jefferson Davis. Both suffered terribly during the war, torn apart over what the country was enduring. Each man also suffered great personal losses during these years of strife, and not surprisingly, both are said to walk among us today as ghosts. In Davis's case, two very different locations in Virginia are associated with hauntings, each connected to tragedies suffered by him during and after the Civil War.

The first location is the home that served as the "White House of the Confederacy," located on Clay Street in Richmond. There is every indication that the Davis family was happy here, despite the pressures of the war and the agonizing hours that President Davis spent working, often until the darkest hours of the night. Davis's only comfort after the long hours of work was his family. He often said that they eased his mind for precious minutes every day, especially his children, whom he constantly indulged.

Davis's special favorite was little Joe, who had just turned five in April 1864. He often remarked that Joe was the hope and greatest joy in his life. Unfortunately, Joe Davis was taken away all too soon. On April 30, 1864, he was climbing on the railing of a balcony in back of the house when he lost his balance and fell to the brick pavement below. The fall fractured his skull, and he died a short time later. Over the next days, cards and letters flooded the Davis home, including a heartfelt message from Abraham Lincoln, returning the gesture that Davis had made to Lincoln when his son Willie had died. Joe was buried in Hollywood Cemetery in Richmond. Shortly after, Davis had the balcony that his son fell from removed from the house and destroyed.

When Federal forces took Richmond on Sunday, April 2, 1865, Davis and his family escaped. At least, his living family escaped.

The same might not be said for little Joe Davis. After the family

Jefferson Davis with his wife, Varina. Inset, Joe Davis's gravestone in Hollywood Cemetery, Richmond.

was barely better than a dungeon. He was kept in solitary confinement for four months, his arms and legs bound in chains, until public sentiment forced his captors to remove them and place him in better quarters. Davis was released on May 13, 1867, after two years of confinement.

Though Jefferson Davis did not die in Fort Monroe, numerous witnesses have reported sighting apparitions in and around the cell at Fort Monroe where he was imprisoned. Most of the sightings have been of strange mists and energy masses of different shapes and forms, but most witnesses believe the ghost seen here is that of Davis, perhaps reliving the ordeal that he suffered. Mrs. Davis is also said to appear on late evenings and has been spotted in the second-floor window of quarters directly across from where her husband was held.

After Davis died in 1889, his body was moved from two different cemeteries before Confederate veterans convinced his wife to bury him in Richmond's Hollywood Cemetery, in 1893. Davis's final burial there resolved the family's other ghostly story. The body of little Joe Davis was also moved and placed beside his father, finally reuniting them. Strangely enough, after being seen in the vicinity of the Confederate White House for over thirty years, the apparition of the little boy who cried, "He's gone!" was never seen again after that.

left Richmond, dozens of witnesses reported seeing the apparition of a little boy who resembled Joe wandering aimlessly near the Confederate White House. The boy was oblivious to passersby and was heard to walk back and forth, muttering, "He's gone! He's gone!" just before vanishing in front of startled witnesses. Would Joe be forever trapped in search of his father?

The Davis family had more immediate concerns. It was during their time of flight that Abraham Lincoln was assassinated, and most believed that Jefferson Davis had somehow been involved. In May 1865, a contingent of Federal cavalry found Davis and quickly arrested him, though he denied being involved in the assassination plot.

Davis and his wife were transported by ship to the country's most escape-proof prison of the day, Fort Monroe. While there, Davis was imprisoned in a cell that

Virginia Battlefield Ghost

The terrible ten-month siege of Petersburg from June 1864 to April 1865 apparently left a host of spirits behind at Fort Stedman, a Union stronghold during the Civil War. The siege was a grueling affair that trapped the Confederate army and left it starving inside the city. On March 25, 1865, the Confederates launched a desperate attack on Fort Stedman. Much to the surprise of both sides, the Southern forces took the fort quite easily. They then turned their attention to nearby Fort Haskell, where the attack fell apart as the Confederate troops began gorging themselves on captured Federal supplies. Four hours after the fighting began, they broke off the attack, just a few weeks before Lee's final surrender at Appomattox Court House.

Despite the fact that the Union actually carried the day at Petersburg, it is said that the ghosts of Federal troops remain behind here. According to a reliable witness who was at Fort Stedman early one summer morning, he noticed a group of Union soldiers on a ridge. They were formed up in a battle line facing the fort. The witness was more than a little surprised to see them, as he knew of no reenactments that had been scheduled to take place there. He stood watching them for several minutes—and then they abruptly disappeared.

A former park supervisor also reported hearing the sounds of music coming from a ridge where a Union corps was encamped during the siege. He swore the music was popular patriotic songs from the Civil War period like the "Battle Hymn of the Republic" and "The Star-Spangled Banner." Although he tried, he was never able to find an explanation for the eerie, and possibly spectral, music.

Lingering Ghosts of Kalorama

The Kalorama estate once occupied a large site in northwest Washington, land that is now the 2300 block of S Street NW. The house had its share of tragedy over the years, but it was not until the Civil War that its walls became a shelter for death and horror—terrifying elements that linger to this day.

General John Bomford purchased the estate in 1812. Bomford was a close friend of naval hero Stephen Decatur and his wife, Susan. Bomford even allowed Commodore Decatur's body to be buried in a tomb on the estate after he was killed in a duel.

But it seems Decatur did not rest happily there. It is said that blood from his wound would sometimes appear on the outside of the tomb and that this is why his wife finally had the body removed to Philadelphia, where his parents were buried. The removal stopped the bloody stains from appearing on the stone walls of the crypt.

During the Civil War, many of the larger homes in the District of Columbia, including Kalorama, became hospitals for soldiers wounded in nearby battles. Hundreds of soldiers were treated and cared for in the mansion and on the grounds of the estate, and some of its ghostly tales come from this time.

When the war ended, in April 1865, many soldiers were still recovering from their wounds and were unable to return home to their families. They lingered at Kalorama for months, and on Christmas Eve decided to throw a party. Unfortunately, a defective stovepipe caused a fire to break out, which spread through the entire east wing of the house before it was brought under control. The building was badly damaged, but most of it was saved.

Within months, tales started to be told about the ruins of the mansion's east wing and about the "sinister

shadows" that were seen there and on the grounds of the estate. It was said that screams and moans could be heard, coming from the darkness. The reports became more prominent as the years passed. Area residents who braved the early evening darkness to stroll among the remains of the estate said they encountered "moving" or "roaming" cold spots. Some of them were described as being accompanied by unexplained odors that seemed to be the smells of blood, morphine, sweat, and gunpowder.

Eventually the growing population of Washington took over Kalorama, and what was left of the house was replaced with a newer home in the early 1900s. There are those who say that even though the estate has vanished, the cold spots and the sickly smells still remain. And that a few former patients of the Kalorama hospital still linger behind.

Ghosts of the Old House Woods

Probably no place has as many ghost stories told about it as the Old House Woods. If even a fraction of the bizarre stories associated with this stand of pine-woods and marshland near Chesapeake Bay are true, then this is undoubtedly one of the most haunted places in the state!

Old House Woods, which is located near the small crossroads town of Diggs in Mathews County, got its name from a wooden frame house that was built in the late 1700s. Once known as the Fannie Knight house, the place was abandoned for many years and fell into ruin. It soon became known by the simple nickname of the Old House.

There are said to be many reasons why the Old House Woods are haunted. According to one legend, the crew of a pirate ship came ashore here in the 1600s and buried their treasure somewhere deep in the woods. They returned to the sea when they were finished, but perished in a terrible storm before they could come back and claim their booty. On dark nights, mysterious figures have been seen digging feverishly in the woods, their work lit by dim lanterns, and many believe these are the ghosts of the pirates, returned from the sea and looking for their treasure.

A second possible reason for the myriad haunts may have also occurred in the latter part of the 17th century, when Charles II of England considered coming to Virginia. The treasure meant to accompany him was somehow diverted to White's Creek, which is near Old House Woods. But before the treasure could be safely hidden, the king's men were attacked by a band of renegade indentured servants. In their rush to escape, the bondmen took only part of the loot, planning to come back later for the rest. Unfortunately for them, their boat capsized during a storm and all of them drowned.

A storm may also account for one of the ghost stories of Old House Woods—the "Storm Woman." She has been described as a "wraith of a woman in a long nightgown, her long, fair hair flying back from her shoulders." According to the oft-told stories, she appears whenever dark clouds gather above this part of the bay, foretelling a coming gale. She moves among the trees, wailing loudly so that those who see her know that they must immediately take cover from the coming storm.

Whether an intrepid ghost hunter believes any of these stories or none of them, it's hard to dismiss the more recent accounts of phantoms in these woods. One of the most celebrated first-person accounts came from a man named Jesse Hudgins, described as a respectable merchant of unquestioned integrity, who ran a store in Mathews Court House in the 1920s. He told his story to a newspaper reporter in 1926 and swore to its authenticity.

Hudgins, who claimed that he had seen ghosts in the Old House Woods at least a dozen times, stated that he had seen his first when he was only seventeen. At that time, he was traveling through the woods at night in his buggy, when he saw a light appear ahead of him, moving along the road in the same direction that he was traveling. He had seen lights on the road before, lanterns carried by men, but this light was different. "There was something unearthly about it," he later said.

As Hudgins grew closer, he saw that the light was indeed carried by a man, but this was a man unlike any he had seen before. This man wore a suit of armor and carried a large musket leaning against his shoulder. As he moved along, he seemed to float, making no noise, despite the bulky armor that he wore.

Hudgins's horse suddenly stopped in the road, frozen in fear, not twenty yards away from the figure. As the buggy slid to a stop, the apparition turned and looked at him. Hudgins was paralyzed with horror, for then he saw that it was not a man inside the suit of armor but a skeleton. The skull, which seemed to be illuminated from within, grinned horribly at him and raised a sword, which Hudgins had not seen before. The specter creaked forward toward the stalled buggy in a menacing manner.

With that, Hudgins fainted. When he came to, it was broad daylight and he was lying on his bed at home, where he had been brought after friends found him. They thought he had fallen asleep. But as Hudgins said, "The best proof that this was not so was we could not even lead Tom [the horse] by the Old House Woods for months afterward, and to the day he died, whenever he approached the woods, he would tremble violently and cower."

Hudgins's tale was corroborated years later by a newspaper story that told of a young Richmond man who had car trouble late one night near the same stretch of road, just outside Old House Woods. As he was standing at the edge of the road, leaning into the hood of his automobile, a voice behind him asked, "Is this the King's Highway? I've lost my ship." According to the account, when the young man turned to look, he saw a skeleton in armor standing just a few feet away. Terrified, the man ran away and did not return to get his car until the following day. When he related this story, he knew nothing of the same figure's being reported years earlier by Jesse Hudgins.

Phantom Ship

Perhaps the strangest phenomenon reported near Old House Woods is the famous ghost ship. It has allegedly been seen by many, both up close and from far away. Ben Ferebee was a fisherman who lived along Chesapeake Bay in the early 1900s, and he often told the story of his encounter with the phantom ship.

One night, while fishing off the mouth of White's Creek, Ferebee saw a large full-rigged ship appear in the bay, sailing in his general direction. Ferebee was surprised, as such ships were rare, but he became increasingly unnerved as he saw it turn and start to bear down directly on him. Lights were blazing all over the vessel, from bow to stern, and he could see sailors standing at the rails, but none of them seemed to notice his small boat.

Convinced that the ship was going to run him down, Ferebee began shouting at the sailors; but none of them looked in his direction. Just when he was sure that the ship was going to strike him, the helmsman apparently put her hard to port. The vessel passed so close to Ferebee's small boat that he was nearly swamped by the wash. "She was a beautiful ship," he later recalled, "but different than any that I had seen. She made no noise at all, and when she had gone by, the most beautiful harp and organ music I ever heard came back to me."

Ferebee recalled that the ship sailed right up to the beach and never stopped. It soared over the sand and then into the forest, finally vanishing into the darkness. He heard the wondrous music trailing on the wind behind the vessel, and then it faded away too.

Ferebee would not be the last to see the phantom ship. One night a young boy who lived in the area was taking a boat from the Mathews Yacht Club over to Moon post office by going up Stutts Creek and then over Billups Creek. Traveling with a friend, the boy set out

just after sunset, and he recalled that there was a fine mist hanging over everything along the water. About a half mile from the mouth of White's Creek, the two young men saw the ghost ship appear. It was floating in the marsh—which the boy knew should be impossible since the water was only about a foot deep—and stayed there for a short while. Then it disappeared.

"I went home and told my mother," the boy later said, "but she just laughed. She said everyone knew about the ghosts in the Old House Woods."

What Harry Forrest Saw

Another man who saw the ghost ship, as well as other haunts of the woods, was Harry Forrest, a farmer and fisherman who lived only a few hundred yards away from the edge of Old House Woods. Forrest died in the 1950s, but shortly before that, he consented to an interview with a local newspaper about his experiences.

"I've seen more things than I can relate in a day," he said in his interview. "I've seen armies of marching British redcoats. I've seen the Storm Woman and heard her dismal wailings, and my mother and I have sat here all hours of the night and seen lights in the woods. We have sat here on our back porch overlooking Chesapeake Bay and seen ships anchor off the beach and boats put in to shore, and forms of men go into the woods. I would see lights over there and hear the sounds of digging."

Forrest also stated that while most of his encounters at Old House Woods were not really frightening, he did have one experience that chilled him to the bone. He went out one night in November to do some duck hunting and came to a little inlet where the pine trees came down to the water. He found a flock of black ducks sleeping there. Forrest raised his gun to fire, but instead of his target being ducks, he saw they were soldiers from what he described

as "an olden time." They stirred before he could lower his weapon and then began marching in formation out of the dark water.

When he recovered from his shock, Forrest ran to his skiff, which was tied up on the other side of the point. When he arrived there, he found a man in a bright red uniform sitting upright and rigid in the stern. Forrest ordered him out of the boat and threatened to shoot him if he did not comply.

"Shoot and the devil's curse to you and your traitor's breed," the man in the uniform replied, and made as if to strike Forrest with the sword that he carried. Forrest raised his gun in defense and pulled the trigger, but it didn't go off. He pulled the trigger again, but it still refused to fire.

Forrest threw down the gun and ran for home, being forced to swim a portion of the creek to get there.

What is it that haunts the Old House Woods? And what secrets are buried here beneath centuries of mud and sand? Many believe it is because of the buried treasure long rumored to be there and that the ghosts who lurk are watching over it, guarding it from beyond the grave. For decades, though, locals have been warning away those who come here hoping to find it.

"A thousand people have been in here after that money," Harry Forrest once said, "but they'll never get it. The trees start bending double and howling. It storms. And they get scared and take off. The woods is haunted, that's what it is."

America's Haunted Capitol

The United States Capitol is home to many secrets, a large number of legends, and, if the stories are true, a multitude of ghosts. The ghost of John Adams is said to haunt the spot on the House Chamber floor where, while in midspeech during his post-presidency stint as a Congressman, he dropped from a stroke. Late at night in the House Chamber, one can hear what may be the shouts of two former House Speakers—Republican Joseph Gannon and Democrat James Clark—as they return from beyond to reenact a fierce 1910 confrontation that forever reduced the powers of the Speaker of the

House. The ghosts of President James Garfield and his assassin were said to have been seen in the Capitol's hallways at the time Garfield's body lay in state there.

But it's not only politicians who haunt the Capitol. The spirit of a stonemason who was killed during the original construction—and perhaps was even accidentally sealed up inside one of the walls—has been seen, with a mason's trowel in hand, passing through a wall in the basement on the Senate side of the building. And a phantom staff member still scrubs the floor that he was cleaning when he died. Late at night, after everyone has left the building except for the maintenance people and the security staff, the sounds of water sloshing from a phantom pail and scrubbing can be heard near the spot where the man died.

Logan's Still Looking for His Horse

General John Alexander Logan, or "Black Jack" Logan as he was affectionately called by his men during the Civil War, was elected to the U.S. Senate in 1871. As a staunch Republican and chairman of the Military Affairs Committee, he used his strong influence to develop Reconstruction policies.

A few years after installing air-conditioning ducts in the Capitol basement, workmen discovered a room that had been sealed off. Inside the room was a stuffed horse that bore a strong resemblance to the horse that Logan sits astride in the famous Logan Circle statue. It was discovered that when the horse died, the general had it mounted and displayed for a time in the Capitol building to remind everyone of his battlefield exploits during the war. Since the discovery, staff workers have claimed that General Logan's ghost roams the basement corridors, still looking for his favorite horse.

The Ghost of the Sneezing Vice President

Henry Wilson was Vice President in the Ulysses S. Grant administration. Since the Vice President's office is in the Senate wing, Wilson could continue a form of relaxation that he and the Senators often enjoyed: tubbing. The lower Senate wing was once fitted with several handcarved marble tubs, and Vice President Wilson enjoyed taking a dip in a hot bath during his lunch breaks. Unfortunately, he caught a tubbing-related congestive chill, resulting in his death in November 1875.

Not long after, Senate guards began to tell stories of seeing the semitransparent form of Vice President Wilson returning from the tubs in the lower chambers. They also claimed to hear him wheezing, coughing, and violently sneezing from the cold chill of the corridors. Since then, there have been reports of mysterious sneezes heard in the hallway leading to the Vice President's office, though no one is in the corridor when the sneezes are heard. There is also sometimes a damp chill in the doorway and the faint scent of the soap that used to be provided for the Senators' use in the basement tubs.

General John Alexander Logan, top, Vice President Henry Wilson, bottom

The Ghost of Honest Abe

There is no doubt that few Presidents left the sort of mark on the White House that Abraham Lincoln did. When he was assassinated, his plans for reconciliation between the North and South were interrupted and his work was left incomplete. In fact, some would say that it remains incomplete, even today. Perhaps this is why his spirit is so often reported at the White House and may explain why he is our nation's most famous ghost.

In the years following Lincoln's death, staff members and residents often reported mysterious footsteps in the hallways. One of the earliest reliable reports from someone who actually saw Lincoln's apparition came from President Theodore Roosevelt, who took up residence in the house nearly forty years after Lincoln's death. "I see him in different rooms and in the halls," the President admitted. In truth, it comes as no surprise that Roosevelt may have "attracted" the ethereal presence of Lincoln, as he greatly admired the former leader and quoted his speeches and writings often.

President Calvin Coolidge's wife, Grace, encountered Lincoln, who she said was dressed "in black, with a stole draped over his shoulders to ward off the drafts and chills of Washington's night air." She also saw him on another occasion in the Yellow Oval Room, which had been Lincoln's library during his tenure in the White House. Poet and Lincoln biographer Carl Sandburg stated that he felt Lincoln's presence close to him in the Yellow Oval Room.

During World War II, Queen Wilhelmina of the Netherlands spent the night in the White House. She was sleeping in the Rose Room when an insistent tapping

> *I sit in this old house, all the while listening to the ghosts walk up and down the hallway. At four o'clock, I was awakened by three distinct knocks on my bedroom door. No one was there. Damned place is haunted, sure as shootin'!*
> *–President Harry S. Truman*

on the door awakened her. Assuming the summons must be important, she quickly opened the door, only to see Abraham Lincoln standing there. The queen passed out, awakening on the floor later. The ghost had vanished.

During his time in office, President Dwight D. Eisenhower made no effort to deny the experiences that he'd had with Lincoln's ghost. He told his press secretary, James Haggerty, that he frequently sensed Lincoln's ghost in the White House. One day, he explained that he was walking down a hallway when he realized the figure approaching him from the opposite direction was Abraham Lincoln. Eisenhower took the encounter in stride—after the horrors of war, the specter of Lincoln was probably a welcome sight.

Despite official denials, members of the First Families continued to encounter Lincoln's specter. When Gerald Ford was in office, his daughter Susan publicly acknowledged her belief in ghosts and made it clear that she would never sleep in the Lincoln Bedroom—or "that room," as she called it. According to one account, Susan actually witnessed Lincoln's spirit.

There were no reports of Lincoln's ghost during the elder Bush's administration. However, during the Clinton years, there were at least two sightings. President Clinton's brother Roger admitted one encounter. In the second instance, a Clinton aide said that he had seen Lincoln walking down a hallway. The story, which was briefly reported in the news, was quickly denied and dismissed by the White House as a joke. As of this writing, no reports of Lincoln's ghost have filtered out of the White House concerning the current President, George W. Bush, but who knows what stories will be told in the years to come.

Does the ghost of Abraham Lincoln really walk in the White House? Some of our country's most influential leaders have certainly believed so. But why does he still walk here? Is the apparition merely a faded memory of another time or an actual presence? Or does the ghost appear, as has been suggested, during times of crisis, when perhaps the assistance of the President who faced America's greatest crisis is most needed?

Grave Matters

Some of the weirdest tales to be heard about Virginia come from places where the residents never utter a single word. We speak of the many storied graveyards and cemeteries found throughout our state and in the District of Columbia. Oh sure, there are plenty of politicians and military heroes interred here, people who wielded considerable power and influence during their lives. And there are famous, infamous, and otherwise noteworthy dead who made Virginia their final resting place. This chapter, however, is not about them. It is instead about certain graves, grave makers, and even body parts whose legends have, well, taken on a life of their own—so to speak. In other words, it is the memorials to the deceased, not the dearly departed themselves, that catch our interest.

Black Aggie

While one of the strangest legends involving mysterious gravestones had its questionable beginnings at the Druid Ridge Cemetery in Pikesville, MD, it ended its strange journey in Washington, DC. One of many spooky statues to be found in burial grounds throughout the region, it is the only one that can claim a deadly curse as part of its legacy!

When General Felix Agnus, the publisher of the *Baltimore American*, died in 1925, he was buried in Druid Ridge Cemetery, right outside of Baltimore. A rather strange statue presided over his grave—a statue of a large black mourning figure called *Grief*. In the daylight, the figure was regarded as a beautiful addition to the mortuary art of the cemetery. But when darkness fell, it showed a different face, and the legends began. For this was a statue whose eyes glowed red at the stroke of midnight.

Those who encountered the Agnus monument in the darkness gave her the nickname of Black Aggie. To these people, she was a symbol of terror. It was said that the spirits of the dead rose from their graves to gather around Black Aggie on certain nights. Living persons who returned her gaze were struck blind. Pregnant women who passed through her shadow (where, strangely, grass never grew) would suffer miscarriages.

Not really believing the stories, a local college fraternity decided to include Black Aggie in its initiation rites. Pledges were ordered to spend the night in her cold embrace. Those who remember the figure recall her large, powerful hands. The stories claimed that the pledges had to sit on Aggie's lap and one tale purports that "she once came to life and crushed a hapless freshman in her powerful grasp."

Other fraternity boys were equally unlucky. One night, at the stroke of midnight, the cemetery watchman heard a scream in the darkness. When he reached the Agnus grave, he found a young man lying dead at the foot of the statue, dead from fright—or so the story goes.

Word of Black Aggie's powers spread and the Agnus grave site soon began to be trampled by curiosity seekers. Although Pikesville was fairly remote at the time, hundreds—perhaps thousands—of people visited and vandalized the site over several decades. Countless names and messages were scrawled on the statue, the granite base, and the wall behind it. Groundskeepers did everything they could to discourage visitors, including planting thorny shrubs around the cemetery, but people kept coming. By the 1960s, the destructive visitors became too much for the cemetery to handle and descendants of Agnus elected to donate Black Aggie to the Smithsonian Institution in Washington.

And here the story takes another strange turn. Although some people recall Aggie being displayed in the National Gallery for a brief period, officials at the Smithsonian claimed they had never shown the statue at all, and in fact were not in possession of her. Conspiracy

solved the mystery. Aggie had ended up in the National Courthouse complex in Washington, in the rear courtyard of the Dolley Madison house. The mysterious statue had finally been found, and can still be seen there today. The graffiti scrawled by the cemetery vandals has been blasted away, although some evidence of the damage remains. Meanwhile, back at the cemetery, the Agnus grave site is well cared for and shows little sign of the desecration of the past. Grass grows now in the place where for many years it could not. The only lingering evidence of Black Aggie is a dark mark on the pedestal where she once rested. At least that's the only presence that can be seen.

These days, Black Aggie's ghostly powers seem to be in semihibernation. She sits quietly in the garden, never disturbing those around her. Does the curse of Black Aggie persist? Or are these legends merely spook tales from the past? If you choose to visit her, we advise you not to taunt her—just in case!

Firsthand Account: Black Aggie

One night, two friends and I came down to Baltimore from Atlantic City for a visit. We wanted to see some girls that we had met while they were in New Jersey on vacation. We went out to see the local sites one night and the girls took us to see the statue of Black Aggie. We got out of the car and went to take a look at her. The girls told us that it was a local tradition for people to put coins in her hands and we wanted to see if anyone had. My friend Freddy, though, thought it would be funny to put out his cigarette in Aggie's hand instead.

We told him not to, but Freddy just laughed. He didn't believe in any of that stuff. . . . About ten years later, Freddy was found in a dump in South Carolina. He had been shot in the back of the head, mafia-style. They never found out who did it.

It's been many years now, but I will never forget the feeling that I had standing in front of Aggie that night . . . as if she knew the future and could see what lay ahead for us.—*Letter via e-mail*

theorists believed that perhaps she was simply placed in storage because of her cursed past. "Maybe, just maybe," wrote a columnist for the *Baltimore Sun*, "they're not taking any chances."

The real answer would not be so strange. Somewhere along the line, the Smithsonian apparently passed her to the National Museum of American Art, where she was put into storage. For years, she would remain in a dusty storeroom, shrouded in cobwebs. Then in the late 1990s, Black Aggie would rise from the dead!

In 1996, a young Baltimore-area writer named Shara Terjung did a story on the statue for a small newspaper. Long fascinated with the legends, she was determined to track down the elusive Aggie. Shortly after Halloween, her contact at the General Services Administration

Copycat "Grief"

Black Aggie is a copy of another statue, one with its own curious story. Augustus Saint-Gaudens, a premiere American sculptor of the late 1800s, sculpted the original for Henry Adams, the grandson of President John Quincy Adams. The statue was a memorial to Adams's wife, Marian, who had committed suicide in December 1885. It was completed in 1891 and placed at Marian's grave site, in Washington's Rock Creek Cemetery. While never officially named, the statue was known as the Adams Memorial and, later, by the more popular name of Grief.

Henry Adams understandably refused to speak publicly about his wife's death, and he never officially named the monument or acknowledged its popular nickname. Thanks to Adams's silence and the fame of his family, many became curious about the monument. Adams furthered this curiosity by refusing to have an inscription placed on the statue and by placing it behind a barrier of trees and shrubs. The challenge of finding it only fueled the public interest, first by word of mouth and later in guidebooks and magazine articles.

Grief was so fascinating that it became the subject of an incredible piracy. Within a few months of the statue's being placed on Marian Adams's grave, Henry Adams reported that someone had apparently made a partial casting of the piece. He wrote in 1907 that "even now, the head of the figure bears evident traces of some surreptitious casting, which the workmen did not even take the pains to wash off."

Who would do such a thing? Bring in sculptor Eduard L. A. Pausch. It was from the original Adams design that Pausch created his own, unauthorized copy in the early 1900s. It was this copy that was purchased in 1905 by General Agnus for his family's grave site and would later come to be known as the infamous Black Aggie—a copy that would go on to become even more famous than the original!

A Stand-up Guy, Even in Death

When folks are laid to rest, usually they are literally *laid* to rest, buried in a supine position. This ensures proper relaxation for the newly departed as they begin their extended sleep, hence the term "rest in peace." Still, we've learned that not all wish to recline during the big dirt nap. In fact, some of the more ornery in life feel a pressing need to oversee matters in death. Case in point: Colonel George Hancock, a two-fisted colonial-era slave owner who wasn't about to lie down on the job when the reaper came calling.

By most any yardstick, Virginian George Hancock was a driven soul. Born on June 13, 1754, this ultra-ambitious man would serve in a number of prestigious positions throughout his life. Beginning as a foot soldier, he would quickly earn the title of Colonel of Infantry while serving in the Revolutionary War. In 1774, Hancock had begun a career in law. In 1787, he would be appointed Commonwealth Attorney of Botetourt County, a springboard position that helped elect him to the Third and Fourth U.S. Congresses (1793–1797). He would later make his home at a southern Virginia estate called Fotheringay, named after the English castle where Mary, Queen of Scots, was beheaded in 1587. There, like most wealthy men of his day, he kept slaves. He would take special pride in his oversight duties and was said to derive much pleasure from the toil and torment of his shackled subordinates.

Hancock ran his plantation himself and kept things in pristine condition. However, whenever military or political duties took him away, he would return to find things in disarray. For this reason, he held a strong distrust of his slaves. He questioned their loyalty and thought they slacked off when he wasn't at the estate. Hancock was said to sometimes take out this frustration on his slaves, and for this reason at least one writer referred to him as "a gentleman of no uncertain temperament." This is clearly true from the perspective of his slaves, who claimed that their treatment at his hand was unusually harsh, even for the era.

Tragically, Hancock's young daughter Julia died unexpectedly in 1820 and the colonel, crushed by her death, died soon after. A double funeral service was held for the father and daughter at Fotheringay. According to legend, at the colonel's request he was placed next to his daughter in a family vault which was located high on a hill above their mansion. However, Hancock's body was placed in a different position from his daughter's, for he had asked to be entombed standing up. The reason for this, he stated, was so that he could watch over his slaves down in the fields below "and keep them from loafing on the job."

A surviving manuscript from his time offers up strong evidence: "High on the hillside overlooking Happy Valley where flow the headwaters of Roanoke River, in a white mausoleum he had himself caused to be excavated from solid rock, the earthly remains of Colonel George Hancock and his daughter, Julia, were laid and to this day the darkies of the region say with trembling, *'De*

Cunnel he set up dah in a stone chair so's he cud look down de valley and see his slaves at work.'"

Over the years, the tomb has been disturbed many times. Curiosity seekers explored the crypt, searching for evidence of the legend's truth, and soldiers even broke into it during the Civil War.

In 1886, the new owner of Fotheringay, Annie Beale Edmundson, decided to see if the long-whispered legend was valid. Since the colonel's tomb had fallen into disrepair, Edmundson and members of her family entered it to learn the extent of the damage. Inside, they found a mass of crumbled bones and stone fragments.

At the top of the pile, they found a skull. This, they assumed, could only belong to Colonel Hancock, as all other family members were accounted for. At the bottom of the heap were bones that appeared to be from his legs and trunk. The position of these skeletal remains in relation to the accompanying stone fragments confirmed their belief that his body had been laid to rest in a *seated* position, not standing as so many had thought. Still, the colonel wasn't lying down; that was proven beyond doubt.

Today, with the mystery likely solved, the stone mausoleum endures. Dense underbrush and wild rosebushes hide the crypt, which has fallen into scattered ruins. Sunny mornings find speckles in its white marble edifice glistening with light, a pleasant circumstance that instills a sense of peace into those peering up at it. A casual visitor to Fotheringay will be forgiven for not sensing the darker moments that occurred here. Whether the colonel was buried in a standing position or seated, this thoroughly odd tale has earned itself a berth in the *Weird* files. The tomb, which is embedded in the hillside behind the estate, is most visible from U.S. Route 460 during the winter months.

The Colonel's Relative Speaks

In the 1980s, my uncle looked into the life of one of our distant relatives, Colonel George Hancock (1754–1820). He was entombed on his plantation, Fotheringay, which is located in Montgomery County, Virginia, between Salem and Shawsville.

The reason I'm contacting you is because of the way he's supposed to be buried. He was said to be placed standing or seated in his mountainside tomb, overlooking his plantation so his slaves would keep it running properly. Hancock was also the brother of George Rogers Clark, the explorer, and an aide-de-camp to Count Casimir Pulaski, the Revolutionary War hero.
—*B. Hancock*

Hollywood Cemetery

One of the most visited tourist attractions in Richmond is Hollywood Cemetery. It is located on the north end of the Robert E. Lee Bridge, just off the Belvidere exit of I-195 (Downtown Expressway). Overlooking the James River, this rural-style graveyard is perhaps America's most beautiful garden cemetery. Visitors will find one of the finest collections of mortuary art, including cast-iron work, angels, and obelisks.

Designed in 1847 and named for the abundant holly trees on the site, this cemetery is the final resting place of many distinguished individuals, including notable Virginians such as Presidents James Monroe and John Tyler, General J. E. B. Stuart, writer Ellen Glasgow, as well as Jefferson Davis, President of the Confederate States. Also buried here are the remains of over 18,000 Confederate dead.

A cemetery is often the subject of ghosts and legends. Hollywood is no exception. Here are some stories associated with the graves of the people buried there. An easy way to see them is to take a driving tour through the cemetery and follow the blue line painted on the road. A map of cemetery highlights is available at the cemetery entrance.

–Lisa Langlinais

Confederate Pyramid

In the Confederate section of the cemetery stands a ninety-foot pyramid made of rough-hewn Richmond granite. It was completed in 1869, and no mortar was used in its construction. The pyramid is a monument to the 18,000 Confederates buried here, including Confederate President Jefferson Davis, J. E. B. Stuart, George Pickett, Matthew Fontaine Maury, and the first Confederate soldier killed during the war, Henry Lawson Wyatt. Twenty-three Confederate generals are buried here, as well as soldiers from battles around Richmond. The Confederate dead exhumed from Gettysburg in the 1870s were reinterred here on what is now known as Gettysburg Hill. In the cornerstone are entombed various Confederate artifacts, including a flag, a button from Stonewall Jackson's coat, and a lock of Jefferson Davis's hair.

When visiting near the pyramid, many people have reported seeing orbs, feeling "cold spots," sensing their energy drain, and becoming ill the next day.

Weeping Winnie Davis

After first being buried in New Orleans, Jefferson Davis was moved to Hollywood Cemetery in 1893. Here he rests with his other family members, including his daughter Winnie. Winnie is said to have died from a broken heart because she unfortunately fell in love with a Yankee. Her young beau, Alfred Wilkinson, was the grandson of a staunch abolitionist and was rejected by

Jefferson Davis when he asked for permission to marry Winnie. Winnie's health began to deteriorate over the next year, so much so that her father changed his mind. But he changed it too late. Winnie died at the age of thirty-four without ever marrying. An angel in mourning stands at her grave and is said to shed real tears.

Iron Watchdog

This cast-iron dog is keeping watch over a little girl's grave. The dog once stood outside a shop in Richmond, the story goes, and the little girl used to pass by it on her way to school every day. She would stop and pet the dog and talk to it. Then the little girl died of scarlet fever. When the storeowner learned of her death, he presented the iron dog to the family so that the dog could keep watch over her grave. It was made by Haywood and Bartlett Iron Company of Baltimore, cast sometime around 1859, and was the company mascot.

Since this dog is said to guard the girl's grave, it supposedly comes to life to chase people from her grave site. It has also been known to move on occasion. Many people have reported seeing it pointed in one direction but, when passing it later, find it pointed in another direction.

Crying for the Colonel

At the grave of Colonel Thomas Branch, who founded Merchants Bank, one will find a most beautiful life-size marble lady. The statue is said to come to life every year on the day of Branch's death and momentarily looks at onlookers with tears in her eyes. She then resumes her position until the next year.

The Richmond Vampire

There are many vaults in Hollywood Cemetery, some of them ornate and finely decorated. The vault of William Wortham Pool is not particularly interesting in design or decoration, but what *is* interesting about this vault is the legend that surrounds the man inside. An accountant, Mr. Pool is rumored to have been banished from England for having a rare blood disease. He died in the early 1920s, and through the years there have been many stories about some kind of being leaving and entering the tomb. There have also been reports that the tomb has been broken into on the equinoxes and at Halloween by Satan worshipers, and the remains of poor Mr. Pool spread around the cemetery, arranged in symbols of the occult. (How they get back into the vault for the next raid is unclear.) The door to the vault is now sealed shut and the gate at the entrance is locked with a chain.

Vampire a Victim of Tunnel Cave-in?

There's a very interesting story concerning a crypt in Hollywood Cemetery in Richmond. It's rumored to be the grave of a vampire or warlock, W. W. Pool. The top of the mausoleum, which is built into the side of a hill, is decorated with carvings above the door that are truly bizarre—children with strange morphing animals. Apparently, shortly after his death, the glass blew from the inside out and has never been replaced.

I've been there many times. The mausoleum has only a single person buried in it, unlike most of the crypts in that cemetery (which have family burials). There's been a lot of conjecture about where the vampire legend came from, and some believe it is connected to the railroad tunnel in Church Hill, on the other side of Richmond, which collapsed about five years after Pool's death. Apparently, a man crawled out of the tunnel, almost scalded to death and looking very unearthly, with skin hanging from all limbs. It has been theorized that this victim became known as the Richmond vampire. I've looked around and tried to figure out who Pool was without any luck. And no one really seems to be able to connect Hollywood Cemetery with Church Hill, which is about three miles away.—*S. Falls*

Tombstone House

If any residence holds the potential for mass haunting, the Tombstone House in Petersburg is surely it. Such fearful probabilities simply have to accompany a home constructed of some 2,200 marble tombstones, particularly since these markers were pulled off *existing* graves. All the headstones used in its 1934 construction were "harvested" from the nearby Poplar Grove National Cemetery. Even more noteworthy is the fact that each one of them came from the grave of a Union soldier who had died at the siege of Petersburg during the Civil War. This last bit adds a devilish touch of retribution to an already bizarre tale.

So how did it happen? Why, simple economics, of course!

It seems that during the Depression era, maintenance costs were strangling the Poplar Grove Cemetery. Petersburg National Battlefield Park superintendent Benjamin F. Moore determined that money could be saved on maintenance if all upright grave markers were cut and laid flush with the ground. Under his orders, the markers were pulled from each individual plot, their bottom portions trimmed off, and the upper portions, replete with inscriptions, positioned flat on the ground, faceup. Since the stones were made of valuable marble, the lower portions were retained for later sale.

This brings us to one Oswald E. Young, who quickly snapped up these lower portions for the anything but princely sum of forty-five dollars. His intent? Why, to build his very own two-story Tombstone House, of course!

This he did, and the rest is pretty much standard history, at least insofar as anything regarding a tombstone house can be seen as standard. As testament to the relative normality involved here, there has been no reported haunting of this house despite the strong implications, and any out-of-the-ordinary bad luck has not befallen anyone. Yet.

But the Tombstone House is not without controversy. There are those who maintain that the markers used in the home's construction were in fact the upper portions that contained the inscriptions—not the lower ones. In this scenario, the written words are said to face inward and wall plaster relegates them to anonymity, for now. Then there are others who say that such a thing would never have been done; it would have been far too ghoulish. Since there is no reliable list of Union dead buried in Poplar Grove during the period of the siege, this question will likely remain with us until Tombstone House reaches its own day of reckoning, and a heavy swinging ball offers up final answers to the mystery.

Today, anyone who walks up the Tombstone House's tombstone path (yes, this too is made out of grave markers) can readily sense the dark playfulness of this morbid idea come to, er, life. And in fact, the home is still in use as a residence, rented out by its current owner.

Strong (Buried) Arm of the Confederacy

Talk about tragic ironies. Stonewall Jackson, the legendary Confederate general known for his role in such Civil War skirmishes as Second Manassas and the Battle of Antietam, was, in the end, removed from this earth not by a Union Army bent on revenge but by his very own troops. History shows this certainly wasn't born of ill will, but rather was a case of mistaken identity. However, it is not this substantial footnote to history that warrants the general's inclusion in his chapter. It is what happened to Jackson's left arm, after the fact, that we find most curious.

The unthinkable occurred on May 2, 1863, during the battle of Chancellorsville. On that fateful night, after a fruitful assault that netted the Confederate general the capture of Union troops, Jackson decided to scout out his defeated enemy, hoping to cut off their line of retreat. He headed out with a small group of soldiers. Later, as they made their way through the dark woods back to their own lines, one of the men in the Confederate North Carolina regiment saw the returning general's horse. Fearing it was the Union cavalry attacking, the man shouted, "Halt, who goes there?" Not giving Jackson's group sufficient time to reply, he fired a shot at the approaching figure. Startled by the sudden gunfire, other Confederates fired blindly into the darkness.

Three musket balls tore into Jackson's left arm during the confusing barrage, destroying arteries and fracturing the bone below the shoulder. The wounded general was placed on a stretcher and carried by his men to a field hospital set up in a nearby drinking establishment called the Wilderness Tavern.

To find out more about the incident, we spoke with Frank O'Reilly, one of the historians at the Fredericksburg and Spotsylvania National Military Park.

Weird Virginia: Frank, doesn't a tavern seem to be an odd choice of place to bring the wounded general?
Frank O'Reilly: Well, you know it was an excellent choice of a hospital at that time. They had various things that they could take care of the patients with. There was a nice creek that ran through here, which was a great water source for the different hospitals. Amputations were a tremendously grisly process. What they would do is simply take a knife and cut a semicircle around the spot where the wound occurred and pull back the skin to expose what's left of the bone. At that point, they would saw across the bone and then tie off the arteries, bring the flap around, and also suture that up.

WV: And what was the usual practice with the amputated limbs? Did they just discard them?
FO: Normally all the limbs would have been placed in a pile and immediately after the battle would calm down they would have buried them in a mass pit.

WV: So who had the foresight to go rescue this limb from the pile so it wasn't buried in a mass grave with all the others?
FO: The person who rescued Jackson's arm was actually Jackson's chaplain, a man named Beverly Tucker Lacy.

He had just joined Jackson a couple of months before and was completely fascinated by the general. He was the right man in the right place at the right time, because he showed up in the field hospital right after they amputated the arm. If he had been there ten minutes later, he wouldn't have even seen the arm.

What he did was actually take it back to the surgeon that amputated the arm, and asked him to identify it. Dr. Hunter McGuire was absolutely certain it was Jackson's arm. He had just removed it a couple of minutes

before, and at that point Reverend Lacy wrapped it up, took it across the fields to his home, Elwood, and buried it in the family cemetery. Burying his arm was just a way for his staff to pay homage to their general. Stonewall Jackson was literally the most famous person in North America at this particular time.

The following day, Jackson was moved to a nearby plantation. Just when it looked as if he might survive his dire skirmish, pneumonia set in. He died six days later, on May 10th. The general's final words were, "Let us cross over the river and rest in the shade of the trees." The Jackson arm still rests on the grounds of Lacy's humble family plantation, Elwood, under a stone that proclaims: ARM OF STONEWALL JACKSON, MAY 3 1863. Frank took us to pay our respects at the small burial ground, located in the middle of a cornfield.

FO: We are in an area that would have had nothing but field hospitals all around us, and Jackson's chaplain walked up on this hill May 4th and buried the arm right here. After the war, another one of Stonewall Jackson's staff officers, a man named James Power Smith, actually put this monument out here so we wouldn't forget this spot.

WV: Didn't somebody try and dig it up once?
FO: Actually, it's been dug up a couple of times.

As it turns out, Union soldiers dug up the arm during another battle, in 1864, but reportedly reburied it right away. The arm apparently rested in peace again until 1921, when a marine corps general named Smedley Butler came across the gravestone while on maneuvers in the area with his men. Butler was quite a maverick. He thought that it was something of a southern myth, so on a whim he decided to debunk the myth and ordered the grave dug up. There's at least one account that alleges that he had a group of marines dig up this spot, figuring that they would get a big open hole and a laugh at the locals, but what they unearthed was actually an arm that had been amputated.

WV: So what did they do with it?
FO: Well, the story goes that they reburied the arm with full military honors.

Washington Vampiress

A strange account appeared in the *Washington Post* in 1923 when a writer named Gorman Hendricks was given quite a lot of space to report on a lady vampire who had been stalking her old North East Washington neighborhood since the 1850s. According to the story, this "creature of the night" had been preying on and terrifying people until just before the story appeared in the newspaper, when her burial vault, located a short distance east of the sprawling Brentwood estate, had been "dismantled and the body entombed there subjected to ghoulish desecration."

The story of the Washington Vampire begins in the 1850s, when a young woman fell in love with a handsome European prince who was visiting this country. The woman was a daughter of a respected local family and lived in the neighborhood where Gallaudet College is now located. The young woman's father, who was well known in local political circles, took her along to a party one evening, where she met the charming prince. She had no way of knowing that this man was a vampire until he got her alone that evening. Her pale body was discovered the next morning, drained of blood. The strange prince was reportedly never seen again.

A funeral service was held for the young woman and she was laid to rest in the family's burial vault, which was located behind the family's mansion. But having been bitten by a vampire herself, the now bloodthirsty girl was eternally doomed to rise from her grave and seek out her own victims.

The first encounter with the newly drained vampire occurred a short time after her funeral. A local laborer was making his way home by cutting through the old family cemetery when he spotted "a white-robed figure of a woman floating through a sealed vault." No one believed his story until the lifeless body of a stable hand was found a few weeks later. Two vivid red bite marks were found on the man's throat. Remembering the laborer's story, the people in the neighborhood were filled with panic. They were so frightened that they hired two heavily armed men to guard the burial vault. This watch was maintained for many nights before the vampire put in another appearance.

On the night of April 22, the guards were startled by the sound of what seemed to be the squeak of rusty hinges. They claimed they were too scared to react as a figure in white crept out and "glided through the woods in the direction of the mansion." The men did not stay around long enough to see if she slipped inside. They ran straight to the home of the man who hired them and told him their news.

The next morning, long after the sun had burned the darkness from the sky, a small group of locals cautiously ventured to the old cemetery to investigate her tomb. Inside, they found that the "huge stone slab that had been over the coffin was displaced." They claimed that the girl was lying in the coffin and, although she had been dead for many months, looked just as she did when she died. Her skin was pale but had not decomposed and her hair appeared to have grown. She looked completely ordinary except for the fact that "sharp wolf-like fangs" protruded over her bottom lip. The sight of the girl brought gasps from the assembled group and they fled the cemetery. They took the time to replace the stone over the girl's coffin but nothing was done to stop her from leaving her grave again. Not surprisingly, tales of her nocturnal journeys continued.

Harassed by the townsfolk, the girl's family moved, but the stories continued. A wraith in a white dress was frequently seen prowling the graveyard and the dark streets nearby. The house where her family had lived sat

an upper room," and they quickly moved out. Neighbors, now generations after the original neighbors of the vampire house, found themselves terrified again. Finally, in 1923, it was decided that something had to be done.

According to Gorman Hendricks, who wrote his vampire article soon after the vigilantes ventured out to the graveyard for the last time, the door of the crypt was hanging on "rusty hinges," and the "hand of time has obliterated the name." He wrote that "large sections of broken sandstone that once covered the tombs of the dead lie about the dank vault given over to the creatures that creep and crawl."

Hendricks did not go

abandoned and empty for years, slowly crumbling into ruin, until a family unfamiliar with the stories finally purchased it in the 1920s. They did not stay unfamiliar with them for long.

Soon after they took up residence, the vampire returned. Apparently, the lure of fresh blood was something she was unable to resist. The new occupants reported a horrible figure "gazing in the window of

into detail as to what occurred in the crypt that night, but the "ghoulish desecration" he described led many people to believe that perhaps a stake was driven into the vampire's heart. Regardless, the woman in white was no longer seen wandering the streets of North East Washington again, peering in windows and terrifying the local populace. The vampire could now, finally, rest in peace.

INDEX

Page numbers in **bold** refer to photos and illustrations.

PICTURE CREDITS

All photos by the authors or public domain except as listed below:

Page 2 top left courtesy Gary Duschl, bottom left © iStockphoto/Michael Knight; top right © Ryan Doan, center © iStockphoto/Hans Culuwaerts; **3** © Ryan Doan; **4–5** © Ryan Doan; **7** © Georgette Sozio; **9** bottom © Joseph Citro; **10** © Ryan Doan; **11** left © Dane A. Penland/1992 Smithsonian Institution, right © Bettmann/CORBIS; **13** © Ryan Doan; **14** © Ryan Doan; **16–24** © Ryan Doan; **25** © CORBIS; **26** © Dane A. Penland/1992 Smithsonian Institution; **28** © Ryan Doan, inset © Pat and Chuck Blackley, Inc.; **29** bottom © Brooklyn Museum/CORBIS; **30** © Ryan Doan; **31** courtesy thecrystalman.com; **36–38** © Ryan Doan, **38** © Chigauhito; **39** Library of Congress, Prints and Photographs Division HABS/HAER; **43** top left © CORBIS, top right © iStockphoto/Hans Caluwaerts, bottom © Evan Hurd/CORBIS; **45** © geocities.com/mikenassau/what.htm; **47** © Evan Hurd/CORBIS; **50** © Bettmann/CORBIS; **53** bottom © iStockphoto; **55** © GlobalSecurity.org; **56** © iStockphoto; **59** left © iStockphoto/Hans Caluwaerts; **61** © wsh.dmhmrsas.virginia.gov; **64–65** left © Ryan Doan, right © Richard Berenson; **67–73** © Ryan Doan; **74** © Digital Art/CORBIS; **76–77** © Ryan Doan; **78** © Richard Berenson; **79–80** © Ryan Doan; **83** © iStockphoto/prozone235; **84, 85, 86** © Ryan Doan; **89** © George D. Lepp/CORBIS; **91, 92, 95, 96, 97** © Ryan Doan; **100** left courtesy Gary Duschl; **101** top © Mark Moran, bottom right © Bettmann/CORBIS; **104–105** courtesy Happy Kuhn; **107** © Bettmann/CORBIS; **108** © Bettmann/CORBIS, inset Hulton Getty Picture Library; **109** © Bettmann/CORBIS; **110** © Bettmann/CORBIS; **112** courtesy www.microsiervos.com; **113–115** © Mark Moran; **114, 115, 116, 117, 118, 119** courtesy Richmond Lucha Libre; **120–121** courtesy Gary Duschl; **128, 129** © Josh Horwitz; **132** © Bob Jones, Jr.; **133** top left © Bob Jones, Jr., top and bottom right © Jim Friedman/bluepelican@columbus.rr.com; **136** © Ted Degener; **137** © Roger Manley; **142, 143** © Ted Degener; **146–149** © Matt Lake; **154** © Debra Jane Seltzer; **157** left © Debra Jane Seltzer; **160** © Mark Moran; **161–163** © Ben Osto; **164** © Ben F. Schumin/Schuminweb.com; **166** left © Rose Johnson; **180–181** © David Schmid, courtesy Palace of Wonders; **182** © James Taylor, courtesy Palace of Wonders; **183–185** © David Schmid, courtesy Palace of Wonders; **186, 187, 188, 189** © Ryan Doan; **191, 192, 193** © Ryan Doan; **194–195** © David Sailors/CORBIS; **197, 198** © Ryan Doan; **199** © Richard Berenson; **200–201, 202** © Ryan Doan; **203** © iStockphoto/Helene Vallee; **205** Library of Congress, Prints and Photographs Division and © iStockphoto/Pascal Genest; **206** © Ryan Doan; **207** © Bettmann/CORBIS; **208–209** © Ryan Doan; **210–211** © Ryan Doan; **213** © Ryan Doan; **214** © Library of Congress, Prints and Photographs Division HABS/HAER; **215** © background Ryan Doan/CORBIS; **216** © Ryan Doan; **217** © CORBIS Stormchasers, **218** © Ryan Doan; **220** © NYPL Digital Library/Mrs. George B. Webb, Humanities and Social Sciences Library/Print Collection, Miriam and Ira D. Wallach Division of Art, Prints and Photographs, inset courtesy Garber Graver; **221** © Richard T. Nowitz/CORBIS; **222, 223** Library of Congress, Prints and Photographs Division; **224, 227, 228** © Ryan Doan; **229** Library of Congress, Prints and Photographs Division; **231** © Bettmann/Brooks Kraft/CORBIS; **232** © Lisa M. Duty; **233–236** © Matt Lake; **236** Library of Congress, Prints and Photographs Division; **239** © Ryan Doan; **240–241** © Lisa M. Duty; **243** Library of Congress, Prints and Photographs Division; **244** © NYPL Digital Library, Humanities and Social Sciences Library/Print Collection, Miriam and Ira D. Wallach Division of Art, Prints and Photographs; **245** © Mark Moran; **247** © Ryan Doan.

EDITORIAL CREDITS

Page 86 Legend of the Wampus Cat © 2001 by PageWise, Inc. Used with permission.

WEIRD VIRGINIA

By
Jeff Bahr, Troy Taylor, and Loren Coleman

Executive Editors
Mark Sceurman and Mark Moran

ACKNOWLEDGMENTS

JEFF BAHR

If shout-outs are to be expressed in their order of importance, my sincerest gratitude must first find its way to those omnipotent Marks (Moran and Sceurman). If not for their considerable generosity, this journeyman would still be dwelling in magazine-writing anonymity. Further credit goes to my parents, Harry and Ruth Bahr, who, while likely saddled with disappointment in hatching a defective, nevertheless lent oodles of support, encouragement, and unconditional love. Thanks a zillion. My amore and deepest appreciation goes to Maria Nicoletta Cirasella. As my much-put-upon girlfriend, this wonderful woman has accompanied me through the best and worst of times. I am eternally grateful for her understanding, patience, and love. Finally, I'd like to thank the following, who in varying ways placed and kept this writer on path— occasionally by force: Brian Rathjen and Shira Kamil, Gayla and Dipesh Alesi, Dave Searle, John Loftus, Jack Sheffrin, Dave Nardone, Howard, Joe, Pete, Ted (a.k.a. The Cracked Pack), Max, Gerard, Nick, and the gang at HBA, Gizzy, Lars.

TROY TAYLOR

This is never a solitary journey and there are many for me to thank along the way, providing information, stories, and reports. These individuals, writers, researchers, and storytellers include Mark and Mark from *Weird N.J.*, L. B. Taylor, John Alexander, Dennis William Hauck, Bobbie & Rick Atristain, Ben Keys, Richard Winer, Joan Bingham & Delores Riccio, my wife, Haven, and, of course, the dozens of people who provided the great information, weird sites, strange stories, and local legends. It's been another weird trip and one that never seems to end!

LOREN COLEMAN

In recent years, my research and intrigue with the cryptozoological and Fortean wonders of Virginia have been stimulated by insights from the founders and members of these groups, based there: International Fortean Organization (INFO), Association for Research and Enlightenment (ARE), and Assassination Archives and Research Center (AARC).

Specifically, for background information shared with me for this book, and permission to use their research or words, I sincerely thank my friends and colleagues: Jerome Clark, Patrick Huyghe, Jim Brandon, Michael Frizzell, Jacques Vallee, Larry Bryant, Sandra Martin, John A. Keel, David Haehn, John Lutz, Mark A. Hall, Robert A. Goerman, Michael T. Shoemaker, Robert Bartholomew, Travis McHenry, Curtis Brooks, George Zug, Jim Trainor, Chad Arment, Bill Grimstad, and Kenny Stewart.

This book is dedicated to my first grandson, T. J.

Contributing Author Chris Gethard

Chris Gethard served as the associate editor of *Weird N.J.* magazine for over four years. He is the author of *Weird New York* and was a contributing author to *Weird N.J.* and *Weird U.S.* Chris is also an actor and comedian. He has written for shows on Comedy Central and appeared on a number of TV programs, including *Late Night with Conan O'Brien.* He is a performer and teacher at the Upright Citizens Brigade Theater in Manhattan.

Chris spent the better part of a year traveling extensively throughout Virginia, sending back reports for us to include in the Fabled People and Places and Local Heroes and Villains chapters of this book.

SHOW US YOUR WEIRD!

Do you know of a weird site found somewhere in the United States, or can you tell us about a strange experience you've had? If so, we'd like to hear about it! We believe that every town has at least one great tale to tell, and we're listening. It could be a cursed road, haunted abandoned site, odd local character, or bizarre historic event. In most cases these tales are told only in the towns in which they originated. But why keep them to yourself when you could share them with all of America? So come on and fill us in on all the weirdness that's lurking in your backyard!

You can e-mail us at: Editor@WeirdUS.com,
or write to us at:
Weird U.S., P.O. Box 1346, Bloomfield, NJ 07003.

www.weirdus.com